Bernard Coulange

Software Reuse

Translation Editor: Iain Craig

Springer

Bernard Coulange
Responsable Technique des Produits, VERILOG, Toulouse, France

Translation Editor
Dr Iain Craig
Department of Computer Science, University of Warwick, Coventry CV4 7AL, UK

ISBN 3-540-76084-9 Springer-Verlag Berlin Heidelberg New York

British Library Cataloguing in Publication Data
Coulange, Bernard
  Software reuse
  1.Computer software - reusability
  I.Title
  005
  ISBN 3540760849

Library of Congress Cataloging-in-Publication Data
Coulange, Bernard,   1953-
   [Réutilisation du logiciel.   English]
   Software reuse   /   Bernard Coulange : translation editor, Ian Craig.
     p.   cm.
   Includes index.
   ISBN 3-540-76084-9   (pbk. : alk. paper)
   1. Computewr software- -Reusability- -Congresses.   I. Title.
   QA76.76.R47C6813   1997
   005.1- -dc21   97-29212

© Springer-Verlag London Limited 1998

© Masson, Editeur, Paris, 1996

Published with the help of the Ministère de la Culture
Printed in Great Britain

The original edition of this book was published in French by Masson, Editeur as *Réutilisation du Logiciel: Légendes et Réalités*

Typesetting: Iain Craig
Printed and bound at the Athenæum Press Ltd., Gateshead, Tyne and Wear
34/3830-543210 Printed on acid-free paper

Software Reuse

3702924650

LEARNING

Springer
London
Berlin
Heidelberg
New York
Barcelona
Budapest
Hong Kong
Milan
Paris
Santa Clara
Singapore
Tokyo

Foreword

We are living through a new development in the art of constructing software. After the languages that were developed to replace machine language programming, after structured languages which improved the readability of programs, after modular languages which allow better organisation, a new technique, object orientation, has achieved the maturity which allows it to be used industrially. We are entering an era in the fabrication of software by assembly of reusable components.

The benefits of such an approach are clear: improvement in productivity, simplification of software maintenance, greater standardisation and therefore better integration of software items.

The profession of developing software will no longer consist of putting lines of code together, but is going to become that of a true architecture of applications.

What must be done to do this? To what really corresponds the concept of software reuse? Where are we today? How can we make the transition?

This book considers all these questions. It rejects received wisdom and identifies the true problems. By reading it, one can form an opinion on what can be expected from reuse and what it is necessary to think about if one decides to become a "software architect."

Contents

Chapter One

Hopes and Myths

1.1 Reuse

Reuse: an old dream which has always haunted information technology people.

Every other profession reuses:

- When constructing cars, motors, body work parts, and numerous other components are reused from one model to another;
- When constructing houses, prefabricated walls, standardised windows are used, as well as prefabricated skeletons.
- Electronic engineers assemble integrated circuits.

With information technology, none of this happens. With each new software project, everything is reinvented: functions to manipulate character strings, lists, stacks, and so on.

If the building industry had the same history as the software of today, to construct a house, the architect would start with designing the bricks and the cement (some would even invent, on the way, the scaffolding).

And yet, if we engaged in reuse.

1.2 Hopes for Reuse

Imagine that you have just constructed some software composed of 50% reused code!

Your productivity would have been incredible; if you had reused 50% of the code, that would mean that you had only developed 50% of the rest of the code. You would have certainly constructed the code 50% more quickly than you would if you had written everything.

The reliability of your software is exceptional. The reused code is used by other software. The greater part of its errors have therefore been corrected. Half of the software that you have just constructed is highly reliable. It can be assumed that it is at least twice as reliable than if you had to construct it all.

The maintainability of the code must be unbelievable. Half of the code has been maintained by other people. What is more, this code has been used in very different contexts from your own. Some errors which perhaps you would only have found later, and with great difficulty, during the development of your code, have been corrected for free. What more could be asked for!

And extensibility! The code that you reused is certainly used as much by demanding people who always want more facilities than you, and wish their software always to be up-to-date. For this, they extend software components which you also use. Your software benefits from this without effort from you, you will even find new possibilities in your implementation. You are always at the forefront of progress in IT.

Choice! While designing your software, you have identified the elements which you need. Going to look in the reusable components, you will have certainly found several things that satisfy your needs. You have been able, without additional load, to test several solutions, indeed even to change a solution while it is being developed. Finally, the solutions which you have retained are the best and you can prove it.

The update of the software has been simplified: your developments have been incremental: in a first version, you have chosen basic components just to construct your application, then, during development, you have refined your choices, so as to produce a final solution. During the development, your client has been able, in an effective way, to follow the advancement of the project, and has had more choice.

Your job has changed. Before, your task consisted of assembling many lines of code. Today, you have become an architect who conceives his software by choosing and assembling components. Your profession has regained its nobility.

Errors have disappeared. Before, your applications had a very different appearance because you developed it at different times using still evolving technologies. The ways of using it were also very different. All of this has stopped. Now, thanks to reuse, all your software has the same appearance and is used in the same way, and, what is more, it is always of the highest technical standard.

Reuse is magic.

It is even, doubtless, too magical because in IT until now, without knowing why, the same things have always been reused: data structures, mathematical functions, graphic interfaces. There is still a long way to go before we can enjoy the benefits just described.

What can be done to make the dream reality?

1.3 Reuse is Object-Oriented

Reuse had always remained an impossible dream until something happened: object-oriented programming appeared (OO to the initiated)—a new magic.

Object orientation is fascinating. Instead of writing lines and lines of code which represent data and routines, you create objects. An object is a set of data associated with all the routines which permit the manipulation of this data. An object provides a set of services. To construct some software, you identify the services your software needs, you assemble the objects which provide these services, and that is that.

Object orientation is the long-awaited key which finally affords the possibility of reuse.

Is it as simple as that?

This isn't the kind of question which should be asked. Everyone knows that

REUSE = OBJECT ORIENTATION

If everyone knows it, that is the proof that it is true! It is useless to attempt to contradict it!

1.4 Getting to the Bottom of the Myths

The magic doesn't stop there: there are other things which everyone knows about object orientation and reuse. For example:

OBJECT ORIENTATION = C++

Ask around you: everyone knows that The Standard for Object Oriented is C++. Every other language which claims to be object-oriented (Smalltalk, Eiffel, etc.) is going to disappear and give way to the majority's choice of C++.

Why is C++ so successful?

Quite simply, because it is compatible with C. Everyone knows that:

C++ = ANSI C + Object-oriented concepts

It is also known that in C++, you can only use object-oriented concepts (this is even advised at the outset). Moreover, a great majority of the users of C++ do not wish to use the object-oriented features and prefer to continue using C (which is more reliable in C++). The true reality about C++ is therefore:

C++ = ANSI C + (optionally, Object-oriented concepts)

And in fact, as the compatibility with C is a major argument in favour of C++, and it is not a bother to ignore the object-oriented features of C++, it is often considered that dealing with C++ is dealing with a C which is acceptable to a C++ compiler:

C++ = C which is compatible with a C++ compiler.

1.5 The Dream Collapses

If we take up all the things that everyone knows, we get:

REUSE = OBJECT ORIENTATION
OBJECT ORIENTATION = C++
C++ = C which is compatible with a C++ compiler

By simplification, this gives:

REUSE = C which is compatible with a C++ compiler

If today, you have maintainability, reliability, and extensibility problems with your code written in C, you need reuse and when you do, very simply: compile all your C code with a C++ compiler.

The reality of this conclusion can be doubted.

When the magic stretches too far, we end up asking questions. Changing the compiler has never changed any code. All the received wisdom about reuse put together produce conclusions that are more than dubious.

1.6 What Reality?

What can be concluded from this? The dream is impossible and never will we be able to engage in reuse in computing, or the dream is possible but reality must be sought.

It is time to reconsider all the dreams, all the legends, and to ask proper questions:

- Is reuse possible?
- If it is, how can it be done?
- What connections are there between reuse and object orientation?
- Is object orientation C++?
- What gains can be had in productivity, extensibility, and in maintenance?
- Does reuse come for free?

The following chapters concentrate on these questions.

1.7 Objectives of this Book

This book has as its objective the creation of a list of all the problems to be taken into consideration if we want to engage in reuse, and to propose ways of solving it. It is not a collection of recipes which are directly applicable to reuse, it is a inventory of ideas. It is for each person to see, from their own perspective, how to adapt what we propose in order to obtain the best results.

1.8 Organisation

Chapter 2 presents different techniques for engaging in reuse. It compares these techniques to a set of criteria which appear essential to successful reuse.

Chapter 3 focuses on software development life cycles and examines the way in which they take reuse into account.

Chapters 4 to 11 consider all matters related to the management of reusable components. These matters include issues such as the classification, identification, construction, certification, storage, search, adaptation and maintenance.

Chapter 12 deals with the problems of organisation in a company which wants to put a reuse policy into operation.

Chapter 13 considers the gains which can result from reuse.

Chapter 14 is about commerce in components (purchase and sale).

Chapter 15 describes a successful attempt of engaging in reuse.

Chapter Two

Techniques for Reuse

In this chapter, we will be interested in all the techniques allowing reuse of information. Some of these techniques are suitable for all types of information, others only suit code. All the techniques are compared on the basis of a set of criteria described at the start of this chapter.

The techniques that we are going to analyse are:

- Copying;
- Pre-processing;
- Libraries;
- Packages;
- Objects;
- Generics;
- Object orientation.

2.1 Introduction

In the introductory chapter, we heard about the various dreams concerning reuse. Starting with these dreams, we can establish a list of criteria describing what we seek to obtain for the software we might reuse:

- Productivity;
- Maintainability;
- Reliability;
- Extensibility;
- Adaptability.

Here is a definition of these criteria.

2.1.1 Productivity

Reuse must increase productivity. To reuse a component must be less costly than developing some specific software. To verify that there is, indeed, an increase in productivity, it is necessary to take all the imponderables into account: a technique can allow us to go very quickly in recovering code, but can, then, require lots of time for its updating. This is the predicted total time for development, updating including, that we are going to take into account along this dimension.

2.1.2 Maintainability

Reuse must increase maintainability. Error correction in reused components must be of benefit, without particular effort, to the software which reuses them. Errors can be introduced into the software during the maintenance phase which are taken into account when comparing techniques according to this criterion.

2.1.3 Reliability

Reuse must increase reliability. If a component is reliable, it must remain so when it is reused. Its functioning must not therefore be disturbed by its mode of use.

2.1.4 Extensibility

Reuse must increase extensibility. All extensions of a component must be able to be used without particular effort by the software which reuses the component.

2.1.5 "Usability"

This criterion measures the independence of components with respect to each other. A reusable component must be able to be assembled, without difficulty, with other reusable components. This must not lead to alternatives.

2.1.6 Adaptability

A reusable component must be capable of being adapted to a new context without affecting its other uses.

The different techniques for reuse are going to be studied as a function of their ability to satisfy these criteria. We are thus going to determine what are the techniques that allow us to expect the objectives aimed at by a policy of reuse.

2.2 Copying

2.2.1 Description

Copying is the oldest, the best known and the most commonly used reuse technique.

The principle is simple (see Figure 2.1). You find a piece of software *{B, C, D}* which suits you in a new development. Using the functions copy and paste in some text editor, you copy *{B, C, D}* into the code which you are currently writing. The piece of software becomes your property. You can then modify it as you want so that it is exactly suitable to your new needs.

For example, you can replace C by C' and thus obtain the software $\{A', B, C', D, E'\}$.

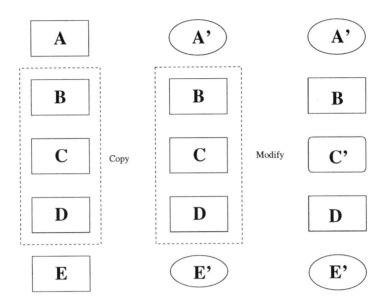

Figure 2.1 Copying

2.2.2 Use

Copying is useable on all types of information: analysis documents, design documents, code, user documentation.

2.2.3 Evaluation according to the criteria

Productivity

A priori, this technique seems to achieve the objective of productivity. At the time when the piece of code to be copied was identified, two simple text-processing commands are enough to replace the capture of numerous lines of code.

In terms of daily reality, things are different. If the portion of the code that we are implementing depends on a context (it uses local or global variables), we can find ourselves confronted by the following choice:

- Either it is necessary to localise this context for it must, itself, be copied, and this can lead us a long way if this context itself depends on another context (Figure 2.2);
- Or, it is necessary locally to reconstruct this context: this is not always a simple task because it is necessary, in this case, to

understand how the retrieved software works (and it is not desirable to go into the details of its design).

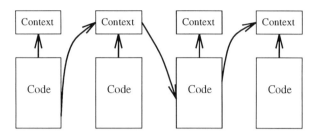

Figure 2.2 Localisation of context.

In the two cases, the integration time of what has just been copied can become longer than the time taken to write it if we take debugging into account.

The risks of manipulation error are also not inconsiderable:

- At the moment the copy is performed, a line is forgotten;

The copy is made one line early or one line late.

- For all these reasons, for the Productivity criterion, copying gets a mark of 3/10.

Maintainability

From the fact that a physical copy is performed on what is being reused, in general, a modification is performed and there is no necessary correspondence between the copy and what was copied. It is possible to imagine implementing an organisation which knows what is copied and who extends it (during corrective maintenance) but this is very difficult to do for two main reasons:

- Copies are in general poorly controlled: we do not know how exactly to identify what has been copied, nor can we easily follow the changes to it (for example, what happens when an error is corrected in one of the copies? How do we know that it is a copy? How do we retrieve the original? How does one know all the other copies?) We can also find ourselves confronted by copies of copies. The nth copy can easily look nothing at all like the original.
- Copied code has, in general, to be adapted. A correction in the original cannot be simply repeated in the copy.

All these reasons cause us to give copying a mark of 0/10 for maintainability according to the definition which has been given at the start of this chapter.

Reliability

The fact that we are taking a piece of reliable code and copying it into another context does not afford us any guarantee of its reliability.

We could, for example, have copied a piece of code which uses global variables into a new item of software which, itself, uses global variables with the same names (the poor imagination of IT people for naming things or for naming conventions for identifiers imply that this case is very often encountered). These variables have, in the new software, a use which can prevent the copied software from working in the same way. This implies, in general, debugging problems which are very hard to control.

For these reasons, on the reliability criterion, copying gets a mark of 2/10.

Extensibility

For reasons suggested in the maintainability criterion, extensions to an original are not reflected in copies (or cost a lot in terms of effort).

For this criterion, copying gets a mark of 0/10.

Usability

Copying gives no guarantee as far as the coexistence of copied code is concerned. One is even tempted to think the contrary if one recalls the comments made about the reliability criterion. Software made only from copies of code taken from other software seems difficult to imagine.

Copying gets a mark of 0/10 on the usability criterion.

Adaptability

After copying some code, it is modified in such a way that it works in the new context in which it is used. Because this is the case, we do not try and verify that we have not done anything to question the original information that we have reused by copying. The connections with the original have been cut.

For the criterion of adaptability, copying receives a mark of 10/10 because, by definition, everything is allowed without modification of the original and thus without causing problems to other users of the same code.

2.2.4 Evaluation

Copying gets an overall mark of 15/60 for the set of criteria which were determined for successful reuse.

It thus seems that the oldest, the best known and the most practical technique is also highly ineffective.

It is necessary to review received ideas: copying is not reuse. It is used to gain (perhaps) some time when the software is written. There is no other advantage to be hoped for from this technique.

2.3 Pre-Processing

2.3.1 Description

The technique of pre-processing is an improvement on the technique of copying. It is a form of copying performed by a particular piece of software called a pre-processor. This technique consists of introducing into a document (code or other kind of document) a set of directives. Among the directives would, in general, include the `include` and `ifdef` directives.

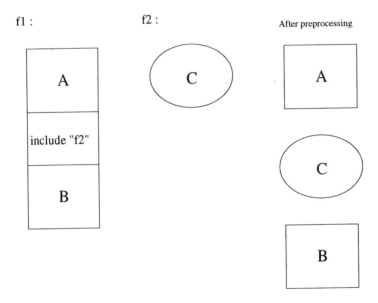

Figure 2.3 The "include" directive.

`#include`

This directive allows us to require the inclusion of a file. For example, if a document (see Figure 2.3) contains the directive:

`include "f2"`

after treatment by the pre-processor this line is replaced by the contents of file `f2`. It is, therefore, just as if at this point we are duplicating the contents of `f2`.

`ifdef ... else ... endif`

This directive allows us to add or to remove text from a document as a function of the value of a variable which is passed to the pre-processor.

For example, if a document contains (see Figure 2.4):

`ifdef v1`

```
part1
else
part2
endif
```

when the pre-processor processes this document with the variable v1 having the value *true* it is as if this part of the document contained part1. On the other hand, if v1 is *false*, it is as if the document contains part2.

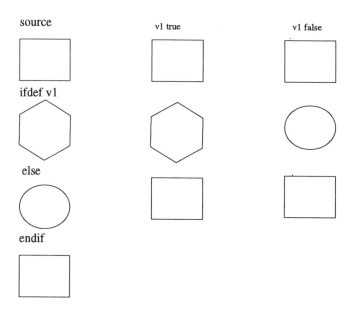

Figure 2.4 The "ifdef" directive.

The best-known pre-processor is *cpp*. It processes C sources prior to analysis by a compiler. The directives include and ifdef are written respectively #include and #ifdef.

2.3.2. Use

This technique is usable on any kind of information.

2.3.3 Evaluation according to the criteria

Productivity

Some problems with copying are removed: we do not risk forgetting lines when we perform a copy.

The operation is faster than that of copy even if a little time is wasted as a result of the operation of the pre-processor. The possibilities for the error due to altering the context from what we are retrieving still exists. We take the risk of including code which uses variables which have another meaning in the software that we are writing or which require copying (or inclusion) of other data descriptions. This technique is frequently used in C but almost only for sharing declarations (of data or of procedures).

Productivity is better with this technique than with simple copy and we can give it a mark of five out of ten.

Maintainability

From the fact that the code which is being used is not copied, every error correction in the code is useful to the code using it.

Some problems can appear if an error correction implies inconsistencies with the reusing codes. Use of variables which have already been declared in the software which is doing the reuse but which are given another meaning, create different side-effects in the reused software. For these reasons the pre-processing receives a mark of five out of ten according to the maintainability criteria.

Reliability

There is no difference at the level of reliability between this technique and copy. Therefore, receives a mark of two out of ten according to this criterion.

Extensibility

With this technique extension of the components that are being re-used is useful. As was indicated under the heading "Maintainability" nothing guarantees that the component is still useable after extension. A mark of five out of ten is given to this technique.

Usability

This technique introduces nothing more than copying as far as usability of components is concerned. According to this criteria a mark of zero out of ten is given.

Adaptability

If a component which we are reusing is not entirely suitable and it is necessary to adapt it, it is necessary to modify the original components. In order not to disturb the other uses of this component, it is necessary to make the changes by using the ifdef directives of the pre-processor if we don't want to duplicate components. In order to do this we define a variable which will serve to identify the change and we have two types of change in the original component:

- Additions of the form:
```
ifdef variable
    additions
endif
```
- Modifications of the form:

```
ifdef variable
      new contents
else
      old contents
endif
```

This technique presents a set of problems:

- If for each use of the component it is necessary to make a change, the component ends up as a result becoming very large and depends upon a great number of variables: its readability diminishes;
- There are non-negligible risks in making errors while modifying the original components (a line might appear in the saved part only if the pre-processing variable is used while this line should figure in every version);
- The distinction between a component in default state and its extended state is not always clear. Some errors can be corrected as a form of modification. They are therefore not corrected in every use of the component.

After some time, and after numerous uses, the components which are generated using this kind of technique end up having the following appearance:

```
ifdef original_version
      code
endif
ifdef extension1
      other code
endif
ifdef extension2
      some more code
endif
```

Indeed, where not by finding components which in fact several independent items of code spread across the same file. Everyone develops their own code without a care for the code of others and without the slightest idea of reuse.

For these reasons we give them marks of three out of ten for adaptation.

2.3.4 Evaluation

Pre-processing obtains a global mark of twenty out of sixty according to the set of criteria which describes good reuse.

This technique can be described as a copy performed by software and has much better results than manual copying. It is difficult to manage when there is lots of reuse as we have seen in the discussion of criteria of extensibility, multiplicity and adaptation.

2.4 Libraries

2.4.1 Description

Use of libraries is also one of the oldest techniques for reuse.

A library is a set of sub-programs.

A sub-program is a portion of code which is referenced by name and which can be used by anybody at any time (or almost), by referring to its name. At the time a sub-program is called, it is possible to pass parameters to influence the processing that it performs.

When a sub-program returns, it is in general possible to retrieve a value called the return value of the sub-program (see Figure 2.5).

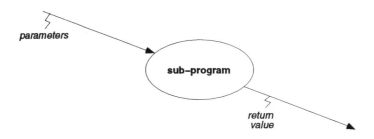

Figure 2.5 Sub-program.

In order to improve the parameterisation of a sub-program without increasing its number of parameters, global variables are often used. These are given a particular value before the call to the sub-program; the sub-program changes its behaviour as a consequence (see Figure 2.6).

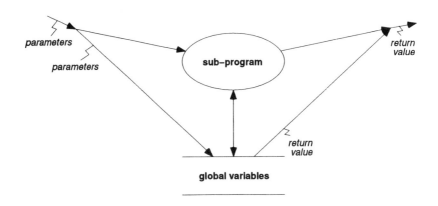

Figure 2.6 Global variables in a sub-program.

On return we retrieve the value which has been returned by the sub-program and we can also retrieve the values of the global variables if their modification by the sub-program has any meaning.

2.4.2 Use

This technique can be used on code. Every language permits the use of this technique.

2.4.3 Evaluation according to the criteria

Productivity

Productivity is very good because we replace the writing of all the lines of code which constitute the sub-program by writing the name of the sub-program and the value of its parameters.

A sub-program can have, in general, its own variables which do not interfere with those of the program which is calling it.

In the case of a sub-program which uses its own variables, productivity is confirmed because, in general, there is no secondary problem. We can, according to this criterion, award a value of ten out of ten for use of libraries.

In the case in which a sub-program uses global variables, productivity can be much less high. Indeed, two phenomena can prevent such high productivity:

- The sub-program reads global variables which the software modifies without knowledge of their meaning to the sub-program;
- The sub-program modifies global variables without knowing that the program uses them.

These two techniques can make global variables inconsistent and can also significantly increase development time.

Another problem can be due to the fact that the sub-program uses global variables which themselves reference other variables and other parts of the codes. Replacing all the necessary code in the sub-program can take much more time than writing the code of the sub-program itself. This is because it is necessary to find all of the other parts and possibly if we don't want to use some useless things, it is necessary to restructure the data.

For these reasons in the case in which a sub-program uses global variables the library technique receives five out of ten as is marked according to this criteria.

Maintainability

If an error is corrected in a sub-program, the correction benefits all software using the sub-program.

This poses no problem if the sub-program does not use global variables. In this case we can award a mark of ten out of ten to this technique according to the criteria.

In the case in which the sub-program uses global variables (because of error correction or otherwise) some problems can appear which prevent the sub-program from functioning any longer in certain software when the errors have been corrected. For example, the sub-program can, after correction of an error, modify a global variable which is used by the software. It does not now function correctly.

In the case of the use of this technique, a mark of eight out of ten is given.

Reliability

If a sub-program does not use global variables and is considered to be reliable, its uses will be reliable as far as the parameters which are passed to it are correct. This technique therefore receives a mark of ten out of ten.

If the sub-program uses global variables interference can be apparent between it and the part of the software which manipulates these global variables. In this case we can only give seven out of ten to this technique.

Extensibility

As far as extensibility is concerned the remarks are the same as for maintainability. The same marks are given;

- Ten out of ten if the sub-program uses no global variables;
- Eight out of ten if the sub-program uses global variables.

Usability

Again, for this criterion, it is necessary to distinguish between sub-programs not using global variables whose introduction into the code poses problems only when the sub-programs have identical names in different libraries. This technique receives the mark of seven out of ten for this criteria (renaming is not always easy to perform), and sub-programs use global variables. It is necessary to add possible risks of incompatibilities between the global variables being used. This technique receives the mark of five out of ten.

Adaptability

If a sub-program does not completely conform to the requirements, we can, in general, use the following techniques to adapt it:

- We add a parameter which indicates that we want a new behaviour; this type of change makes the software which is using the sub-program subject to a change in order to add the new parameter at the time of call (even if the language being used does allow the default value of parameters);

- We use a global variable which must have a certain value so that we obtain the new behaviour; by default this variable has a value which gives the old component the old behaviour; this solution poses problems from the point of view of debugging (the initialisation of the variable can be forgotten, for example) and the solution also requires that we get the same problems with sub-programs which manipulate global variables as we discussed above;
- We add to the code pre-processor directives, in this case it is no longer possible to have the component in a library and it is harder to use;
- We have the ability to pass parameters to sub-programs, one of which is the address of one or more sub-programs which also allow this specialisation of its behaviour.

None of these techniques is satisfactory. For the criterion of adaptability, the library technique receives the mark of two out of ten.

2.4.4 Evaluation

We arrive, with relatively few problems, for libraries of sub-programs not using global variables at a mark of forty-seven out of sixty. The only weak point is adaptability: a sub-program must be appropriate, otherwise it is necessary to write something else.

On the other hand, if sub-programs use global variables the score is much less at twenty-five out of sixty. This bad mark is due essentially to the potential risk of interference between the global variables which it uses.

2.5 Packages

2.5.1 Description

The idea of a package derives from the comments that can be given a study of libraries:

- Problems with sub-programs using global variables are due to inconsistencies in the uses of the global variables.
- We obtain good results for reuse if we write sub-programs which do not manipulate global variables.

A first idea for taking into account these thoughts consists of deciding never to use global variables in sub-programs. This is not very realistic because very often sub-programs co-operate and need to save information.

The approach using packages consists of managing the use of global variables and not allowing them to be visible only by a clearly identified sub set of sub-programs which are the only ones which are committed to operate on them.

A set formed from sub-programs and global variables necessary for their functioning is called a package.

The modification of global variables is only possible by means of a call to one of the sub-programs of the package (Figure 2.7).

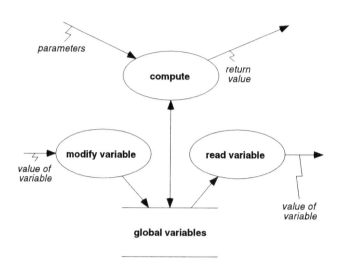

Figure 2.7 Access to variables in a package.

Some languages possessing the concept of package distinguish the package interface (lists of sub-programs which form the package with the description of their parameters and the type of their return values) and the implementation of the package (way in which the sub-programs are written). From this fact, a package can have several implementations.

The servers in client-server systems are really similar to packages. They manage their own variables and are activated by requests.

2.5.2 Use

This technique is useful for code. It requires using a language which allows limitation of the visibility of global variables (Modula-2, C, Pascal, etc.). The Ada language possesses, as standard, the concept of package. This notion is now to be introduced to C++ in the form of name spaces.

2.5.3 Evaluation according to the criteria

Productivity
Productivity is that of sub-programs which do not use global variables: ten out of ten.

Maintainability

Maintainability is the same as for sub-programs which do not use global variables: ten out of ten.

Reliability

Reliability is the same as for sub-programs which do not use global variables: ten out of ten.

Extensibility

Extensibility is the same as for sub-programs which do not use global variables: ten out of ten.

Usability

Usability is the same as for sub-programs which do not use global variables in languages which do not use packages (the problem of identical names in different packages exists) and for this reason, a mark of seven out of ten is given for to this criterion.

For languages which support the notion of package (like Ada) some visibility rules for sub-programs allow packages to contain sub-programs with the same name and this causes no problem. The only possible conflict is produced when two packages which are different have the same name. It is then necessary to rename one of them in the software which uses it. This type of language receives a mark of nine out of ten, according to this criteria.

Adaptability

If one of the sub-programs in a package is unsuitable and if we don't want to create a new function which duplicates but modifies the unsuitable one, we can use the value of a package variable to indicate which sub-program must have new behaviour and to modify the sub-program to take this variable into account. We add to the package a function which is charged with setting this variable to new behaviour or old behaviour. The value by default is old behaviour. We run the risk of the user forgetting to set this variable when they want the new behaviour. Another technique consists of writing a new function with the same parameters as that which is unsuitable. This new function sets the variable to new behaviour, calls the function and then resets the variable to old behaviour. This technique prevents forgetting but has the disadvantage of increasing the sub-program's cost in terms of development. All of this is not really satisfactory and leads us to attribute a value of three out of ten to packages as far as adaptability is concerned.

2.5.4 Evaluation

We get the same results as the technique for libraries of sub-programs not using global variables: fifty out of sixty.

If, furthermore, the language being used offers visibility rules for contents of packages, the mark increases to fifty-two out of sixty. The weak point still remains adaptability.

2.6 Objects (or Modularity)

2.6.1 Description

Objects resemble packages. The essential difference between an object and a package is the fact that the concept of package is a static notion while that of an object is dynamic (we will not speak here of concepts of inheritance or of genericity which are treated in object-oriented systems).

An object resembles a package because, like a package, it is formed of data and of sub-programs for manipulating this data. The difference is that the data is not static but is dynamically allocated during the execution of some software.

If a package P *contains*

> A variable V
> A sub-program S

the programs which use it can contain only one package P and therefore can only have a single variable V (except, certainly, if the programmer has foreseen that V is a reference to information which is dynamically allocated). If an object O contains

> A variable V
> A sub-program S

it will be possible to have several exemplars of O in software, and, therefore, several different values assigned to the variable V (see Figure 2.8).

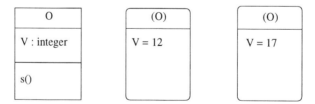

Figure 2.8 Instances of objects.

For an object to be a true object, it must not be possible to modify its variables without calling one of its sub-programs. Respect for this rule is called the respect for encapsulation.

An object is therefore a data structure to which a set of sub-programs is associated. The sub-programs allows the manipulation of the structure of the data. They have, in general, as their first parameter, a reference to the structure data.

The description of the composition of an object is called its class. The data which constitute it are called attributes and the sub-programs it contains are called methods. Objects are instantiated by programs; instantiations are called instances.

2.6.2 Use

Many languages allow the definition of objects, provided a particular kind of programming discipline is introduced: objects. For this, it is necessary to allow the creation of structured data types (structures in C, records in Pascal and Ada, for example). It is necessary to add to these structures a set of sub-programs which manipulate them.

Object-oriented languages allow, certainly, the concept of objects and it is possible to restrict oneself to using only languages with objects. It is necessary to distinguish two types of object languages:

- Those which impose a discipline of encapsulation (as in Smalltalk and Eiffel),
- Those which allow disrespect for encapsulation (as in C++).

2.6.3 Evaluation according to the criteria

Productivity

Productivity is the same as for packages (if encapsulation is respected) and receives a mark of ten out of ten. In the case in which encapsulation is not respected, we encounter again the problems of libraries which use global variables. The object which is being reused and whose attributes are being modified can itself modify the attributes of other objects which are being manipulated. When the changes are undesirable, this fact makes the error very hard to correct. In this case this technique gets a mark of five out of ten according to this criterion.

Maintainability

Maintainability is the same as for packages when encapsulation is respected, and for this criteria we award a mark of ten out of ten.

In the case of a language which allows the direct modification of object attributes, correction during maintenance can lead to the modification of the content of other objects and to incorrect behaviour of the software.

It can also happen that in the maintenance cycle, one is led to add behaviour which must be performed each time a particular attribute is modified. If encapsulation is respected, the processing is added to the method which encapsulates the attributes. If it is not respected, it is necessary to find all the software which modifies and to change them, a process which is not simple and which often leads to the introduction of errors.

Without respect for encapsulation, this technique has the same performance as libraries which use global variables and that is eight out of ten.

Reliability

Reliability is excellent if we respect encapsulation: ten out of ten.

In the case of programs which authorise the direct modification of attributes, nothing guarantees that a reused object will function correctly in the presence of other objects. Untidy modifications of object attributes can lead to errors in functioning. This leads us to award a mark of seven out of ten for this technique.

Extensibility

The remarks are the same as above and lead us therefore to the same marks: ten out of ten if we respect encapsulation and eight out of ten otherwise.

Usability

If we respect encapsulation, the only possible problem is the attempt to reuse different, but identically named, objects into the same application. We encountered the same problem as with packages, and for this reason this technique receives a mark of nine out of ten.

If we do not respect the principle of object encapsulation, we again find the same problems as with libraries which allow the manipulation of global variables, together with their attendant risks. Therefore, for the latter, we give a mark of five out of ten.

Adaptability

As for packages, opportunities for the adaptation of objects (according to the definition used here) are slight and we award a mark of three out of ten.

2.6.4 Evaluation

Use of objects according to the rules of art give us a mark of fifty-two out of sixty.

The case of objects which do not respect encapsulation receive a mark of twenty-eight out of sixty.

Adaptability is also the weak point in simple approaches to objects.

Lack of respect for encapsulation loses every benefit gained from adopting objects.

2.7 Genericity of Objects and Packages

2.7.1 Description

Genericity is the capacity for creating a package or an object class whose types are not completely defined. The exact definition is made at the moment of use. There exist two types of generic: static and dynamic generics.

Static Generic

Static generics are found in languages such as Ada and C++. They allow the association of a package or object and set of parameters (data types and general). This allows us to have several instances, perhaps with different contents, in the same software of a package or object.

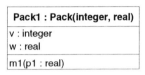
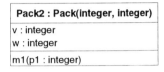

Figure 2.9 Static generic.

For example (see Figure 2.9) if a package is declared by:

```
Package Pack (U,V)
     v: U;
     u: V;
     m1(p1: V)
```

then this notation means that the package Pack is generic and associated with parameters U and V. The use of this package has the form:

```
Package Pack Pack1 : Pack(integer,real);
Package Pack Pack2: Pack(integer,integer);
```

and allows the creation of two new packages. The first, Pack1, corresponds to the following description:

```
Package Pack1
     v: integer;
     w: real;
     m1(p1: real);
```

and the second, Pack2, corresponds to:

```
Package Pack2
     v: integer;
     w: integer;
     m1(p1: integer);
```

In the final software there are as many copies of the code of m1 as there are instances of the package with a different type parameter. This is equivalent to tightly controlled duplication of code.

Dynamic Generic

Dynamic Generic is found in a language like Eiffel.

This allows the creation of classes of objects whose description is dependent on one or more types of information. The difference between static generic and dynamic generic is that there is no duplication of code. The generic class exits in software in one and only one instance and it is its behaviour which is different according to the different uses to which it is put.

Figure 2.10 Dynamic generic.

For example, the following declaration (Figure 2.10):
```
Class Obj[U]
     v: U;
     m1(p1: U)
```
corresponds to a generic class whose name is Obj, which depends upon a generic parameter. It is possible in some software to declare objects by:
```
x : Obj[integer];
y: Obj[real];
```
These objects will have different behaviour but the code for m1 will only exist in a single instance.

2.7.2 Use

Generic is directly available in some languages (Ada, C++, Eiffel).

It can be simulated in languages which use a pre-processor.

To evaluate it we make the assumption that it is used with respect to encapsulation (which is preferable if we want to avoid severe problems).

2.7.3 Evaluation according to the criteria

Productivity
Productivity is the same as packages and objects: ten out of ten.

Maintainability
Maintainability is the same as packages and objects: ten out of ten.

Reliability
Reliability is the same as packages and objects: ten out of ten.

Extensibility
Extensibility is the same as packages and objects: ten out of ten.

Usability
Usability is the same as packages and objects: nine out of ten.

Adaptability
This technique affords the possibility of a slightly better adaptability for reuse of an existing component. We can therefore give it a mark of four out of ten.

2.7.4 Evaluation

The result is a mark of fifty-three out of sixty for generics.

A beginning of a solution to adaptability is presented.

These good results take account of the fact that if we assume that the principles of encapsulation are respected. If this is not the case performance of this technique is comparable to that of libraries.

2.8 Object Orientation

2.8.1. Description

The basic principle of object orientation is the use of objects and the ability to use three techniques called inheritance, polymorphism and dynamic binding.

animal
head
body
paws
eat
walk

Figure 2.11 An object.

Inheritance allows the definition without code duplication of a new class of object on the basis of the definition of one or more other classes. For example (Figure 2.11) if we have defined the animal class by:

```
class animal
     attribute head
     attribute body
     attribute paws
     method eat (food)
     method walk()
```

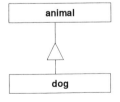   

Figure 2.12 Inheritance

We can define a class dog by (Figure 2.12):

```
class dog
        inherits from animal
```

Without needing to write anything else, dog has a head, a body and paws, and it knows how to eat and how to move.

If inheritance were only to do this, its use would be severely limited. We can, in one class which inherits from another, add attributes and methods. We call this specialisation of a class.

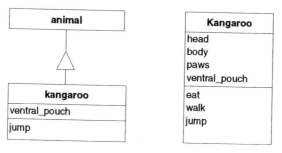

Figure 2.13 Specialisation.

For example (Figure 2.13):

```
class kangaroo
```

inherits from animal:

```
attribute ventral_pouch
attribute jump()
```

This description signifies that a kangaroo is an animal and, therefore, has a head, a body and paws, it knows how to eat its food and how to move, but, furthermore, it has a ventral pouch and it knows how to jump.

We say that there is multiple inheritance if a class inherits from several other classes.

Another interesting possibility for object orientation is that of allowing the redefinition of methods. For example, if in the animal class, the content of the move method were:

```
move ()
```

put one paw down in front of the others; for a kangaroo we would redefine its contents by:

```
move ()
jump;
```

An animal will put its paws one in front of the other to move while a kangaroo will jump.

A great advantage of object orientation is that between the classes kangaroo and animal there is no duplication of method code. Kangaroo only contains the description of jumping, the new description for movement and the other methods references those for animals.

Polymorphism is a technique which completes inheritance. Its principle is to allow the use, in the place of an instance of one class, of the data of a subclass. This is logical because by definition of inheritance everything which is accessible in one class is equally accessible in its subclasses.

For example, if the variable `an_animal` references an animal, it is possible to make it reference kangaroo:

```
an_animal: reference to animal;
a_kangaroo: reference to kangaroo;
an_animal := a_kangaroo;
```

By the principle of dynamic binding, every object always executes the methods which correspond to its true type. If we had the following description:

```
an_animal: reference to animal;
```

and if `an_animal` was really associated with an animal and requiring that `an_animal` move, you would use the move method in the animal class, and therefore the animal puts its paws one in front of the other. If we change `an_animal` to reference `kangaroo`:

```
an_animal := kangaroo;
```

by requiring `an_animal` to move, we would use the move method from class kangaroo and therefore the animal would jump. We do not have to modify the existing code to take account of the particularities of the new objects which it will manipulate. This is fundamental in simplifying the development of software.

2.8.2 Use

Using this technique requires a language which is object-oriented. It is another question of compiling or drawing up the lists of existing languages and making a choice. Therefore, we crave the pardon of those who designed CLOS, objective C, Java and other languages. We are going to describe three languages amongst those which are the best known: Smalltalk, Eiffel and C++.

Smalltalk (Goldberg '83) is an interpreted language. Everything is an object in Smalltalk. When we ask an object to execute a method, it searches among the methods of its class, then among the methods of its ancestor classes to see if there is one with the required name. If this is the case, it executes this—otherwise an error is signalled. This language is not typed. It imposes respect for the encapsulation principle (attributes are not accessible to other classes). The redefinition of methods is very flexible since the methods are characterised uniquely by their names. Smalltalk only offers simple inheritance.

Eiffel (Meyer '92) is a compiled language. A program written in Eiffel is formed from a set of classes and only from a set of classes. In order to execute a method in an object, tables are used which allow indirection to be used in finding the address of the correct method. This language is typed. It requires that encapsulation be respected (attributes are read accessible to other classes which are not write accessible). The redefinition of methods can be made on condition that certain consistency rules at the interface level are respected. Eiffel allows multiple inheritance.

C++ (Stroustrup '92) is a hybrid language. It is C to which has been added object-oriented constructs (therefore, correcting certain faults and making it more strongly typed). A C++ program is, in general, composed of a set of classes and a functional part which does not involve classes. C++ uses techniques similar to Eiffel, although a little more obscure in its rules for determining which methods are actually to be activated. It is strongly typed. It does not impose the principle of respect for encapsulation. Redefinition of methods are possible on the condition that the interface does not change. It allows multiple inheritance.

2.8.3 Evaluation According to the Criteria

Productivity

Productivity is the same as as given by objects and gets a mark of ten out of ten if encapsulation is respected or five out of ten otherwise.

Maintainability

Maintainability is that of objects and receives therefore ten out of ten if encapsulation is respected and eight out of ten otherwise.

Reliability

Reliability is that of objects and therefore receives ten out of ten if encapsulation is respected and seven out of ten otherwise.

Extensibility

Extensibility is the same as for objects and receives ten out of ten if encapsulation is respected and eight out of ten otherwise.

Usability

As for object languages, usability is nine out of ten if encapsulation is respected and five out of ten otherwise.

Using Eiffel, name conflicts between classes are resolved by a particular directive. So, according to this criterion this language receives ten out of ten.

Adaptability

Adaptability is much better supported by object-oriented languages with respect to other techniques. This adaptability differs according to the language being used.

If the alteration we want to make is a change to the contents of a method but which does not change its interface, the change is possible in all the object-oriented languages. It is enough to create a subclass of the class that we want to reuse and redefine the method which we find unsuitable.

If the alteration consists of changing a method and its interface yet, still keeping things consistent, only Smalltalk and Eiffel can do this. For example, if the class animal has a method reproduces declared as:

```
method reproduces (): animal;
```

This method has a return type animal. What we want is, that in the class kangaroo, reproduction of kangaroo gives a kangaroo and not simply an animal. This is possible in Smalltalk and Eiffel, but not possible C++ (if we do this, it corresponds to overloading, and from the point of view of sub-classes, it is not a redefinition of the reproduces method in the ancestor class).

If adaptation consists of reusing several classes at the same time, Eiffel allows this in every case: it is enough to inherit from all of the classes. C++ allows this in certain cases: it is necessary to inherit from all of the classes but this is only permitted if they are not common ancestors in which some methods are redefined in different ways. Smalltalk doesn't allow this (the language only allows simple inheritance).

If we give a mark out of five for the ability to change the content of a method, we award three for the ability to change the interface of method, and two for the ability to inherit from several objects, Eiffel receives ten out of ten for adaptability, Smalltalk eight out of ten, and C++ seven out of ten.

2.8.4 Evaluation

The global mark is:

- Sixty out of sixty for a language of the Eiffel type,
- Fifty-seven out of sixty for a language of the Smalltalk kind;
- Fifty-six out of sixty for a language similar to C++ if we use objects and we respect encapsulation, and forty out of sixty for C++ if we use objects but we don't respect encapsulation.

Let us hope that the proponents of C++ and Smalltalk are not too offended. These marks compare the language with respect to a criterion defined for successful reuse. If we want to make a complete comparison between the languages, we must certainly take into account other factors such as:

- Readability;
- Ease of learning;
- Number of users, number of existing compilers;
- Libraries and tools available;
- Stability;
- Etc.

It is not part of the objective of this book to make this kind of comparison.

Object-oriented languages therefore hold promise for us. They allow the satisfaction of all the criteria which afford suitable opportunities for reuse.

There is no miracle: if we do not use the object-oriented techniques, we do not have the advantages even by using an object-based language.

2.9 Conclusion

The following table recapitulates all of our results:

	Prod	Main	Rel	Ext	Use	Adap	Total
Copy	3	0	2	0	0	10	15
Preproc	5	5	2	5	0	3	20
Lib (minus glovars)	10	10	10	10	7	2	49
Lib (glovars)	5	8	7	8	5	2	35
Sim. pkgs	10	10	10	10	7	3	50
Ada pkgs	10	10	10	10	9	3	52
Obj+encaps	10	10	10	10	9	3	52
Obj-encaps	5	8	7	8	5	3	36
Generics	10	10	10	10	9	4	53
C++ +encaps	10	10	10	10	9	7	56
C++ -encaps	5	8	7	8	5	7	40
Eiffel	10	10	10	10	10	10	60
Smalltalk	10	10	10	10	9	8	57

If we establish a classification for techniques the result is the following -

- Object-oriented techniques:
  - Eiffel sixty points;
  - Smalltalk: fifty-seven points;
  - C++ with use of objects and respect for encapsulation fifty-six points;
- Packages and objects:
  - with generic objects and package: fifty-three points;
  - packages with visibility rules and objects which respect encapsulation: 52 points;
  - packages without visibility rules: 50 points;
- Libraries;
  - Libraries not using global variables: 49 points;
  - + with objects, but not respecting encapsulation: 40 points;
  - Objects not respecting encapsulation: 36 points;
  - Libraries using global variables: 35 points;

- Copying:
  - Using a pre-processor: 20 points;
  - Manual: 15 points.

This is no fairy story: object orientation allows us to obtain the best results for reuse. Its great power, with respect to other techniques, is that it allows the alteration of components for new requirements thanks to inheritance and to method redefinition. The differences between languages relate to their ability to make these opportunities for adaptation more difficult.

It can also be noted that using an object-oriented language is not enough on its own; if the concepts of object orientation are not respected (concepts such as encapsulation), the results are less good.

Those approaches using objects or packages produce good results. These can be used with almost any programming language on condition that a certain implementation discipline is respected.

The limits of libraries or closely related techniques can be seen. It can be noted, in particular, that a use that does not respect the elementary rules of C++ gives the same results as the use of any other structured language.

Copying is certainly the worst of the techniques available for reuse. It should be avoided at all costs.

2.10 Back to the Myths

Some of the myths in the introductory chapter can now be re-examined. Certainly , hopes for reuse are technically feasible.

The statement:

REUSE = OBJECT ORIENTATION

is particularly justified. To obtain good results from reuse, it is necessary, at least, to have objects or packages. The fact that we have object orientation is a plus which will allow us to go even further.

The second statement:

OBJECT ORIENTATION = C++

is, on the other hand, far from being reality. Among the object-oriented languages, the possibilities of Eiffel and Smalltalk are better than those of C++. Moreover, if for C++, we do not take certain precautions in use, we will not be engaging in object orientation, but in classical programming (something which is not possible with Smalltalk or Eiffel).

It is therefore useless to take your C sources and to compile them with a C++ compiler to make them reusable: this will not work. You should, rather, try to design your software in terms of objects, and, if you can, using object-oriented techniques. The results are better.

2.11 Chapter Summary

In this chapter, we have examined the techniques which allow reuse:

- Copying;
- Pre-processing;
- Libraries;
- Packages;
- Objects;
- Generics;
- Object orientation.

Some criteria have allowed us to compare the different techniques.

The result of this comparison is that object-oriented techniques give the best results. They are closely followed by the use of packages and objects.

The worst results are obtained from copying which is, however, the most commonly used technique.

Nothing prevents us, in the same piece of software, from mixing the different techniques that we have examined. For example, in C++, we can very often combine pre-processing, libraries, objects, generics and object orientation.

Chapter Three

Development Cycles

Having reuse techniques is good. But being good is not enough if we do not know when and how to use them.

In this chapter, we are going to determine how the development cycles for software allow the implementation of component reuse.

We are not going to make a systematic study of all the cycles which exist. The reader who wants to know more about the different development cycles can consult [Boehm 88].

3.1 The V Cycle

The best known software development cycle is the V cycle (which is also often called the cascade model). It is presented in [Royce 70]. It is, in general, described by the schema shown in Figure 3.1.

The way in which the cycle operates is as follows. To develop some code, we employ a series of phases which are the specification (called in French "analysis"), general design, detailed design, coding, unit tests, integration and validation. The passage from one phase to another is determined by a set of rules.

3.1.1 Specification phase (or analysis phase)

The goal of the specification phase is the identification of what the software must do.

- What information does it manipulate?
- What services does it provide?
- What are its interfaces?
- Which constraints must it respect (memory size, performance, etc.)

The specification phase is the one in which the problem to be solved is described.

At the start of this phase, a requirements document is received. This document outlines the needs that the constructed software must.satisfy.

There exist different methods and techniques for producing specifications. We will describe the main ones in a subsequent chapter.

In the specification phase, technical problems connected to the software to be produced must not be considered. The focus should be the description of the be handled should be the focus.

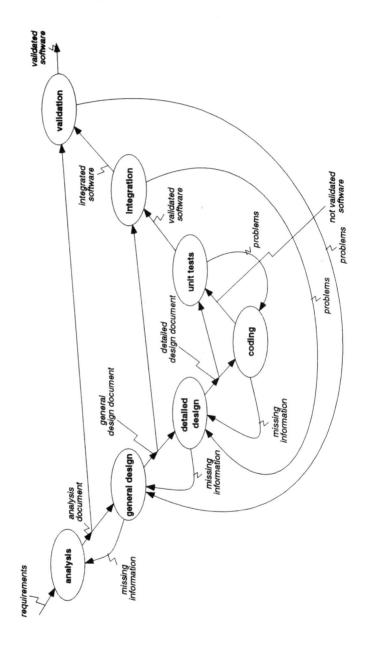

Figure 3.1 The V Cycle

The result of the specification phase is generally composed of (Figure 3.2):

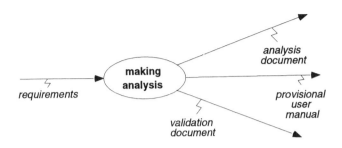

Figure 3.2 Specification phase.

- A specification document which describes (in a formal or informal fashion) the information manipulated, the expected services, the user interfaces, constraints, desired performance, the volume of information to be handled, external interfaces;
- A provisional user manual which outlines in broad terms who will use the software to be constructed;
- A validation document which consists of lists of tests to be performed when the software is finished; these tests check that the software conforms to what was specified.

3.1.2 General design phase

The goal of the general design phase is to identify the organisation of the software so that it is able to satisfy the specification produced in the previous phase.

The specification phase is that in which the problem is analysed, while the general design phase is the phase in which the solution is analysed. The different elements of the problem are re-examined and which information-processing solutions to use to solve the problem are sought.

As inputs to this phase, we have:

- The specification document;
- The provisional user manual.

The software architecture is invented, then its different components are detailed. For each of these, the following is given in detail:

- The information that it receives (what sorts of information? what is their origin?);
- The processing it performs;
- The results it produces (result types and the components which receive them);
- The constraints it must respect (size, performance, etc.).

As for the specification, there exist different techniques and methods for general design which we will talk about in a later chapter.

It can happen during the general design phase that some aspects of the problem being attacked are insufficiently precise. In this case, it is necessary to return to the specification phase in order to make matters as precise as possible.

The result of the general design phase is usually composed of (Figure 3.3):

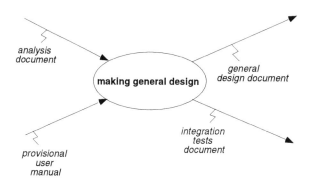

Figure 3.3 General design phase.

- A general design document which describes (either in a formal language or not) the architecture of the software to be constructed and its different components, detailing the connections with the associated information derived during the analysis phase;
- A document describing integration tests which identify the tests that must be performed on each component of the software to verify that they conform to what has been defined.

In the case of a very large project, some software element descriptions can be very complex. The project, therefore, divides into several sub-projects, and the general design elements become the requirements for the sub-projects. They then produce architectural choices and a general design.

3.1.3 Detailed design phase

The goal of the detailed design phase is to prepare for the software's coding phase.

At the start of this phase, the general design document is received; it describes, for each component, what it takes as input, the processing it must perform, the results that it must provide and the constraints it must respect.

The work in this phase consists of defining all the data structures and determining the algorithms which will allow the coding of the different components of the software to be constructed.

It can happen that some information is lacking and this prevents the determination of how to code one of the software components. In this case, it is necessary to return to the general design phase in order to provide the necessary details.

The results of the detailed design phase are generally formed of (Figure 3.4):

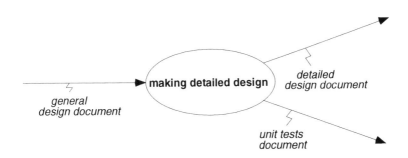

Figure 3.4 Detailed design phase.

- A detailed design document which describes the different choices which were made for coding the components and which describes the connections with the general design document;
- A document describing the unit tests which describes how to verify that all the code correctly implements the constituent functions.

3.1.4 Coding phase

The goal of the coding phase is to code the set of components in the software; this must be code so that it conforms to the decisions taken in the detailed design phase.

At the start of this phase, the detailed design document is received. This document contains indications about how the coding of each of the components it identifies should be done.

The work of this phase consists of coding the software.

It can happen that some information that helps in the coding of one of the components can be missing. In this case, it is necessary to return to the detailed design phase in order to make things more precise.

The results of the coding phase are generally composed of (Figure 3.5):

- One or more programs which represent the software components;

- A programming document which explains how the code is constructed.

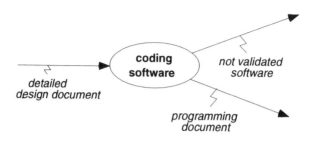

Figure 3.5 Coding phase.

3.1.5 Unit test phase

The aim of the unit test phase is to verify that all the functions in each software component function according to the definitions stated in the detailed design phase.

At the start of this phase, the unit test document and the implemented software are received.

The work of this phase consists of passing each component of the software through the set of tests defined in the unit test document. To do this, it is sometimes necessary to develop test programs.

When errors are detected, there is an error in the coding phase. It is necessary therefore to return the software development phase to this phase as long as errors are detected in the unit test phase.

The result of the unit test phase (Figure 3.6) is a unit test document which has been augmented by new tests identified during the phase and a set of tested software elements.

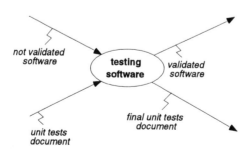

Figure 3.6 Unit test phase.

3.1.6 Integration phase

The goal of the integration phase is to verify that each component of the software conforms to that which was defined in the general design phase.

At the start of this phase, the integration tests document and the software to be integrated are received.

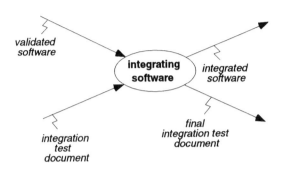

Figure 3.7 Integration phase.

The work in this phase consists of passing each of the components in the software through the set of tests defined in the integration tests document, then putting these elements together. To do this, it is sometimes necessary to develop programs to help perform integration tests.

When errors are found, an error from the detailed design or from the coding phase has been detected. The development process must then return to the phase which produced the error. This is done as long as errors are found in the integration test phase.

The result of this phase (Figure 3.7) is a piece of integrated software and an integration test document which is completed by the inclusion of new tests which have been identified during the phase.

3.1.7 Validation phase

The goal of the validation phase is to verify that the implemented software conforms properly with what was defined in the specification phase.

At the start of this phase, the validation document and the integrated software are received.

The work in this phase consists of passing the software through the set of tests defined in the validation document. When errors are detected, there is an error that derives from the general design, detailed design, or from the coding phase. It is necessary to go back to the phase in which the error occurred as long as errors are found in the validation phase.

The results of this phase are (Figure 3.8):

- A validation document completed by new tests which have been identified during the phase;
- The software ready to be delivered;
- The definitive user documents.

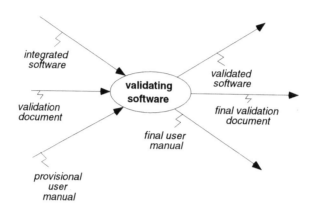

Figure 3.8 Validation phase.

3.1.8 And reuse in all of this?

Yes, in the description of the V cycle, the word 'reuse' does not appear. It can be assumed that new software is constructed each time.

In reality, there is, however, reuse, but it is not formalised:

- There is reuse in the general design phase when an architecture used in another project is employed;
- There is reuse in the detailed design phase when algorithms that have been proven in other projects are employed;
- There is reuse in the coding phase when sub-program libraries are used.

It is up to each person to know whether there is reuse and to know how to do it. Nothing is provided by this cycle to help those who want to engage in reuse.

3.2 Spiral Cycle

One of the principle criticisms made of the V cycle is that it is necessary to wait until the end of the development before one can have any software. There are no intermediate phases which allow use is to have an idea of what the software will be when the project is finished.

In reality, it is rare that software development proceeds in this fashion. Prototypes are sometimes developed during the specification phase in order to validate certain ideas. The development of the software is undertaken in a piecemeal fashion. Some parts are finished while other parts are still being designed.

To take this reality into account, B. Boehm proposed a spiral cycle to describe the development cycle for software [Boehm 88].

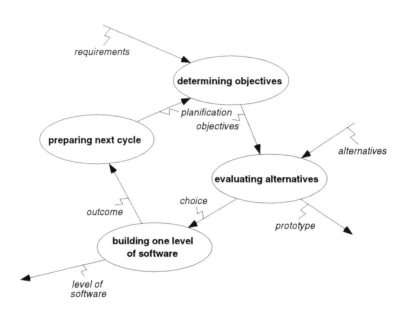

Figure 3.9 Phases of the spiral cycle.

The principle of the spiral development process is to consider that the implementation of a piece of software is composed of a succession of cycles in four phases (see Figure 3.9):

- Determination of the objectives of the cycle (performance, functionality, for example), alternatives (design, reuse or purchase, for example) and constraints (costs, delays, for example);
- Evaluation of the different alternatives, taking the risks into account;

- Development of the software or of a prototype according to the choice made in previous phases and the establishment of evaluation criteria;
- Preparation for the next cycle.

In an early cycle, for example, a prototype can be constructed to demonstrate the problems to be solved and to evaluate global risks.

A second cycle sees the creation of specifications (using a second prototype).

A third cycle supports design by prototyping some chosen solutions.

A fourth cycle sees the coding of the final software.

The number of cycles through which development runs depends on the application under consideration.

This type of development cycle is the basis for what is called incremental development. In this method, the prototype is gradually transformed into the final application.

The phases of the development take place according to that for the V cycle: detailed design, coding, unit tests, integration and validation.

The cycle is even closer to reality because it takes into consideration the fact that some software development tasks can be worked on without having started others. The construction of successive prototypes allows implementation to be followed better and to be controlled more easily.

In the description of the spiral, there is little reference to reuse. This word appears in the test describing the cycle in more detail. We can see that, among the alternatives to be evaluated at the start of a cycle, we can have: design, reuse or purchase.

The assumption is thus made that the decision to reuse is made before starting a new step in the implementation. This does not conform to the kind of reuse which is usually practised. We saw for the V cycle that architectures can be reused during the design phase and code can be reused in the coding phase. It is not possible to determine before the completion of the specification whether code is going to be reused during the coding phase. This can only be decided after the detailed design phase has been completed. Reuse, as far as this cycle is concerned, is macro reuse. The question that is being asked is: does the kind of reuse that I want to make already exist within this cycle?

Nothing is said about how to answer this question, nor about the way in which possible candidates for reuse are constructed or stored.

We will look at another cycle in order really to take the aspects of reuse into account.

3.3 The X Cycle

The X cycle was proposed by Ralph Hodgson [Hodgson 91]. It allows the introduction of reuse in the V development cycle.

What is proposed here is an adapted version of this cycle aimed at introducing the considerations required for the implementation of a reuse policy.

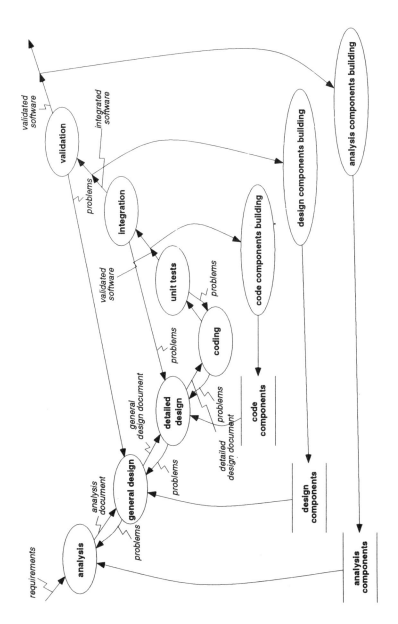

Figure 3.10 The X Cycle.

The X cycle is represented by the scheme in Figure 3.10.

The upper phases of the cycle have, for initial development, the same significance they had in the V cycle.

A first big difference between this and the X cycle is that the end of the validation phase does not signify the end of the work on the software that has just been constructed. There remain two phases to be effected:

- The acquisition phase, and
- The archiving phase.

The acquisition phase is that during which those parts of the project which are to be reused are identified.

The archiving phase is that during which the components identified during the acquisition phase are stored so that they can later be retrieved.

In order to take reuse into account, the specification, general and detailed design phases of the cycle are modified.

The upper part of the X cycle represents everything that is specific to a particular development. The lower part represents everything connected with reuse.

3.3.1 Acquisition phase

This phase is divided into three parts:

- Acquisition of analysis components;
- Acquisition of design components;
- Acquisition of code components.

Acquisition of analysis components

The acquisition of analysis components consists of returning to the specification documents to try to extract from them information which appears to be of a general nature. In practise, the implemented software covers one or more domains of expertise (already acquired or yet to be acquired) in the company. During specification, it has been necessary to identify information and processing which are perhaps standard for the problem being studied. It is necessary to identify the parts of the specifications which cover this information and these processes. A document (or several) can be obtained from the specification which is potentially reusable in the particular domain. Below, this will be called a component domain, a specification component.

Acquisition of design components

The acquisition of design components is identical to the acquisition of analysis components. The difference comes from the fact that it is applied to the general design components. To handle the problems in the domain of the software to be constructed, an architecture and a division of the software into components has been imagined. Some of these components are general. They can possibly be reused in other software; it is necessary to isolate their designs. These components are called service components, services, or design components.

Acquisition of code components

The acquisition of code components is identical to the previous acquisitions, but it addresses detailed implementations. The goal is to identify among the code that which has been used to code the software's services, and those which are of a general character and which could be reused in other developments either for coding the same service or for coding others.

Results of the acquisition phase

At the end of the acquisition phase (and note that this is not always possible), one or more analysis components have been identified, as have one or more design components, as have one or more code components. It is then necessary to store them in order to be able to reuse them later (after possibly modifying them to make them more general).

3.3.2 Archiving phase

The archiving phase is formed of three parts:

- Archiving of analysis components;
- Archiving of design components;
- Archiving of code components.

Archiving of analysis components

Archiving of analysis components consists of storing them in a library of domains in order to allow their later retrieval and to use them on a new problem.

The techniques to support searches at a later date are covered in another chapter.

So that these components are subsequently usable, it is necessary to store them together with a collection of information which must allow the determination during new developments of whether they are appropriate to these later implementations. Here is an example of the associated information which characterises an analysis component:

- The requirements document which served as the basis for the specification;
- The specification documents.

To obtain the best results, other information can be added such as the user manuals for the corresponding application.

So that the analysis components can be reused in the most efficient manner, it is necessary to store:

- The corresponding validation document;

- The associated design;
- The possible services that might be associated.

Archiving of design components

The archiving of design components consists of storing general designs in a library of services so as to permit their later retrieval and use in subsequent projects.

To judge the relevance of a service to a new general design, a set of information is needed:

- The specification documents which served as the basis of the design;
- The general design documents.

So that the design component can be reused in the best way, it is also necessary to store:

- The description of the architectures in which the component has been used;
- The corresponding integration test document;
- The associated detailed designs;
- Possibly, the associated code components.

Archiving of code components

The archiving of code components consists of storing in a component library detailed designs and code elements in order to retrieve them later so that they can be used in the coding of a new general design.

To know how to evaluate the relevance of a code component for a new implementation, a set of information is needed:

- The design documents which served as the basis for the coding;
- The detailed design documents;
- Commented code.

To be able to maintain the code component, it is necessary to store the corresponding unit tests document.

3.3.3 Adaptation of the specification, general and detailed design phases

The other major difference with the V cycle is the taking into account of reuse in the specification, general and detailed design and coding phases.

Specification phase

In the specification phase, having set the problem, it is advisable to consult domain libraries in order to find out whether a specification dealing with the same kind of problem has already been effected. If there is one, those parts appropriate to the new problem will be reused after possible modification. The techniques for reuse and modification are considered in a later chapter.

During the specification, it is also advisable regularly to consult the domain libraries to determine whether some new aspects which have been identified as a problem, are already known.

General design phase

If a part of the specification has reused analysis components, it is perhaps possible also to reuse the associated design components. This must be verified.

As the general design progresses, service libraries should be consulted in order to determine whether certain components of the software which are being designed are already known and reusable. This also permits the discovery of architectures which can be reused.

Coding phase

For reused services, it is possible, sometimes, also to reuse, during coding, associated code components.

During detailed design, code libraries should be consulted in order to find possible code components which can be reused in the new context.

3.3.4 Incremental development

The X cycle can also be used in the phases of the spiral development cycle. Reuse of an application does not necessarily start with specification and end with the storage of components. It is quite common to consider that development is often in the form of several nested X cycles. Some cycles can have as their objective the construction of code components. Then, other cycles serve to construct services. Finally, several cycles serve to construct the application by constructing prototypes that are progressively closer to the final result.

Object-oriented techniques lend themselves particularly well to this approach. The application is designed in the form of a set of communicating services. These services are constructed in different forms:

- A simple form in which communication of their existence is all that is wanted;
- A more developed form in which they perform part of the processing which they will have to perform;
- The complete form which implements the service completely.

Thanks to object-oriented techniques such as inheritance, polymorphism and dynamic binding, and conditional upon using a language that supports these techniques correctly, it is possible incrementally to develop applications by analysing them successively by parts.

3.4 Ingredients for Reuse

The rest of this book depends on what we have said about the X cycle to identify all the problems that need to be considered in order better to lead to a policy of reuse.

Among these problems, in the light of what was presented here, we can mention:

- The identification of components: how does one find in a specification, a design or some code, elements which could be reused at a later date?
- Construction of components: what rules must be followed to guarantee that components are reusable?
- Component certification: how can one guarantee that the components are reliable and that additional difficulties do not arise because of their reuse?
- Component archiving: what should be archived and what techniques must be used so that whatever has been stored can be later retrieved?
- Component search: how does one describe what is to be searched for? How does one know if what is retrieved is appropriate?
- Modification of reused components: how does one modify the components so that they become useful in a new context?
- Component maintenance: how does one correct the errors in components while extending them?
- Organisation: how does one organise in order to reuse?

3.5 Chapter Summary

In this chapter, we have examined the way in which reuse is taken into account in the V and spiral development cycles. These cycles hardly take reuse into account.

The X cycle completes these cycles by introducing specific phases for handling reuse: acquisition and archiving of, and search for components. The examination of these phases has helped in the compilation of a list of themes to consider when engaging in reuse.

Chapter Four

Characterising Reusable Components

From the above, we now know what the techniques are which allow reuse. We have identified, using development cycles, the moment at which to reuse. It is now time to define precisely what a reusable component is.

To do this, we are going to examine different methods and notations used in analysis, design and coding and determine, for each of them, which is able to characterise reusable elements.

So as not to lose the reader in different, but equivalent, notation, only the notation used by the OMT method [Rumbaugh 91] will be used for the examples in this chapter (where possible) and in the following ones (this notation is the basis of that used in UML).

4.1 The Different Types of Reusable Components

A reusable component is an entity which can be used, possibly with modifications, in a new software development.

There are reusable components for:

- Specification;
- Design;
- Code.

From the moment when a piece of software is implemented by retrieving parts of other software, it is highly probably that a part of the documentation of the reused software will be appropriate to the new software. The user documentation thus forms a part of the information associated with a reusable component. In a general fashion, all information which has a meaning for the development process must be kept.

In this chapter, we are going to determine which information characterises reusable components. This will allow us, in what follows, to know how to identify reusable components, how to construct them and how to adapt them to new uses.

4.2 Characterisation of Specification Components

We have seen in the previous chapter the description of the specification phase for software. The result of this phase is the production of a document called the specification document. This document describes:

- The information manipulated by the software to be constructed;
- The services provided by the software;
- The user and environment interfaces (other software items, systems, media).

If it is complete, the specification document also describes the constraints connected with the software to be constructed (maximum memory size, response time, etc.)

The specification document is generally accompanied by a user manual which shows in outline the way in which the software will be used (user interface) and a validation schedule which indicates how to validate the software after implementation in order to determine that it conforms to its specification.

There are several techniques for writing a specification document:

- Some structure the document in the form of informal text without using any particular method;
- Some use a method which helps them to organise an informal specification text;
- Others use a method which is associated with a notation which allows them to formalise part of the specification.

There are numerous methods to formalise specifications:

- Methods which emphasise data, such as entity-relation;
- Methods which emphasise functions, such as Structured Analysis;
- Methods which deal with dynamics, such as Statechart;
- Object-based methods;
- Object-oriented methods;
- Methods which combine several methods.

4.2.1 Methods emphasising data

These methods suggest describing problem-related information in such a way that they can be handled by entity-relation diagrams. In these diagrams, we represent the different information for what is being handled and the relationships which exist between this information.

For example, the diagram in Figure 4.1 can be read thus: a person lives in a house and owns a dog. They can be the owner of zero or more houses. The houses are their property. A house can be inhabited by zero or more people. A person owns zero or more dogs. They are the master of the dogs and the dogs are their companions. A dog has only a single master. A person has a name and a forename. A dog has a name and belongs to a particular breed.

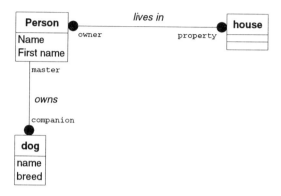

Figure 4.1 Entity-relation schema.

Person, house and dog are entities. Name and breed are attributes (sometimes we also say properties) of the entity person.

The connection between house and person is called a relation. A relation has a name. Each end of the relation plays a role in the relation. A name can be given to roles to clarify the diagram. House plays the role of property and person plays the role of owner in the relation *lives in*. The fact that a relation has, at one end, zero, one or more entities, is indicated by a symbol on the ends of the relation. We call this the cardinality of the role. In the case of OMT methods, for example, there exist pre-defined symbols for cardinality such as that shown in Figure 4.2.

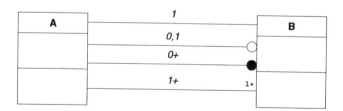

Figure 4.2 Cardinalities.

In the diagram in Figure 4.1, the OMT method's notation is used [Rumbaugh 91]. Different notations exist for drawing entity-relation diagrams. The most famous are those described by [Chen 76] and [Martin 89]. The principal differences between these entity-relation notations are derived from the different ways of notating the names of relations (in many notations, it is indicated in an ellipse in the middle of the relation), from the fact there are or are not names for roles, and from the way in which cardinalities are indicated. With OMT, the cardinalities of an entity with which something is in relation are indicated beside that entity. With other notations, they are indicated by the side of the source entity. It is therefore necessary to pay close attention when we read an entity-relation model with an unfamiliar notation.

In an entity-relation model, a reusable component is formed of a set of entities and relations which have the character of exhaustiveness and generality which makes them reusable in other contexts. Generality is given away by the fact that only entities and relations which are indispensable are present.

An entity -relation component can reference entities in other entity-relation components.

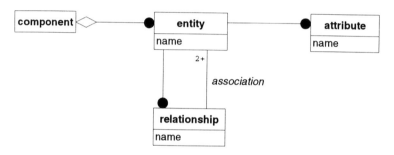

Figure 4.3 Characterisation of entity-relation components.

Using this kind of method, a component which is reusable or not is composed of a set of information and relations which associate them. The names associated with the information, the names of the relations and the roles characterise the component. Figure 4.3 shows in the form of an entity-relation diagram that which characterises this type of component (the losange indicates a relation of composition).

4.2.2 Object diagrams

The methods underpinning object diagrams take up again the principle of entity relation diagrams but allow the use of objects as entities. An object is an entity composed of attributes and methods (also called operations). The inheritance notation is available. It allows us to indicate that one object is derived from one other while keeping all of its characteristics (attributes, methods and relations).

Entity-relation diagrams (Figure 4.1) can be transformed into object diagrams as indicated in Figure 4.4.

Some extra detail is given on the entity *person*. It can walk, work, sleep and eat. Its house is a particular kind of habitat structure (inheritance between house and dwelling). It lives at a certain address. The relation *lives_in* is given between person and dwelling and makes it more general. *House* inherits from *habitation,* and in this way, it inherits from the relation with *person.* The relation *possesses* which existed between *person* and *dog* is generalised by a relation *possesses* between *person* and *animal.* *Dog* is a type of *animal.*

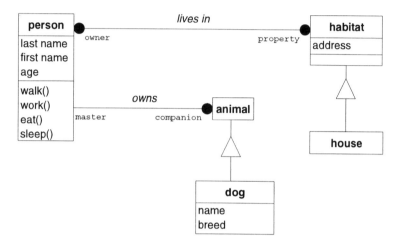

Figure 4.4 Object diagram.

The diagram in Figure 4.4 uses OMT method notation (and the UML notation). The triangle represents inheritance.

In an object model a reusable component is formed of a set of objects and relations which have the characteristics of exhaustiveness and generality in the same way that we saw in the case of entity-relation components.

A reusable component of this type can reference other types of components. Objects of such a component can inherit from objects in another component.

Reusing a component of this type is to relate objects of a new application with objects of a component and/or create sub-classes of the objects in the component.

With this type of method, a component is characterised by a set of objects and a set of relations between objects. Among the possible relations, there is the inheritance relation. An object is characterised by a set of attributes (names and possibly types) and methods (names, possibly parameters and return value types) (Figure 4.5).

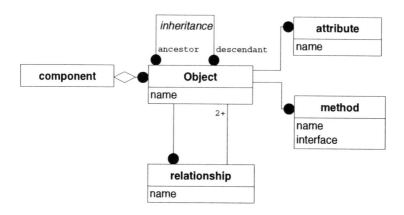

Figure 4.5 Characterisation of an object diagram component.

4.2.3 Methods emphasising functions

Function-based methods allow the description of the operation of software by an analysis in terms of data flow diagrams (we also use the term functional diagrams). In these diagrams, we represent the different functions of the software being analysed by indicating for each one of them the information which is received, and the information which is produced. In some methods a function can be refined by its sub-functions.

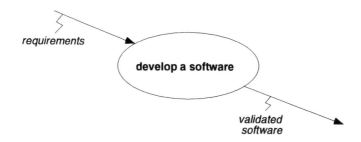

Figure 4.6 Functional diagram.

For example the development of a piece of software can be described by a functional diagram as shown in Figure 4.6.

The function implementing some software takes as an input (as a parameter) a set of requirements and produces validated software. We can decompose this function with the functions indicated in Figure 4.7.

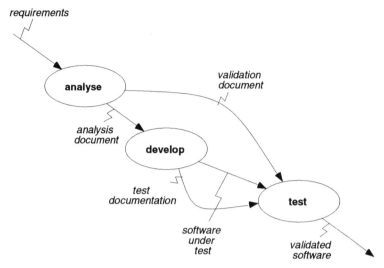

Figure 4.7 Decomposition of a function.

The data produced by a function has three possible destinations (cf. Figure 4.8):

- Another function;
- The space where data is stored (which we call a store);
- The function's environment.

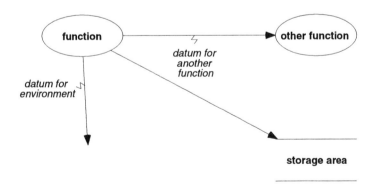

Figure 4.8 Data destinations.

The data emitted into the environment of the function corresponds to information which is produced by the software (which is accessible outside the software as a result).

Information transmitted to a function can have, in the same way, three different origins; another function, a storage space for data, or the environment.

The principle methods of functional analysis are SA [DeMarco 78], [Yourdon 89] and SADT [Marca 88]. The notation used in this chapter is that of SA as used in OMT.

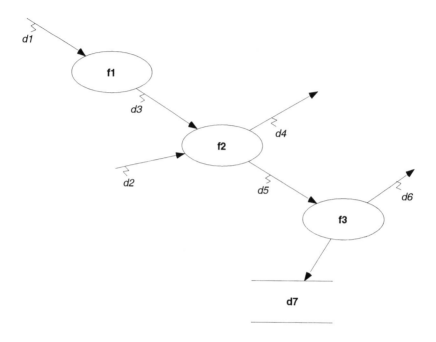

Figure 4.9 Content of a future component.

In a data flow analysis, a reusable component is formed instead of functions which consume and produce data. As far as the notation which we are using allows the description of hierarchies of functions, it is possible to synthesise such a component by a single function whose decomposition is composed of component functions. The input data to these functions are data which come from the environment and which are input to the functions in the component. The data output from this function are the data which are produced by the component functions and are sent to the environment. In the case of which some functions of the components have stores as their source and destination, this can be indicated at the level of the component; they represent persistent data manipulated by the component.

By way of illustration, the component in Figure 4.9 can be synthesised by the function (Figure 4.10).

A data flow component can use another data flow component. In order to do so, it is enough that in its decomposition there is a function representing another component.

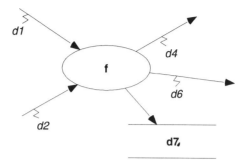

Figure 4.10 Synthesised content.

For the component to be reusable, it is necessary for its description to have a general character. This indicates that the sub-functions and their connections must be general.

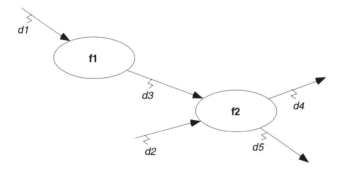

Figure 4.11 Non-specific content of a component.

In the example in Figure 4.9, if function *f3* is too specific, it is necessary perhaps to consider that component *f* is constituted only of the functions *f1* and *f2* as in the diagram in Figure 4.11, and is therefore synthesised as indicated in Figure 4.12.

Our model in Figure 4.9 represents then the use of component which we can simplify as indicated in Figure 4.13.

To reuse a functional component, we have to provide it with data which it waits for as inputs and to recover the data that it produces (it is certainly necessary that the processing that it performs is appropriate).

With this type of method a component is characterised by a set of functions and a set of information consumed or produced by these functions (Figure 4.14). A function can be refined into several functions.

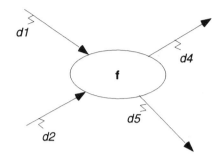

Figure 4.12 Non-specific synthesis.

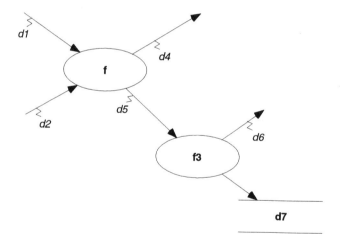

Figure 4.13 Reuse of a functional component.

4.2.4 Methods emphasising dynamics

Methods which emphasise dynamics suggest modelling the software to be analysed in the form of a set of automata. An automaton describes one or more states of the software. A state corresponds to characteristic values of a set of data for the software. In a given state, the software can receive information (an event), this leads to the execution of a set of actions and the passage to another state (where other events can be received).

A classical example of the analysis by automaton is that of the elevator (see Figure 4.15). This has three states, stopped, ascending and descending. When a call arrives and the elevator is at rest, if the floor demanded is higher than the current floor, the elevator passes to the state

ascending and starts the motor working. We say there is a transition
between the states halted and ascending. This transition is fired by the call
event. It is conditioned by the fact the requested floor is above this current
floor. The starting of the motor is performed during this transition.

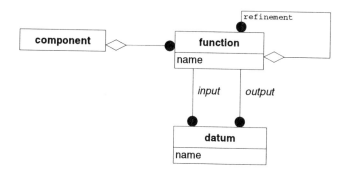

Figure 4.14 Characterisation of a functional component.

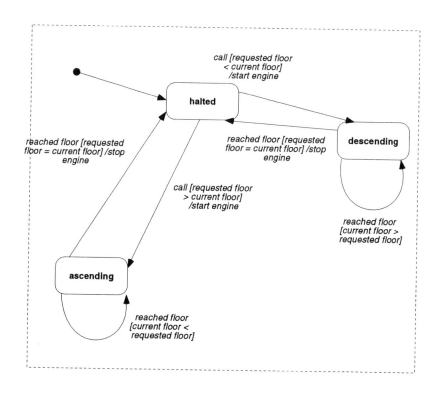

Figure 4.15 Automata

Figure 4.15 uses the OMT/UML notations (which include Harel's Statecharts). States are described by rectangles with rounded corners. A transition between two states is indicated by an arrow which goes from the start state to the final state. The text which accompanies the arrow gives the name of the event which triggers the transition, then, between brackets the possible condition associated with the firing of the transition, then the action to be performed. A black disk denotes the start point of the automaton. The transition which goes from this point indicates the state in which the automaton must be when it is started.

In this diagram we can see the processing of another event which corresponds to the fact that a sensor signals that a floor has been reached and we find the transitions which lead to the stopping of the elevator once the desired floor has been reached. This diagram is not complete. It does not indicate what happens when a call is received while the elevator is in the middle of ascending or descending, when the floor reached is lower than the floor required while the lift is descending, etc. A good analysis by automaton must indicate what is to be done in every case.

The principle method in this character is the Statechart [Harrel 87]. Numerous other notations exist and formalisms which use automata. Amongst all of these we can mention SDL [CCITT 88] and Petri nets [Reisig 89].

In an analysis using automata, the component is constituted of a set of states and a set of transitions. The reusable part of the transitions corresponds to the event which is being treated and the list of actions which are executed. The automaton exits (final state) when particular events occur.

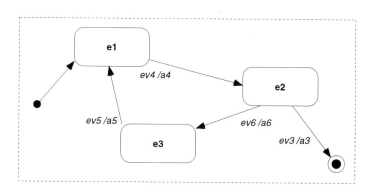

Figure 4.16 Content of an automaton.

Every automaton can be synthesised and informed of a macro state whose decomposition gives the state which is constituted. For example, the automaton in Figure 4.16 can be synthesised as that shown in Figure

4.17 (the ring with the central black disk represents the exit from the automaton). Event *ev3* makes the automaton halt. The automaton accepts events *ev4*, *ev5* and *ev6* which are processed by actions *a4*, *a5* and *a6*.

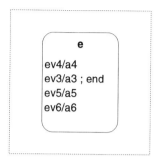

Figure 4.17 Content synthesis.

For this type of component to be reusable, it is necessary to provide a relatively general description of the events which it accepts and the associated actions. In particular, the arrival of an event causes a transition which can cause the execution of a set of actions which also causes a change of state. This change of state corresponds to changes in certain data. If we do not give the decomposition of the automaton, we must not forget (in the actions with the events) to describe those things connected to the state change. In the same way, an event can be accepted only in certain states. It is then necessary to indicate this by an acceptance condition for the event at the level of the macro state resulting from the synthesis.

To reuse an automaton component is, in a new application, to make one or more events leading into the automaton and at its termination, re-enter one of the application's states.

With this kind of method, a component is characterised by a set of events which are accepted under given conditions and a set of actions associated with these events (Figure 4.18).

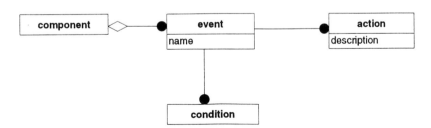

Figure 4.18 Characterisation of an automaton.

4.2.5 Object-oriented methods

These methods appeared at the end of the 1980s. They use the capabilities of the different methods described above in order to analyse a problem.

They offer, therefore, in general object diagrams, data diagrams, and automata. The principle of these methods is to play on the overlap between these different approaches in order to allow us to obtain an analysis which is as complete as possible. The principle diagram for these methods is the object diagram (from which is derived the name which is associated with them: object oriented methods. In what follows we will use also the term composite methods). As we have seen above, information from this diagram is in the form of objects (which therefore have attributes and methods). The behaviour of the objects is refined by automatons. The exchanges of information between the methods are on objects and the actions of the automatons are described by data flow diagrams.

Using an object oriented analysis method, we can complete the automata in Figure 4.15 which represents the behaviour of an elevator using the description of the elevator class as in Figure 4.19.

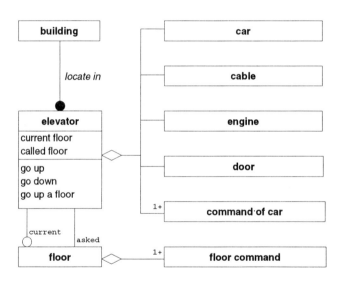

Figure 4.19 Object diagram for the lift.

The operation go to a floor of the elevator can be described as a function diagram which can start in the way indicated in Figure 4.20.

Figure 4.20 Detail from an operation.

This function has as its perimeters the elevator and the requested floor and produces a diagnostic as a result.

The principle methods of this type are: OMT [Rumbaugh 91] Shlaer and Mellor [Shlaer 88] [Shlaer 91], Coad and Yourdon [Coad 90], Fusion [Coleman 94], Relation-Class [Desfray 92] and UML.

With this type of method, a component is characterised by:

- The characteristics of the object model;
- The characteristics of the dataflow model;
- The characteristics of automata;
- The connections between these different kinds of information.

In fact, to obtain a component which is simplest to use, you would be advised to concentrate on just one of the diagrams which will be the one that is really going to be used. The other diagrams will then provide the additional information that helps to describe the components better.

If we consider (as is often the case) that the principle diagram is the object diagram, the functional diagrams serve to detail the exchanges of information between the methods of the objects and the automaton diagrams will serve to show the internal functioning of the objects. The different stages are characterised by sets of values of the attributes and the relations of the objects.

Nothing prevents us, *a priori*, from having a functional diagram as a principle diagram. In this case, object diagrams serve to detail the data exchanged by function.

In the same way a component can be constituted of an automaton. The object diagrams allow the description of the data manipulated by the automaton and the functional diagrams show the exchanges of data between the functions used in these transitions.

4.2.6 Characterisation common to the analysis components

There exist a number of tools which allow us to treat the analysis using these different methods. In this case, a specification document is accompanied by a model describing, using the chosen method, certain aspects of the problem under consideration.

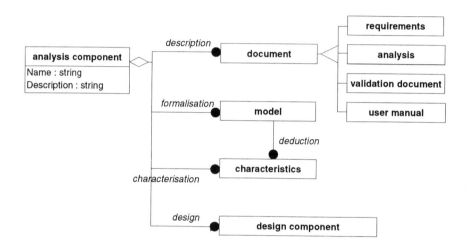

Figure 4.21 Characterisation of a specification component.

To characterise a component of a specification we have, in general, the following information (Figure 4.21):

- A specification document (or the reference to extracts of these specification documents);
- The corresponding model if the specification is formalised using a particular notation;
- The characteristics of the specification if it is realised with a method of a type described above (these characteristics can be deduced from the model);
- The associated user manual;
- The corresponding test schedule description.

To complete this information, we can add:

- A short description of the component (a few lines);
- A short description of the information manipulated in the specification;
- A short description of the functions treated by the specifications;

- The requirements document which led to the creation of the specification;
- The list of design components which have led to the design of the software corresponding to the specification (in order also to be able to reuse the associated design if it is decided to reuse the specification).

You will see in a subsequent chapter how to choose information in order really to allow the reuse of components.

4.3 Characterisation of Design Components

The result of the design phase for software is the production of a document which is called the design document. This document describes:

- The architecture of the software which is to be implemented;
- The different elements which will compose the software.

The design document is generally accompanied by a suite of integration tests which indicate how to verify that the different parts of the software conform to what has been described.

As with specification, there are several techniques used when writing a design document:

- Compiling the document in the form of informal text without using any particular method;
- Using a method which helps in organising the informal text describing the design;
- Using a method with an associated notation which allows the formalisation of part of the design.

Design methods allow the identification of the different elements which will compose the software to be created. They formalise the description of each of these elements and describe the way in which they are associated. The majority of the analysis methods can be used in the general design phase. We are interested in the description of the software which is going to be realised rather than in describing the problem to be treated. We can therefore use entity-relation diagrams to describe the data manipulated by the software, data flow diagrams to describe its functions and automata to describe its behaviour. So we find in design those methods which have already served us in analysis.

The more precise the design becomes, the more we need notations which aid us in being precise about the content of the software. Some methods offer the possibility of identifying processes and the organisation of the software. There is a number of different design methods and different notations. We can cite the methods of Booch [Booch 91], the OMT method [Rumbaugh 91], the Coad and the Yourdon Method [Coad 91], the SDL Formalism, the Hood method, the UML notation, and so on.

Some notations are abstractions of languages used to describe the software. For example, a part of the notation used in the HOOD method can be viewed as an abstract form of the Ada language.

A design component is one of the elements identified during the design phase.

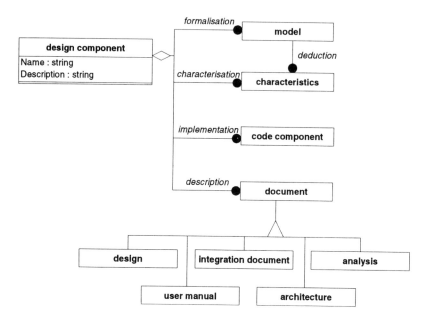

Figure 4.22 Characterisation of a design component.

In order to characterise a design component, we can use the following information (Figure 4.22):

- The design document (or a reference to extracts from the design documents);
- The corresponding model if the design is formalised using a particular notation;
- The characteristics of the design if it has been created with a method (the characteristics can be deduced from the design model);
- The description of the architecture in which the component will be used;
- The corresponding user manual (possibly);
- The corresponding integration test document.

To complete this information, we can add:

- A short description of the component (a few lines);
- A short description of the information manipulated in the component;
- A short description of the function treated by the component (description of the interfaces, conditions for use and the usage protocols);
- The associated specification;
- The list of the code components and the code which were used in the construction of the component (a single design component can have several implementations either in different languages or with different algorithms).

According to the kind of information used, this can be made more precise. For example, if the design is performed using the object notation in the OMT/UML method, a design component will be characterised by:

- A set of classes (with indications of their attributes (typed) and their methods (with parameters and return types));
- Relations between classes.

A design performed using the SDL formalism (which supports the descriptions of real time systems) will be characterised by:

- Blocks (which will contain processes) and their interfaces;
- Processes;
- Types of abstract data.

If the analysis and coding domains are clearly identified, they are not the same as design. The design phase is a more or less precise phase situated between specification and encoding which is necessarily precise. In what follows, we will usually only consider designs as the intermediaries between analysis and coding. In order to treat the components of design, we will use therefore either techniques for design components, or those for coding components.

This difficulty in characterising the design components is reinforced by the fact that programming languages can, in a reduced form, serve to support the description of design components. Some languages like Eiffel [Meyer 92] and C++ [Stroustrup 92] allow the possibility of describing different classes (we also use the term abstract classes or capsule classes). These classes contain the description of a set of functions whose interfaces are fixed but whose content is not yet known. For example, a method can be described in Eiffel by:

```
method (parameters): return_type is
    deferred
end
```

This means that, for this method, we have indicated what the parameters are, and what is the type of the value to be returned is, even though the code is not written. The code will be inherited and inheritance will be used to make this work.

We cannot dream of a better formation for the design because it is directly usable by the final code (we can even have classes used from the design and classes associated with them that derive from the coding in a single piece of software).

In the majority of the cases when we speak of a design component, we will be able to imagine a set of objects related to each other. An object of the set can correspond to a process, a code file, a package or to a class. The attributes must be typed and the interfaces for the methods must be known (Figure 4.23).

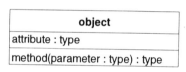

Figure 4.23 Synthesised design component.

The characteristics of such a component are those of the object diagrams.

4.4 Characterisation of Code Components

The result of the detailed design phase and of the coding of software is the production of some code and a detailed designed document which describes different constituents of the software and the algorithm used in coding them.

Different languages can be used to code the software:

- Unstructured languages (Fortran, Assembler, etc.);
- Structured languages (C++, Pascal, Fortran in the structured form, etc.);
- Modular languages (Ada, etc.);
- Object oriented languages (Smalltalk, C++, Eiffel, Ada95, Java, etc.)

The design document is generally accompanied by a set of unit test documents each indicating how to verify that the code conforms to what was expected at the start of the detailed design phase.

To characterise a code component we can use the following information (Figure 4.24):

- A detailed design document (or reference to extracts from the detailed design documents);

- The code corresponding to the component (that is the representation of the component in one or more programming languages);
- The characteristics of the component (which can be deduced from the code);
- The corresponding user manual (perhaps);
- The corresponding document containing the unit tests.

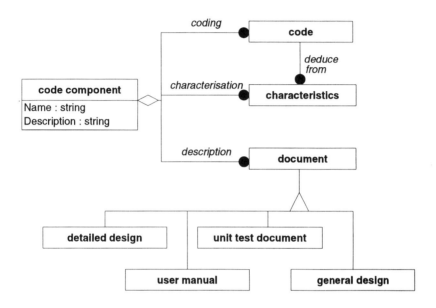

Figure 4.24 Characterisation of a code component.

In order to complete this information we can add;

- A short description of the component (some lines);
- A succinct description of the information manipulated by the component;
- A succinct description of the functions treated by the component;
- The associated design.

The characterisation of the code depends upon the language which has been used.

4.4.1 Languages that are not structured, languages that are

A code component implemented in a structured language or an unstructured language is characterised by:

- The global variables it manipulates (with an indication of the role for each variable and its type of use: read or modify);

- The subprogram which it contains (with an indication of the role of the subprogram, description of its parameters and meaning of its return value if one is present);
- The subprograms which it uses (or rather the code components which it uses);
- The logic for using these subprograms (order of use for example, initialisation subprogram, termination subprogram).

We can represent this information perfectly in the form of an object;

- The global variables are its attributes ;
- The subprograms are its methods.

The methods which offer an object notation can then be used to abstract, at the design level, the component described in a language whether structured or not. Such a component can use other components (see Figure 4.25).

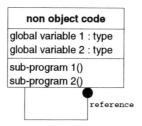

Figure 4.25 Abstraction of a code component.

4.4.2 Modular languages

Code components implemented in a modular language are characterised by:

- The name of the corresponding package;
- The list of the services offered (subprograms) with, for each one, a description of its role, of its parameters and its return value;
- The list of packages which it uses;
- The logic for the use of services which it offers.

Such a component can also be represented in the form of an object which only possesses methods (see Figure 4.26) and which will be in relation with other objects.

4.4.3 Object-oriented languages

A code component written in an object oriented language can be characterised by:

- The names of the object which it contains;

- For each object, a list of its attributes and methods (with all the associated information);
- The names of the objects from which it inherits;
- The names of the objects which it uses.

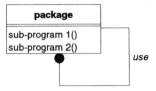

Figure 4.26 A component in a modular language.

Object diagrams are well suited to representing components written in object-oriented languages. In the case of languages requiring the description of objects in different files, information of a much more synthetic nature can be obtained.

4.5 Other Types of Components

We can identify other types of components than those which have been described above. We can mention for example:

- Code generators;
- Servers in a client-server system.

Code generators, such as their lexical analysers or man-machine interface generators, for example, can be assimilated to components or rather to the generators of reusable components. Starting with a description, they generate code which is always used in the same way. By giving a symbolic representation of the generated code, we can foresee the use of the code right at the start of the design phase. The generated code is then a particular implementation of the component.

If we implement an application as a client-server architecture, the servers that we are going to use can be viewed as reusable components right at the beginning in the design phase. If we develop an application under OLE, the components that we reuse are tables, databases and text processors. The data acceptable by these components is perfectly defined and the services that we can demand of them are also so defined.

4.6 Examples of Reusable Code

4.6.1 Code components

Code is the part of the software in which you find most reusable components. Here are some examples which are amongst the most famous.

String Library

String
strcat(s1 : string, s2 : string) : integer
strchr(s : string, c : char) : integer
strcmp(s1 : string, s2 : string) : integer
strcpy(s1 : string, s2 : string) : integer
strcspn(s1 : string, s2 : string) : integer
strlen(s : string) : integer
strncat(s1 : string, s2 : string, n : integer) : integer
strncmp(s1 : string, s2 : string, n : integer) : integer
strncpy(s1 : string, s2 : string, n : integer) : integer
strpbrk(s1 : string, s2 : string) : integer
strrchr(s : string, c : char) : integer
strspn(s1 : string, s2 : string) : integer
strstr(s1 : string, s2 : string) : integer
strtok(s1 : string, s2 : string) : integer

Figure 4.27 A string component.

The string library in the C language is a set of sub-programs;

- *strcpy*; copying of character strings;
- *strcmp*; comparison of strings;
- *strlen*; calculation of the length of the string;
- etc.

In the manuals, this library is characterised by the description of the names of the subprograms, their interfaces and their use.

This library is represented in Figure 4.27.

String_object
strcat(s2 : string) : integer
strchr(c : char) : integer
strcmp(s2 : string) : integer
strcpy(s2 : string) : integer
strcspn(s2 : string) : integer
strlen() : integer
strncat(s2 : string, n : integer) : integer
strncmp(s2 : string, n : integer) : integer
strncpy(s2 : string, n : integer) : integer
strpbrk(s2 : string) : integer
strrchr(c : char) : integer
strspn(s2 : string) : integer
strstr(s2 : string) : integer
strtok(s2 : string) : integer

Figure 4.28 A string component object.

An object oriented language would not have the first parameter in each subprogram fixed because this is the string to which the subprogram will be applied, as shown in Figure 4.28, in the class *string_object*.

Mathematical libraries

Mathematical Libraries offer in every language, the indispensable *sqrt*, *log*, *sin*, *cos*, etc. An example of such a component is given in Figure 4.29. By removing in a systematic way the first parameter of each operation, we regain a part of the object *real* that we would have in completely object-oriented languages.

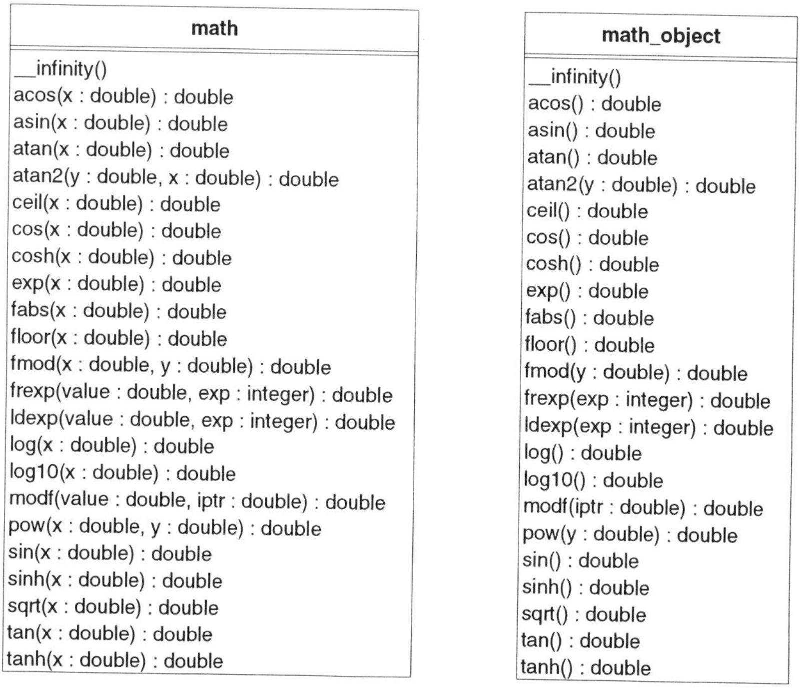

math
__infinity()
acos(x : double) : double
asin(x : double) : double
atan(x : double) : double
atan2(y : double, x : double) : double
ceil(x : double) : double
cos(x : double) : double
cosh(x : double) : double
exp(x : double) : double
fabs(x : double) : double
floor(x : double) : double
fmod(x : double, y : double) : double
frexp(value : double, exp : integer) : double
ldexp(value : double, exp : integer) : double
log(x : double) : double
log10(x : double) : double
modf(value : double, iptr : double) : double
pow(x : double, y : double) : double
sin(x : double) : double
sinh(x : double) : double
sqrt(x : double) : double
tan(x : double) : double
tanh(x : double) : double

math_object
__infinity()
acos() : double
asin() : double
atan() : double
atan2(y : double) : double
ceil() : double
cos() : double
cosh() : double
exp() : double
fabs() : double
floor() : double
fmod(y : double) : double
frexp(exp : integer) : double
ldexp(exp : integer) : double
log() : double
log10() : double
modf(iptr : double) : double
pow(y : double) : double
sin() : double
sinh() : double
sqrt() : double
tan() : double
tanh() : double

Figure 4.29 Mathematics component.

4.6.2 Analysis Components

Nowadays, we have access to libraries of components such as the Booch library (Booch 87) or the Eiffel libraries (Meyer 94).

In Eiffel there exists a list class which describes the concept of lists (Figure 4.30). This class is described in the notation of the concept of first element, last element, subsequent element, addition and deletion of an element. The interfaces of the different methods are described, indications are given on the context in which these methods can be used, and what must be expected as the return value, but no code is defined. There exist several code components which are the implementation of the design component list: singly linked, doubly linked, fixed size lists, etc.

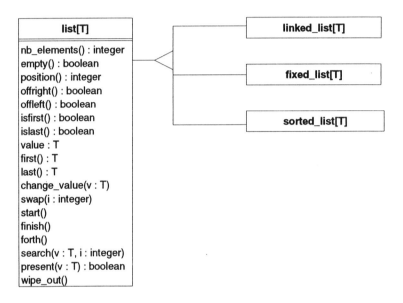

Figure 4.30 A list component.

The specifications of Ada packages or header files in C or in C++ can be assimilated to design information which indicates how the associated code is constituted.

4.6.3 Design Components

Design components are specific to the particular work area. For example, a company which produces operating systems will produce, in the form of design components, general descriptions of the different elements which comprise an operating system by insisting on the expected services from these different elements.

4.7 Chapter Summary

In this chapter, we have examined the different forms which can be taken by analysis components, design components and code components. For each of these we have identified a set of information which allows their characterisation.

This chapter has also given some examples of components.

Chapter Five

How to Identify Reusable Components

5.1 Introduction

One of the major problems with a reuse policy is to know how to identify reusable components. To answer this question, we are going to examine the different periods during development when it is possible to find reusable components.

So as not to forget anything, we are going to take into account the following times:

- During development, i.e.:
  - Before development, or:
  - During development;
  - After development.
- Unrelated to development.

We will determine, during the course of these periods, which components are identified and how.

As with the previous chapters, all illustrations in the chapter use the OMT/UMLnotation.

5.2 Identification before Development

To be capable of identifying components which will be necessary for future development, there are two principal techniques:

- The first consists of appealing to the specialists of the domain in which the software is being developed (see Fig 5.1). From their acquaintance of this type of development, they will be able to identify the components likely to be of use in the future. In general, these components will be components of design or code. Possibly, architectures can be proposed as satisfactory for new implementations.

This technique is not formal in the slightest. Nothing guarantees that the components that are implemented will really be reusable. Too much effort in generalisation (by trying for example to construct a component *a priori* usable in several contexts) increases the risk of having components that are too general and therefore unsuitable for new software.

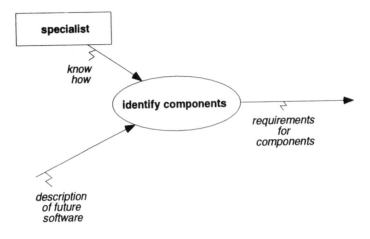

Figure 5.1 Identification of components by specialists.

- The second method consists of analysing the needs of several projects which have to be run at the same time (Figure 5.2). It is also possible to identify the common needs and thus to describe the specification components which will be reused by the different projects. Then, when the projects have started, it will be possible also to identify that which is not common in design and in code and therefore to construct reusable components in several projects.

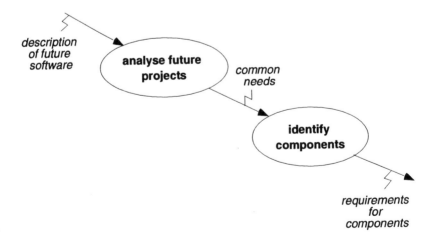

Figure 5.2 Search for common requirements.

This technique also presents a number of risks, the greatest of which is to disrupt several projects (maybe even all the projects). If the fabrication of a common component gets behind schedule, all the projects will get behind. If a common component is faulty, all the projects will be faulty. Another problem is for one project strongly to influence the implementation of components and to obtain components ill-suited to the other projects.

5.3 Identification during Development

It is very difficult to identify analysis components that are reusable. In general, during the specification phase, one concentrates on the problem to be studied and generalisations are not sought. This is done in the later phases of development.

The identification of components can be made during the general design phase or during the detailed design phase.

During the general design phase, the architecture of the software to be constructed is established and the different elements that will constitute it are described. One or more of these elements can be identified by specialists as having general interest and give way to fabrication of the components. In this case, the construction of these components begins at the same time as the rest of the project.

During the detailed design phase, one can identify an implementation for one of the parts of the software as being general and can decide to implement the corresponding component.

For these techniques, we do not have the risk cited above of building a component that does not suit because the component specifications are inferred directly from the project requirements. At worst, we run the risk of building a component which will only be used once.

On the other hand, we always run the risk of putting the project into difficulty. Constructing a component is, in general, more difficult than building the corresponding specific software. A poor estimate of the overhead can lead to spending more time than predicted in fabricating components and can also lead to making the project run behind schedule.

Another technique for identifying reusable components during design consists of organising design reviews at which component specialists participate. During these reviews, a technical presentation of the progress of the project is given. The specialist auditor of the components can detect identical choices in different projects. They can suggest the implementation of components which will be used by the different projects which share this particular need. The specialist can also guide the project towards the use of existing components for some parts of the software.

This technique allows the identification of components which will be really reused. It does run the risk of making several projects encounter difficulties at the same time as the realisation of components poses problems.

5.4 Identification after Development

When identifying components after development, we no longer run the risk of endangering projects because of the desire to construct things in a reusable way.

After a specific software development, we can call upon the specialists to identify the reusable parts of the analysis, design or code,. If they are used to the type of development which has just ended, they are capable of identifying the usual elements in this category of software and thus can also determine what is likely to be reusable. This technique contains no formal element and is reliant upon experienced people.

In the case of post-development component identification, we can use much more systematic techniques. These are highly dependent upon the methods used in the different phases of the project and are described below.

5.4.1 Identification of specification components

The identification of specification components is more or less straightforward, depending upon whether the specification is formal or not. The methods used have an impact on the techniques for identifying components.

Informal analysis

In the case of an informal analysis, there are no systematic techniques for identifying reusable components. If this technique is used, it is advisable that a domain analysis is made (see the end of this chapter). This analysis allows the identification of the themes which are often treated in the company and by classifying the analyses by type.

Entity-relation methods

An analysis performed using an entity-relation method contains a number of entities (sometimes several hundreds) and many relations.

To simplify matters, we are going to consider those entities that do not have attributes. The case of entities with attributes and methods is handled by object diagrams.

In the previous chapter, we saw that a reusable component, in the case of an entity-relation analysis, is a set of entities and relations which have the properties of exhaustiveness and generality. In any analysis, to find such sets, it is first necessary to localise the connected subsets of entities. To do this, it is necessary, for each entity, to identify all the entities with which it is in a direct or indirect relationship. A specialist then examines the sets thus found in order to determine those which have a general character and which can also be transformed into reusable components.

For example, in Figure 5.3, there are two possible components: the sets *{A, B}* and *{D, E, F}*. The application represented in the figure is then formed of the entity *C* and two components.

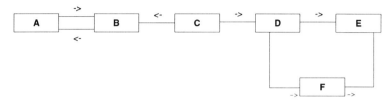

Figure 5.3 Search for connected subsets.

This determination of the potential components is eased because the relationships are oriented. We can see in the figure that there is a relation from *C* to *B* but that there is none from *B* to *C*.

If the notation used does not allow one to indicate the orientation of relations, it is necessary to find a convention to indicate a sense of direction for relations if we want to identify reusable subsets. This can be done by annotating relations to indicate their sense, or, if there is a concept of role, by considering how a role orients a relation.

Figure 5.4 Orientation of a relation.

For example, the relation in Figure 5.4 can be considered as being oriented because of the presence of a role name on the relation named street. The street plays the role of address for house. On the other hand, house plays no role for street. The orientation is thus from house to street. This orientation is reinforced by cardinalities: a house's association with a street is obligatory (relation of cardinality 1), while a street can have no houses (cardinality 0+).

When relations are oriented, we can look in the diagrams for connected subsets of entities. These are formed of entities such that whatever is the entity in the subset, its relations are directed towards another entity in the subset. A connected subset can contain connected subsets. To detect the reusable components among the connected subsets identified in a specification, we appeal to the knowledge of a specialist.

This decomposition of an entity-relation model in the form of components in relation to each other forms the basis for better structuring of the model and making it more comprehensible.

Object diagrams

For object diagrams, we can use the same techniques as in the entity-relation method for finding reusable components. Here also we determine the strongly connected subsets linked to objects.

The definition of a connected subset is the following. For any object in the subset:

    A. The objects with which it bears a relationship are elements of the subset (modulo the direction of relations);

    B. The objects referenced by the parameters and its operations are elements of the subset;

    C. The objects which are the return types of its operations are elements of the subset;

    D. Its ancestors are elements of the subset.

    E. In the case in which the sets thus obtained are too large, we can try to reduce this definition to the single points (A) and (D).

The objects referenced by the operations are then the basis for identifying new components that the current component uses. This is imperative for it is inconceivable to have components in a base which refer to information which does not represent components; such components will be unusable.

If inheritance is available in the formalism being used, it is possible to identify reusable components by looking for possible factorisations between objects.

Figure 5.5 A model to be factorised.

For example, in Figure 5.5, we can factorise a part of person and a part of dog by creating a class living being as in Figure 5.6.

The class living being is more general than the classes dog and person, and has without doubt more chances of being reused. We note in passing that it is an error to call this class living being. Indeed, its characteristics are to have a name and to be associated with a date. It would be preferable to maintain its generality by renaming it dated entity and thus this class will be useable as the definition of book, for example (if the language used later permits it, we will even be able to rename name in title and date in date of publication so as to have an entity that more closely resembles what we want).

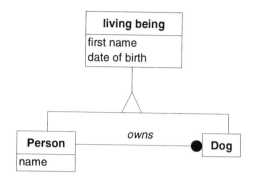

Figure 5.6 Factorised model.

The component is formed of the class which allows the factorisation to be performed and of the associated connected subset. The daughter classes serve as a base for identifying components which are specialisations of the component that has been constructed.

Another useful technique for object diagrams rests on the following observation: a simple object is easier to reuse than a complex object. It is necessary to define what must be understood by simple. To do this, we can start with the number of possible manipulations for each object. This is a function:

- Of the number of attributes of the object because we can read and modify them;
- Of the number of methods of the object because they can be invoked;
- Of the number of methods of the objects with which it is in some relation because they can be used.

In this calculation, one should not forget to take into account the ancestors of the objects.

On this basis, a complexity metric can be computed for each object in a diagram. The less complex objects must be examined for they are candidates to become the basis for reusable components. The components are formed by the connected subsets created on the basis of these objects.

We can also, by combining the techniques of search for connected subsets and complexity measure, measure the complexity of the connected subsets: it is equal to the sum of the complexities of the elements which form it. We can thus next analyse the subsets in increasing order of complexity so as to find reusable components.

Data flow

Data flow diagrams contain a set of functions which consume and produce data. Some functions in the diagram are inseparable. For example, a first function produces a datum which is consumed by another function. As with entity-relation diagrams, we can determine the connected subsets of functions. Such a subset is characterised by the fact that, no matter what the function of the subset:

- It consumes data coming from the environment, of a data storage space or of another function in the set;
- It produces data that goes into the environment, a data storage space or another function of the set.

In Figure 5.7, we have a set of functions which conforms to the definition which has just been given.

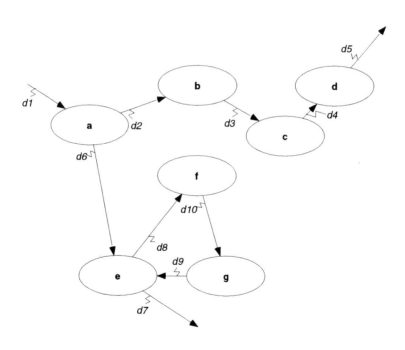

Figure 5.7 Search for connected subsets.

We can, in fact, identify in the environment two connected subsets in this figure. If we remove the function *a* and consider that *d2* and *d6* are data coming from the environment, we have identified the subsets *{b, c, d}* and *{e, f, g}*. In the original figure, *a* is a function which uses the two subsets.

We can restructure Figure 5.7 as indicated in Figure 5.8.

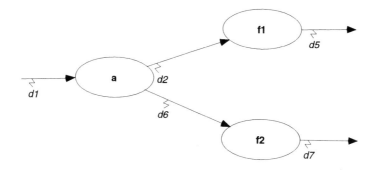

Figure 5.8 Restructuring of the diagram.

In this diagram, *f1* is decomposed as indicated in Figure 5.9.

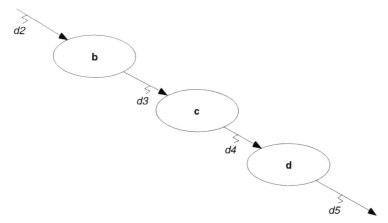

The function *f2* is decomposed as indicated in Figure 5.10.

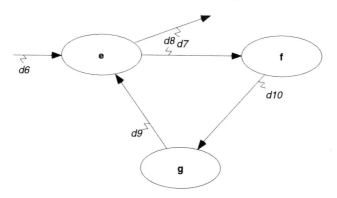

Figure 5.10 Contents of f2.

The diagrams describing *f1* and *f2* are candidates for becoming reusable components.

Another technique allowing the identification of reusable components in the case of a functional model consists of analysing the decompositions of different functions. This decomposition allows the structuring of the analysis and each level corresponds to a reduction in complexity. The levels which now contain only functions which are not decomposed are good candidates for becoming reusable components. It is also useful to examine their generality with a specialist.

Figure 5.11 A general function.

For example, let us assume that a function such as that in Figure 5.11 is refined into three sub-functions as is shown in Figure 5.12.

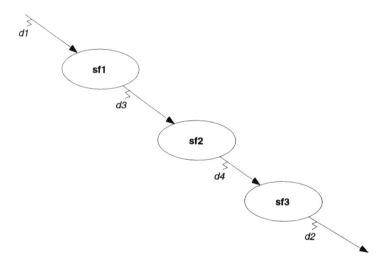

Figure 5.12 Refinement.

If the sub-functions *sf1*, *sf2* and *sf3* are not refined, it is necessary to see if they do not have the property of generality which would make them candidates for reuse.

If a function is refined into several functions which are judged to be reusable, it is itself, perhaps, at top level, a reusable function. This is to be verified.

In every case, a specialist will have to evaluate whether what has been identified as potentially reusable actually is so.

Automata

To find reusable sub-automata in an automaton consists, in fact, of identifying subsets of stable states. Such a set is formed of states and events so that whatever the event in the set, its processing remains in one of the states of the set. For this subset to be useful, it is necessary to complete it by identifying events which allow it to exit.

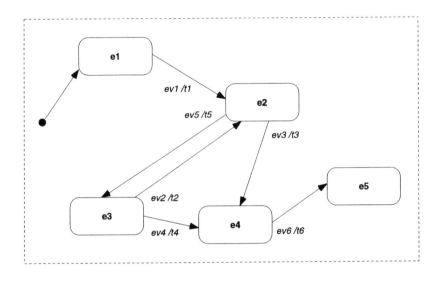

Figure 5.13 An automaton to be simplified.

Consider, for example, the automaton in Figure 5.13.
We can simplify it as indicated in Figure 5.14.

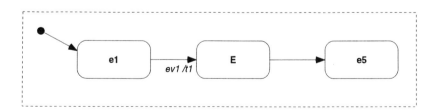

Figure 5.14 The simplified automaton.

To do this, we create a state E which is described by Figure 5.15.

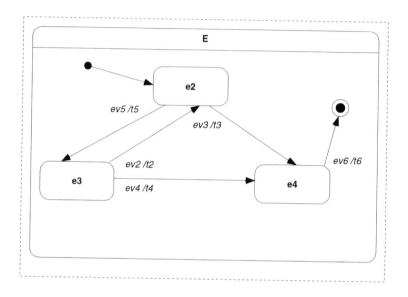

Figure 5.15 Decomposition of the state E.

The events *ev2*, *ev3*, *ev4* and *ev5* make the automata settle into states *e2*, *e3* or *e4*. The event *ev6* makes an exit from this set of stable states. E is a candidate for becoming a reusable component.

A specialist must be consulted to judge the generality of what has been found.

Composite methods
The identification of reusable components in the case of the use of composite methods uses everything which we have just seen in object diagrams, automata and data flow. The identification of a reusable component based on one type of diagram must be confirmed and/or completed by studying other diagrams.

5.4.2 Identification of design components

As for specification, in the case of an informal design, the identification of reusable components can only be made by specialists.

In the case of a design performed using a general formalism, we use techniques which have just been described. While a design contains more details than a specification, it is advisable, therefore, to abstract from the design in order to facilitate the identification of components.

If the formalism used is an abstraction from code, the techniques described below relating to code are useable.

5.4.3 Identification of code components

Depending upon the language used, there are several techniques for identifying reusable components. The procedures mentioned here offer equally the possibility of helping in the reconstruction of the code which must allow the simplification of the maintenance process.

In what follows, we only cite component identification techniques which can be automated. It is always possible that specialists might be needed as a complement to the use of these techniques.

Languages without data structures

Sub-programs are all that are reusable in a language that does not allow structured data to be defined, provided that their global variables have been properly identified. A reusable component in this type of language will, therefore, be composed of a set of sub-programs and their associated variables.

To identify these components at the start of the development of an application, we can use the following technique:

- For each sub-program in the application, we calculate the number of times which it is called;
- We also calculate the complexity of each component [McCabe 76];
- We determine an average of the number of uses of sub-programs and an average complexity;
- We classify the sub-programs in four subsets:
  - S1: those which are used more than the average number of times and are less complex than average
  - S2: those which are only used the average number of times and are more complex than average
  - S3: those which are used less than the average and are less complex than average
  - S4: those which are used less than average and are more complex than average. We can also set complexity and

usage thresholds to classify the sub-programs if we judge
that the use of averages is inappropriate.

- On the basis of this classification, we can determine (Figure 5.16):

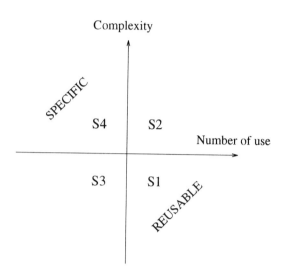

Figure 5.16 Different types of candidate.

- Sub-programs which are doubtless reusable (set S1)
- Those which have little chance of being so (set S4)
- Those which need closer examination (sets S2 and S3). The sub-programs in S2 and S3 which are considered to be reusable are transferred to S1.
- We are now only interested in set S1. We determine for each of the constituent sub-programs that constitute it the set of global variables that it uses.
- We group together the sub-programs of S1 which manipulate the same global variables.
- The components which are candidates for reuse are identified. It only remains to complete the sets thus obtained by adding to them the sub-programs in the sets S2, S3 and S4 which manipulate the same variables. During process, we can modify the code of those considered too complex so that they are simplified.

We obtain a set of global variables and a set of sub-programs. It is necessary to appeal to a specialist to identify the global variables which are not general (with their associated sub-programs) and the sub-programs that are too specialised.

We have therefore some objects (data and associated functions). It is then advisable to restructure the code around these objects to improve maintainability.

Languages with data structures

The techniques for the identification of reusable components described for languages without data structures can, certainly, be used.

Another technique for the identification of reusable components consists of assuming that the data structures correspond to declarations of objects none of whose attributes is known. By analysing the set of sub-programs, we can determine those which have a parameter referencing a data structure and those which return a data structure. These sub-programs are identified as potential candidates for becoming methods of the object associated with the data structure. The analysis of the consistency between these associations of data structures with sub-programs allows the validation of the discovery of objects. To find out if they are candidates for becoming reusable components, the techniques described below for modular languages can be used.

In the case in which the objects are really identified, a regrouping in the code of everything connected to these objects allows the simplification of the final maintenance of the software.

Modular languages

To identify reusable components in code written in a modular language, we can use the technique described in the case of identification of specification components using the entity-relation analysis method. The relations between objects are oriented by considering that an object which uses another object has a relation which goes from it towards the other object. We can thus detect strongly connected sub-sets of objects which must later be analysed in detail to determine those which are reusable.

Another way of identifying reusable objects consists of calculating the complexity metric for each object. These metrics are based on:

- The number of attributes of the object;
- The number of methods on the object;
- The complexity measure for the object's methods;
- The number and the complexity of the methods of the classes referenced by the object's attributes.

By also computing the number of uses for each object, we find, as for languages without data structures, four sub-sets of objects as a function of their number of uses and complexity.

We can immediately identify as potentially reusable the sets composed of one or more objects strongly connected and whose use is greater than the average and whose complexity is lower than average.

We will also later appeal to a specialist for determining if these sets have a meaning and are of interest at the level of reuse.

Object-oriented languages

For object-oriented languages, the identification techniques for reusable components is the same as for modular languages. During the calculation of the object's complexity, it is necessary to take into account all the attributes and methods of the object (including those which are inherited).

Among the objects identified as reusable, it is possible to perform simplifications using the technique of inheritance. Objects now containing the same information are reconstructed using inheritance allowing duplications to be removed (to the extent that the language to be used in coding correctly supports inheritance).

5.5 Identification without Reference to Development

Can one identify components outside the development process? The answer is yes. There even exist several techniques for doing it.

The first, and simplest, technique is to buy components. When you buy a library of graphic components, for example, you buy components that are judged useful for certain developments. In this same library, there are other components that you are unaware of, and that appears to be very useful.

Another means of identifying reusable components outside of development is reading books describing existing libraries [Booch, 87; Johnson, 88; Meyer, 94; Korson, 93].

A third method, much better targeted on the real needs of a company, consists, when using a library of reusable components, of keeping a history of failed searches. By regularly analysing this information, we can find searches for the same types of component. Where these components do not exist (for the searches have failed), we use a description of an unsatisfied requirement expressed in several developments. This description is no more than the requirements document for a component that is yet to be implemented.

Finally, we can use the technique of domain analysis. This consists of collecting the maximum information in a company (saving specification, and design documents, code, interviews with software developers). From the analysis of this information, we can compile a list of domains which characterise the company's activities. Hypotheses are formulated for the choice and the description of these designs. They are validated by software developers. After finalisation, we have a list of activity domains with their precise description. It is then possible to identify, domain by domain, general, repeated, and elements which serve as the basis for the construction of reusable components.

The reader who wishes to know more about this approach can consult [McCain, 85; Nighbors, 84] or [Prieto-Diaz 90].

5.6 Chapter Summary

In this chapter, we have swept over a set of techniques which are intended to identify what can be reused. It is clear that what is given here is not exhaustive. Other procedures exist; it is important to think about them so as to find the most effective techniques.

There exists no technique allowing us instantaneously to find reusable components. We can find potential candidates: it is for specialists to determine if they are suitable or not.

A general rule is that it is necessary to avoid being too original. There are already components in the majority of domains. If we identify new components, it is necessary for us to attempt to rely on existing components rather than be innovative. In doing this, we can retain possibilities for more substantial reuse at a later date.

Chapter Six

Building Reusable Components

6.1 Introduction

We have seen, in the last chapter, some techniques which allow us to identify reusable components in different phases of the life cycle. The question arises, having found such components: how to construct them so that they really are reusable in other applications.

To be reusable means, first of all, that we are able to understand the component in order to judge whether it is suitable or not in a new development. It then must be constructed using techniques which will allow it to be reusable in other contexts.

Given that there exists no universal way to construct reusable components, but just techniques suited to the type of components to be obtained, we will, as in previous chapters, distinguish components according to the phase in the life-cycle where they occur and according to the methodology being used.

We will not consider here the problems of organising to make reusable components. These are considered in another chapter.

6.2 Construction of Analysis Components

6.2.1 Informal analysis

Failure to use analysis methods makes the construction of analysis components very difficult. The only things about reusable components that are written that we can suggest are presentation rules.

An analysis is characterised by the identification of a set of data manipulated and by the description of a set of functions which are handled. To make an informal analysis document reusable, it is necessary to make these different kinds of information rapidly accessible.

It is therefore advisable to start an analysis document with a quick summary of its subject matter. This summary is aimed at helping future users to know as quickly as possible if the component is near to their needs or not. This summary must be followed by two glossaries: one for the data processed and one for functions.

The data glossary gives, for each type of data, a short description of its role. The function glossary gives, for each function, a short description of its use.

References to the pages where the data and functions are described in more detail allows us to make the document more usable.

As far as possible, it is better to isolate as much as possible: if a set of data and functions is autonomous, it is necessary to devote a separate section in the analysis to it and to add to it its own summary and its own glossary. This will later help someone understand the section more easily.

To construct a reusable component when formal analysis methods are not used, it is essential to extract general information from existing documents and complete it using a summary and indices. By respecting the rules for presentation and for the organisation and phrasing of the document, subsequent use is made easier.

6.2.2 Entity-relation methods

If we use an analysis method of the entity-relation type, a component is composed of one or more entities with associated relations.

To construct a reusable component is to construct a model with only the essential entities and relations. We must therefore remove all the entities which are not of a sufficiently general character.

To do this, it is sometimes necessary to call into question the model we use to construct one or more components. Here is an example of this.

If we have designed a data structure which is supposed to be represented graphically, it is necessary to avoid mixing in a single component the data and the graphic representation of this data. If we do not take this precaution, we cannot use the component in batch applications which are only concerned with data.

Figure 6.1 Mixture of information.

Let us assume that we have a diagram on which to base the construction of a component of the type shown in Figure 6.1.

The information is associated with their graphical representation. If we directly use this representation to construct the component, we then will not be able to use it in non-graphical applications, nor even in applications which do not use the same type of graphical interface (application operating on different systems, for example). The graphics themselves can be relatively general and cannot be used if there is no need for the associated information.

To construct a reusable component, in this case, it is necessary to cut what we had into two independent parts in the form of two components:

one which corresponds to the information and one which corresponds to the graphical representation.

Applications which wish to use the information and the graphical representation will use intermediary entities which will make the connection between some data and a graphical representation such as is shown in Figure 6.2.

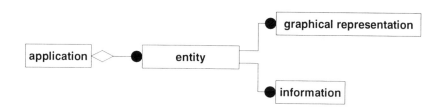

Figure 6.2 Separation of information.

The intermediate entity must serve to extract the information which is necessary to drive the graphics (and conversely).

Another rule to be respected when constructing reusable components is that of always using the most general possible names for entities and relations. It is necessary to avoid specialising the diagrams.

For an entity-relation component really to be reusable, it is necessary to enrich it. To do this, it is necessary to associate with the mode a brief explanatory text commenting the entities and the relations. Every entity, every attribute and every relation must be accompanied by a comment explaining their role. Certainly, this is simplified if the method used (and the tools supporting the method) allow the association of comments with the model, the entities and the relations (some methods suggest the establishment of a data dictionary which plays the role of the glossaries described in the case of informal models).

6.2.3 Object diagrams

To construct components using object diagrams, it is necessary to work in the same way as for the diagrams constructed with an entity-relation method. The only difference comes from the fact that, instead of having entities, we have objects.

For the component thus obtained to be reusable, it is necessary, in addition to the comments associated with the objects and relations, to put comments on attributes and methods. It is necessary only to keep, on objects, the attributes and methods which are useful for understanding the component.

We can envision the synthesis of a set of objects and relations into a single object, whose attributes and methods represent the principal attributes, methods and relations of the objects in the component. This makes understanding the component easier.

In the reuse phase, we will use this general view to show the objects which use the component. In a more detailed view, we will be able to show which sub-objects of the component are used.

During the construction of this type of component, it is necessary to examine each of the possible factorisations of objects under inheritance (these factorisations might be made with components which already exist in the base). A factorisation can be the departure point for the discovery of a new component that is far more general than had been imagined.

It is necessary also to verify that the different objects which form the component are not already known. If this is the case, the new component uses another component. This fact should be indicated.

6.2.4 Data flow

To construct a reusable component using a functional approach, is, in particular, to synthesise, as a single function, a diagram in which several functions are. It is enough to place all these functions in a single, more general, encompassing function and to indicate what the information that it receives from the outside is (that is, information which only passes between component functions) and those which are produced for output (by the same definition). For this to become possible, it is necessary to use a notation which allows a hierarchy in the functions.

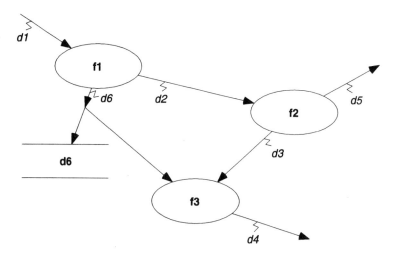

Figure 6.3 Contents of a component.

The reusable component formed from the functions in Figure 6.3 is represented by the function in Figure 6.4.

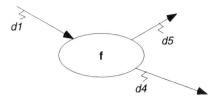

Figure 6.4 Representation of a component.

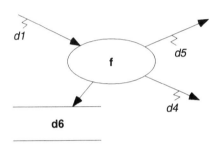

Figure 6.5 Another possible representation.

In the case in which intermediate results are stored by the function (as is the case in our example for datum *d6*), we must indicate in the description of the component that some persistent data is used and to describe it. We can perhaps represent the component such as that shown in Figure 6.5

Its subsequent reuse will be simplified.

In order that the component can be reused in appropriate conditions, it is necessary to describe the role of the function and the role of each of its input and output data.

In an analysis document, it is useless to describe the sub-functions. The component's user will only be interested in the global behaviour of the component.

To reuse the component, it must be provided with the data which it expects in a new diagram (either from outside of the system or via an information storage zone, or from another function) and we connect the data which it produces (either going outside the system, or through an information storage area, or sent to another function). An example is shown in Figure 6.6.

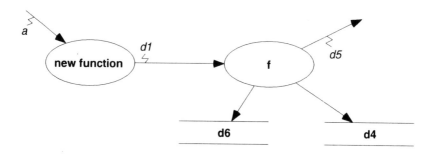

Figure 6.6 Reuse of a component.

The names of the functions and of the data must be the most as general as possible. The description of the component must be precise while being simple.

6.2.5 Automata

An automaton component is formed of a set of states in which it remains after the processing of a certain number of events. The general form of such a component is the same as that which was proposed in a previous chapter and is shown in Figure 6.7.

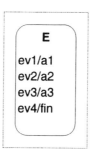

Figure 6.7 Automaton component.

The automaton in this figure processes events *ev1*, *ev2* and *ev3* using actions *a1*, *a2* and *a3*. The occurrence of the event *ev4* causes the automaton to halt.

As we have also seen, this automaton is composed of sub-states as shown in Figure 6.8.

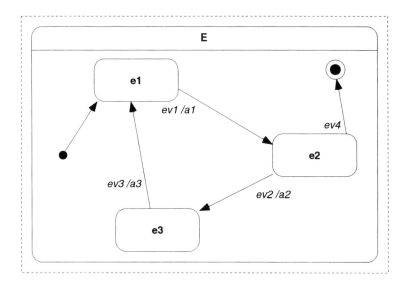

Figure 6.8 Contents of an automaton component.

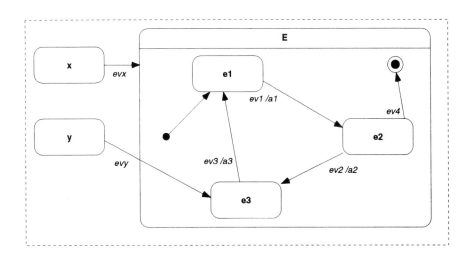

Figure 6.9 Input to an automaton.

The most subtle part of constructing this kind of component from an existing one is to determine what the start state is and how to halt the automaton.

If there are several possible start states, it is advisable to choose one of them as a default. When a user wants to use the component, they will be free to activate the automaton using the default state or to activate it using another state of their choice. Figure 6.9 illustrates these two possibilities. From state *X*, we use the automaton via its default start state, and from state *Y*, we exit state *e3*.

Halting the automaton can be performed using one (or more) given state(s) on the acceptance of a particular event such as is represented in Figure 6.8 (possibly *ev4*).

We can also choose to have a list of events which make the automaton exit no matter which state it is currently in. This is shown in Figure 6.10 using events *evx* and *evy*.

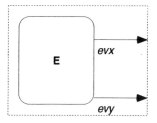

Figure 6.10 Output from an automaton.

To make reuse of this type of component easier, the associated documentation must give a global idea of the role played by the automaton. It is necessary to make clear which processing is triggered by each accepted event and what the acceptance conditions for this event are.

It is useful to describe the sub-states only in the case in which we can reuse the automaton on the basis of one of these sub-states.

6.2.6 Composite methods

Composite methods, in general, favour objects. A component, for this type of method, is a set of objects related to each other as we saw with object diagrams.

Each object of such a component must be examined in order to determine if it is appropriate to complete its description using one or more data flow diagrams which will make clear what data exchanges between the objects' operations are. We must also determine if it is necessary to complete some objects using an automaton which shows their behaviour in a detailed fashion.

The joint use of different notations allows us to obtain components from the most precise descriptions. The documentation must state the diagrams used to complete a description.

6.3 Construction of Design Objects

A design component must allow the description, in the most complete way possible, of a set which is (or will be) coded using one or more different algorithms in one or more languages.

The ideal form for a design component is an object. This object possesses a set of attributes which correspond to the data handled by the component and a set of methods which correspond to the functions which the component can handle. All this information must be commented.

In order for the component to be usable, the types of data it manipulates, as well as the interfaces of the proposed methods must be stated.

So that the component can be really reused, it is necessary to avoid making choices which reduce its generality. For example, if the component has to manipulate several data of the same type, it must not fix on a choice of implementation by deciding to use a table, a list or a stack. It is preferable to state that a set (of some kind) of data is being manipulated. The actual choice will be made later.

An ideal design component has a clearly defined interface which allows us to fix the way in which the implementations of this component are useable. Despite this, it is necessary to allow the greatest possible freedom for these implementations.

For example, to take a famous example due to Meyer [Meyer 88], the list: it is necessary not to make choices too early. A list is characterised by:

- A set of elements that can be sequentially traversed;
- The ability to insert an element after a given one;
- The ability to remove an element.

From these observations, to construct a list component, we must be content with declaring the existence of this information.

Figure 6.11 A list component.

The theoretical list component has, then, the form shown in Figure 6.11.

To have a reusable component, it is necessary to fix the interfaces of the methods. Meyer suggests that we imagine a list as a set of elements along which a cursor can be moved. The list component corresponds to this cursor. The insert method means that an element can be added after the current element (in fact, after the cursor). The remove method indicates that the current element can be removed. For this list to be useable, it is necessary to add a head method which places the cursor on the first element of the list, the tail method which moves to the next element of the list and a method which tests if we have gone off the end of the list.

In Eiffel, the list class is written in the following way:

```
class list[T]
    -- position on the first element of the list
    head () is
        deferred
    end;

    -- position on the next element
    tail () is
        deferred
    end;

    -- test to see if we have gone off the end of
    -- the list
    too_far_to_right () is
        deferred
    end;

    -- add an element to the right of the current
    -- one
    add (an_element: T) is
        deferred
    end;

    -- remove the current element
    remove () is
        deferred
    end;
end list;
```

This class is generic: it manipulates the elements of a type which is to be identified when the class is used.

The greatest property of this class is being what we call a capsule class: all of its methods are declared as being deferred. This means that we have not yet described their functioning in detail. Providing the method bodies is the responsibility of the subclasses of this class and depends on the way their implementations are built. Indeed, this class is going to have several sub-classes: singly linked lists, doubly linked lists, fixed-length lists, circular lists, sorted lists. Fixed-length lists will use an implementation that uses a table. Singly- and doubly-linked lists use elements with different chaining methods.

In this case, the design component list will therefore be composed of the capsule class list and will suggest several implementations which are code components. Although written in a programming language, we can consider that this list component is a design component. We again find here the difficult problem of the dividing line between design and code, a line which is hard to establish.

A program which has to manipulate lists will have to declare that it manipulates instances of the list class and not specify the type of the list that is to be used. It will also be able to operate on all types of list.

This rule is general: so that a component written in an object-oriented language increases its chances of being reusable, it must declare the information that it manipulates using the most general possible type. It is then useable with every type derivable from this general type.

The equivalent in C++ of deferred is the declaration of a null address for a virtual function. The technique described above is also valid in C++. The only limits are due to the limitations C++ imposes on inheritance (no redefinition of attribute type, operations or parameters).

The fact that we are using abstract descriptions requires that we do not bother with implementation details and allows us to construct components that are easiest to reuse along the way. It is useful to have this type of representation when we want to think of reusing code during the design phase.

Tools exist which allow us to obtain a representation of existing code using a notation for a design method. We can find, in particular, tools which allow us to have a representation in OMT/UML notation of code in C++ or Smalltalk.

To keep the design components as general as possible, it is also advisable that one does not choose to have data when it is not absolutely necessary. For example, if a component represents a quadrilateral, it is not necessary to store the perimeter as an attribute, but in the form of a function. In the same way, the number of elements of a list must not be an attribute but a function. All these choices can, certainly, be changed during the implementation of the component. For example, in Eiffel, we can redefine a function as an attribute in a subclass, and in C++ we store the function as an inline operation which returns the value of the attribute.

The design of the component must not stop at a simple statement of requirements. It is necessary to try to imagine all the other possible uses of this component and remove everything which seems to be a restrictive choice.

We find in [Gamma 94] a description of a set of techniques which allow the construction of reusable components. Each component model is called a pattern. The ways of constructing and reusing 23 types of pattern are described.

6.4 Construction of Code Components

Comments are also very important for code components. To obtain good results in the implementation of a policy of reuse, it is advised that each software item (or rather component) begins with a commentary formed of three parts:

- Keywords: these will help in the classification of the component at a later stage. Here can be put all the words which bear some relationship with the component (domain of use, functions handled, for example);

- Summary: this is a brief description of what the component does;
- Description: the complete directions for use which explains how to use the component.

These different information levels are then used in the following way:

- Keywords allow the component to be found in a quick search;
- The summary allows one to determine whether the component is appropriate;
- The description allows us really to reuse it if it is chosen.

This information can be subsequently used for the storage of, and to search for, the component.

The description of the component must be genuine for the reuse of the component. It must not be limited to describing what the component does and how it is designed. It must clearly indicate what must be done to reuse it.

6.4.1 Languages without data structures

In order to be reusable in an optimal way, a code component written in a language without data structures, must resemble an object as closely as possible; it must group in the same source the functions which we want to reuse and the global variables which they use.

This job can be simplified by tools which produce cross references or by tools which help in finding all uses of the data.

Having chosen a set of sub-programs that can be reused, we can determine, for each one, the global variables which are used. These variables are grouped together in the component. We can then determine the list of sub-programs which manipulate these variables (there are not necessarily in the list of sub-programs that have been identified as reusable). All those which modify the component's variables are a part of the component or must be transformed to use a sub-program, forming part of the component, which modifies the variable. In fact, but this is to the detriment of performance, the ideal is to use these variables by having, for each one, only a single sub-program which performs the modification.

At the level of documentation, each global variable must be commented. It is necessary to indicate what its purpose is, and to give the list of the sub-programs in the components which use it (either reading or writing).

The sub-programs must be commented. The comments must state the use of the different parameters, the meaning of a possible return value and give a list of global variables read or written.

It can happen that there is an order imposed on the use of sub-programs. It must be indicated in the general comments associated with the component and must be recalled at the level of each sub-program concerned in this ordering.

Certainly, to ease the readability of the component, it is essential to have some kind of structure (not to use gotos anywhere, but to respect a certain logic in the program).

To improve the opportunities for extension of the component, it is necessary to leave open points so that the user can personalise the component with their own code. To do this, we can provide, at specific points, or at various points in the code, calls to functions which the user of the sub-program must write. For example in C:

```
sub_program () {
/* call a user-supplied initialisation
function.*/
     user_init();
                /* sub-program code */
     ...
/* call a user-supplied termination function.
*/
     user_end();
}
```

The user of this component can add, when editing some lines of their own, functions user_init and user_end if they wish.

Here is another example. If errors are detected by one of the sub-programs of the component, it is not necessary directly to write the error message in the sub-program for it will not be useable in every context (for example, it will not be useable in every graphic application which needs an error message displaying in a particular area). It is preferable to call an error sub-program. A default version of this sub-program (which displays the error message) must be available in the component. The user of the component writes their own sub-program for the treatment of errors either by calling the standard method or by using what is already provided in their application.

6.4.2 Languages with structured data

What has been said for languages without data structures is also applicable to the languages which support it.

With these languages, the use of structured data is preferred to the use of global variables (we thus minimise possible name conflicts when using several components).

In the case where the language used allows the hiding of global variables or structured data, it is necessary to use this facility (the static directive in C, for example). The update of these variables is then performed via intermediary sub-programs which support the reuse of components with less risk as we saw in the chapter on reuse techniques.

To allow the extension of components and to simplify their use in some cases, a good trick consists of adding a field in the component's data structures that is reserved for user. This field is declared as being of some neutral type (void * in C, for example). The user will employ this field to store information about their application and not the component. For example in C:

```
typedef data_struct{
    void *user_hook; /* reserved for the user*/
    ...
} data;
```

A single data structure can thus support several types of manipulation without needing to be modified.

6.4.3 Modular languages

Modular languages offer, as standard, everything that is necessary for making reusable components. Certainly, for it to work, it is necessary to use the facilities on offer by these languages to construct objects: classes or packages.

We can simulate perfectly an approach using objects using languages which are not object-oriented. It is enough, to do this, to group in the separate compilation units data items and the sub-programs which use them.

6.4.4 Object-oriented languages

Object-oriented languages have all the facilities of modular languages for the construction of reusable components. With inheritance, they offer a big plus for the specialisation of components.

The ideal component in the object-oriented framework has a clearly defined interface and offers several implementations in the form of subclasses.

We have seen in the chapter comparing the different techniques for reuse the fundamental role played by encapsulation. Even if we use an object-oriented language which tolerates lack of respect for encapsulation (as is the case in C++), it is imperative to respect this principle when constructing reusable components.

We generally say, as an excuse for directly modifying the objects, that we do not want to degrade performance by adding an intermediate sub-program. This is a poor excuse. Every user of C++ knows inline functions allow us to respect encapsulation without altering the performance and that in languages like Eiffel, the compiler makes optimisations which avoid the overhead when it is useless.

In general, we only avoid encapsulating data through laziness: it is necessary to write a function, this takes some time, and we prefer to do this later (i.e., never). For the lazy, let us recall that there are tools which generate the code corresponding to the objects and to all the encapsulation functions necessary from a simple description of objects. Why deprive yourself?

On the other hand, if some data is not encapsulated and it is discovered, some processing is needed each time the data is modified; it is necessary to find all the sources which refer to the data and add the call to the processing or the data needed for encapsulation. The lazy then regret not having been more courageous at the start.

What was said for languages with structured data concerning the benefit of adding a field that is reserved for users in the data structures is ill-advised in objects. It increases the size of objects and is useless if the user wants to personalise an object, and it is then sufficient to create a subclass to which new information is added.

There is a limit to writing reusable components in object-oriented and object-based languages: it is the problem of freeing memory when it is no longer used.

Some languages like Eiffel, Java and Smalltalk have a garbage collector which has, as its purpose, just the recovery of all the blocks which are no longer used. In the case of a language like C++, it is necessary, each time we create an instance of an object, to ask the question as to whether we know who will free it. The answer to this question is fundamental if we do not want to construct applications consuming increasing amounts of memory over time. It is therefore necessary to add indications in the component documentation on how to free objects allocated by the object or passed as parameters. The general rule is that whatever allocates an object frees it.

6.5 Backing Up and Restoring Information

If we construct a reusable component which has to backup and restore data, it is important when it is designed, to take into account the fact that the data being manipulated can change its structure over time and that the applications which use the component do not use the same version.

It is therefore imperative to foresee a backup system for the information which affords upward and downward compatibility.

Upward compatibility means that components must know how to read the data which was backed up by one of its old versions. Downward compatibility means that this component must know how to read data that will be backed up by one of its subsequent versions.

For this to be possible, we should not be content with only backing up data values. It is necessary also to indicate what information is backed up in order to be able to retrieve it in one version rather than another.

There exist standards, such as ASN.1, for example, which permit the inclusion in backup files of a description of the data and the values of these data. A program which must restore such a file analyses the description of the information. It knows then how to read the data part of the file. It only saves the data which concerns it (it does not bother with, for example, information added by a new version) and determines the default values for the data which has not been found (data which does not appear in older versions).

6.6 Chapter Summary

In this chapter, we have seen how to construct reusable components depending on the different types of formalism and methods being used.

The construction of reusable components is highly dependent on the type of component being constructed. At the level of code components, the rigour of the object approach should be used even if an object-oriented language is not used.

A successful component will be one which:

- Is easy to understand;
- Is easy to use.

It is useless to claim as reusable components which are poorly documented or which require too complex a parameterization.

Chapter Seven

Component Certification

7.1 Definition

To certify is to perform a set of checks on reusable components in order to guarantee that they are error-free (or at least without major error) and that their reuse will not lead to problems for those who have kept them.

To certify software, is to verify that everything goes as intended, that it has the expected performance and that it is resistant to malicious use.

To certify is also to verify the documentation, to ensure that it is up-to-date, that it conforms to what the software does and that it indicates possible restrictions.

Why and how to certify reusable components is what is covered in this chapter.

7.2 Why Certify?

To certify reusable components allows the avoidance of a good number of problems:

- Failure of a reuse policy;
- Waste of time during development;
- Risk to several projects at the same time.

7.2.1 Failure of a reuse policy

In a later chapter, we will see that it is not at all in the nature of computer people to engage in reuse. From this fact, it follows that introducing a policy of reuse in a company is very difficult because the developers find every conceivable pretext to demonstrate that they cannot reuse that which is proposed, and that it is preferable to reconstruct it. By making unreliable components available to them, we reinforce the argument that one is only certain of what one has done oneself. It is therefore essential for the success of a component policy to start with the provision of components of extremely high reliability. It is worth more to offer few, but reliable, components, than many components of which some contain errors.

Component reuse must be easier than the corresponding development of specific components. It is therefore also necessary to ensure that the documentation for the components is reliable and clear.

7.2.2 Waste of time during development

If we make the assumption, in a development, that we are going to engage in reuse, we can reduce the development time for the parts where reuse is performed. If what is being reused is not appropriate to what we want to do because the documentation of the component is not reliable, we waste time before accounting for the problem. Then it is necessary to devote time to implementations that were unpredicted.

If what is being reused is suitable, but unreliable, it is necessary to fix it. It takes more time than a simple act of construction. This can even, sometimes, take more time than the construction of the corresponding component, because it is necessary to understand how the component being reused is designed, how to localise the errors and find the means to correct them without, in the meanwhile, introducing other errors.

7.2.3 Risking several projects at the same time

In the case of unreliable components, one of the greatest advantages of reuse is using the same code in several applications, yet this advantage can turn against those who engage reuse. If a grave error is detected in a heavily used component, this will be of concern to many applications. If the correction of this error takes a long time, several projects can be put at risk at the same time. This occurs, in particular, when one engages in extending of existing components. If all necessary precautions are not taken, we take the risk of having old implementations which no longer work.

One of the important rules for reuse is that the more a component is reused, the more one must be careful when altering it. Never risk modifying the string component in your component library without taking infinite precautions: you will regret it for a long time.

7.3 How are Components Certified?

As for the techniques studied in previous chapters, it is necessary to note that there do not exist universal techniques for certifying components. It is very difficult even to certify analysis or design components. We are going to sweep up the different types of component and identify the potential faults which can apply to these components and the techniques employable for their certification.

7.4 Certification of Analysis Components

Analysis components are those which are the most difficult to certify. The major problems which an analysis component can present are:

- Not corresponding to reality;
- Containing inaccuracies.

The fact that this does not correspond to reality can have several causes. The first is that it might have been created for a particular application and that in the implementation phases of this application, modifications have been made so that parts (or all of the component) of what is described in the analysis documentation of the component has never been implemented. Another reason can be that during update or maintenance phases, developments have taken place which are not reported in the analysis. We are using, in this case, an analysis component which certainly has design and implementations associated with it, but whose description is not good.

An analysis component can contain errors if, for example, we have imagined several functions and that only some of them have been implemented. We do not know, therefore, if the analysis of the other functions is correct.

An analysis component can also work very well in the particular case for which it was imagined, does not work when used in another context. The lack of indications about its domain of use can lead to its use in contexts to which it is not suited.

To avoid these problems, we can cite some simple rules:

- Always update the analysis documents;
- Make precise those contexts in which the analysis is used;
- Obey the rules recommended by the methods being used.

By taking the precaution of always updating analysis documentation for a project, we guarantee that this documentation conforms to something real. To update, is certainly to modify what has changed between the moment in which the analysis was performed and the moment the implementation ends. It also removes from the description everything that was not implemented or, at least, indicate that it is still being analysed and has not been validated by an implementation.

From the moment where software corresponding to a given analysis functions correctly, we can consider that this analysis is good for the context of implementation. It is therefore necessary to make a note of which applications this analysis has been used in so as to allow other possible users to determine if they are in the same context or if they need to take precautions.

It is very difficult to guarantee that an analysis does not contain errors. In the case of an informal analysis, the only technique for detecting possible errors consists in having the analysis documents re-read by readers who have backgrounds that are different from the original ones (domain specialists and non-specialists). In the case of analyses using formal methods, respect for the rules given by these methods allows the reduction of the risk of error. Despite all of this, errors can never be completely eliminated by these methods. Here, too, alternative readers are strongly advised.

In the case of the analysis, we cannot really speak of certification. We must, at most, verify whether certain rules have been respected.

Below, for the different analysis methods we have already cited, are some examples of rules.

7.4.1 Entity-relations

There must not be isolated entities. If this is the case, they must form a separate component.

There must not be two entities with the same name.

Figure 7.1 Disjoint entities.

There must not be a disjoint set of entities. For example (see Figure 7.1), if a component is formed of entities *{A,B,C,D}* and *A* is associated with *B* and *C* is associated with *D* and there exists no relation between *{A,B}* and *{C,D}*, then we have two components. They must be separated.

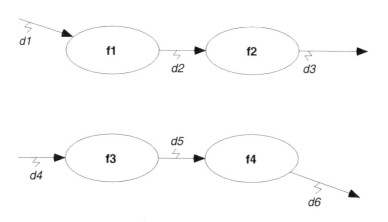

Figure 7.2 Disjoint flows.

7.4.2 Data flows

There must be no functions which receive no data.

There must be no functions which do not produce data.

All input and output data of a refined function must appear in the refinement.

There must not be isolated functions, that is such that all the data they receive and produce lead to no other functions. These functions, if they exist, are components.

There must not be disjoint sub-sets of functions (Figure 7.2). This occurs if in a functional model of functions, some functions communicate data without other functions being involved.

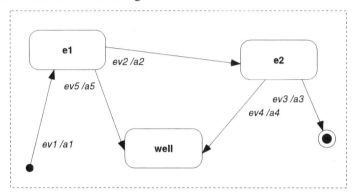

Figure 7.3 Well states.

7.4.3 Automata

There must not be states from which there is no exit (well states, see Figure 7.3).

There must not be a disjoint sub-set of states (Figure 7.4).

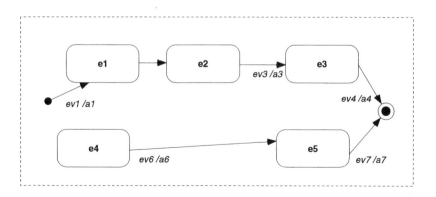

Figure 7.4 Disjoint states.

There must not be unprocessed events.

There must not be inaccessible states.

The behaviour must be made clear for all possible events.

7.4.4 Object diagrams

There must not be isolated objects.

There must not be circular inheritance.

There must not be disjoint sub-sets of objects (see the case of entity-relations).

7.4.5 Object-oriented methods

There must be consistency between the different types of diagram. A good component in this type of method must have a description which shows it in other types of diagram.

7.5 Certification of Design Components

Design components can present two of the same problems as analysis components; lack of conformity with reality or an error.

Lack of conformity with reality is generally due to a lack of update of the design after software update. The documentation now corresponds only partially (if at all) with reality.

Errors are in general rather due to forgetting: we cannot think of a particular use for the component or of a predicted use, but in an unforeseen context.

To avoid the problem of the component's non-conformity with reality, here too, it is necessary systematically to update design documents at the end of the implementation. Some designs with formal methods even lend themselves to automatic update of the design on the basis of the corresponding code. Each technique can be used every time that it is possible.

To avoid errors, the technique of using different people as readers of the design documents can also bring results. It is the only technique useable in the case of informal design.

In the case of a design depending on a programming language (or a formalism close to a programming language), the technique of programming by contract proposed by B. Meyer [Meyer 88] gives very good results during the design phase.

This technique can be very well applied to object languages (but it is still completely useable with other types of language if a pre-processor is used, for example). It consists of indicating at the level of the object classes the invariants and at the level of methods the pre- and post-conditions.

Invariants are conditions which must always be true for some sets of information. These conditions are established during the design phase because they correspond, in general, to the choices which are made during this phase. Every implementation corresponding to this design must conform to the invariants for them to be acceptable.

To fix ideas, here are some invariants:

- In a list, the number of elements of the list is always positive or zero. During design we decide not to treat lists with a negative number of elements (which simplifies matters, let us not hesitate to say).

- To push an element onto a stack and then remove one from the same stack is a process which retrieves the element that was stored. This is the definition of the stack itself and constitutes an invariant.

A pre-condition is a constraint which must be satisfied when we call a sub-program or a method on an object. For example, the square root method can have a precondition which requires that we must pass it a positive or zero parameter. A precondition is one way of indicating in which context a method can be used.

A post-condition is a constraint which must be satisfied after the execution of a method. It is, thus, in fact, a summary of what the method must have performed. For example, in a method which updates a datum, a precondition will verify that the datum actually has the value which was supposed to be assigned to it.

One speaks of programming by contract because it is really a contract which is established between the component and those who use it. If you respect its contract by calling its methods in the foreseen context, it will respect its contract by doing the expected processing. If you do not respect the contract, the component will signal you in the finalisation phase.

Invariants, pre- and post-conditions are, in general, identified in the design phase. It is advisable to state them in the code. It is not necessary then to use thereafter an object-oriented language in order to use this technique. All the design techniques lend themselves to this kind of approach.

One of the checks to be performed when one verifies a design component is to ensure the presence of pre- and post-conditions and invariants.

Object-oriented languages offer a more interesting property to help in the final testing of implementations of a design component: dynamic binding. If we use the technique of capsule classes to describe design components and if the implementations are realised in the form of subclasses of these capsules, we can associate with the capsules the test suites which verify everything predicted in the design. Later, when we implement the capsule component, it will be enough to launch this test sequence, feeding it with the objects which have just been created.

For example, let *C1* (figure 7.5) be a capsule class. We add to this class a test method which verifies all the class methods (for example, in Eiffel syntax):

```
test () is
-- test the class and its implementations
do
   ...
   m1();
   ... verification of m1's processing
   m2();
   ... verification of m2's processing
   m3();
   ... verification of m3's processing
end;
```

All the sub-classes of this class inherit this test method. When it is executed in an instance of a subclass, it tests it.

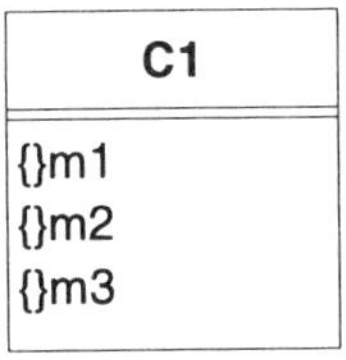

C1
{}m1
{}m2
{}m3

Figure 7.5 A capsule class.

A design component is thus able to judge the validity of its implementations.

7.6 Certification of Code Components

The validation of code components is easier to implement even if there are no techniques giving a guarantee that a component is 100% reliable.

The problems originating in code can be of several orders:

- The code does not correspond to its documentation;
- There is an error in the code;
- The code functions badly in some contexts;
- The code is too complex

The code does not correspond to its documentation if we do not take the precaution of updating this documentation after the implementation of the software.

Errors in code are due to coding errors that have not been identified during testing.

Poor functioning in certain contexts comes from the lack of explicit definition of the contexts in which the code must be used.

7.6.1 Code does not correspond to its documentation

To avoid this problem, there exist several techniques:

- The first is discipline in the organisation of the project: after the finalisation phase (or during), the phase in which the documentation is updated is foreseen and is considered as a function of the changes which have been made;
- The second is to cross-read the code checking it with reference to the available documents;
- The third technique (which is without doubt the most effective while being the most simple to implement) consists of automatically extracting the documentation from the code;
- Another technique consists of saving the design documentation ensuring that coding and design can be effectively traced.

Automatic documentation of code can take several aspects. For example, among the commands available in the Eiffel environments, we find the short command which automatically extracts documentation from a class. This documentation contains the name of the class, the names of its ancestors, declaration of its attributes with associated comments, declarations of methods with associated comments, and contracts. There is the same kind of command in Java environments.

In the case of coding in C++, the header files containing descriptions of the classes can, if they are commented, act as documentation.

For this technique of automatic documentation to work, it is completely necessary to comment the code and to update the comments as soon as modifications have been made. Comments must respect some rules so that tools can be automatically extracted by them (the tools are generally simple to implement). In C, for example, we decide that everything appearing between comment /* B */ and comment /* E */ must appear in the documentation. In this case, the following code:

```
/* B  */
/* General comment about software */
/* E */
lines of no interest to documentation

/* B*/
/* Global variables */
int var; /* comment about var */
other variables
/* E */
other declarations of no interest to the
documentation

/* B */
sub_program (p1,p2)
```

```
/* description of sub_program */
int p1;
float p2;
/* E */
{
    contents of sub_program
}
```

will have the following documentation:

```
/* General comment about the software */
/* Global variables */
int var; /* comment about var */
other variables

sub_program (p1, p2)
/* description of sub_program */
int p1;
float p2;
```

Implementing a tool which extracts this documentation is simple.

We can, by the same principle, integrate documents intended for different uses: one type of comment to frame design documentation and another type to frame code documentation and to help in the job of maintenance.

The last technique that we can cite for having a coherent documentation with respect to code consists of using methods and associated tools to design and then use a code generator, through these tools, to obtain the skeletons of the application being coded. The code thus obtained is complete and up-to-date. Changes are possibly performed. When the code is finished, we can perform an update of the design to make it coherent with the code (the ideal is to have a tool capable of doing this update by retro-analysis). The differences introduced in the design are indicated and we make use of them to add comments. The implementation details are signalled as far as possible in the design and do not interfere with reading.

This technique of retro-analysis is equally useable for code which has been produced by rapid prototyping (RAD). These tools encourage the rapid development of applications. Something complex can be constructed very quickly without documentation. The fact of having a more synthetic view from that which was realised makes for clearer documentation.

7.6.2 Code errors

A first technique for avoiding numerous errors in code consists of using a strongly typed language. Such a language allows one to detect, during compilation, numerous errors. It is necessary, certainly, to avoid passing its type in typing information. For example, the abusive use of casts in C or C++ leads to the introduction of errors that are often difficult to detect.

To remove the maximum number of errors from code, it is necessary to verify the functioning of all the possible paths through this code. There exist, to do this, different techniques.

The fact of testing reusable components adds nothing in particular to the ways of testing. It is just to be more rigorous because an error in a component does not entail problems in a single piece of software, but in several.

Among the numerous techniques for testing reusable components which exist, the most famous are those which are linked to the amount of code covered by the test: we run test sequences over some software and we look at how many paths we have followed out of those which are possible.

Let us mention some techniques. The measure of coverage of blocks of instructions and the measure of coverage of paths from decision to decision. To explain these two notions, let us take an example.

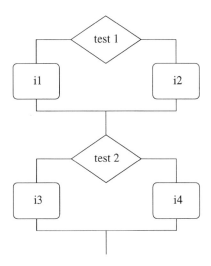

Figure 7.6 Code to be tested.

Let a portion of the code be formed from a test with two branches which join up at a new test with two branches as in Figure 7.6.

To measure the coverage of the instruction blocks consists of examining how many instructions in the software one has passed. To have complete coverage of the software means passing through all its instructions. In the case of figure 7.6, it is enough to perform two tests to do this. A first test which passes through *i1* then *i3*, for example, then a second test which passes through *i2* and *i4*. This type of verification allows us to discover a great number of the errors in software. It does not guarantee that everything is correct. Indeed, if in branch *i2* we modify a variable and that this alteration causes a problem in the execution of branch *i3*, we will not detect it with the two tests that have been performed. It is for this reason that there exist other measures of test coverage: the coverage measure for paths from decision to decision. The principle of this measure is to try to run over all the instructions in the software with all the possible contexts in the test instructions.

In our example, the set of possible paths is formed from:

- (i1, i3)
- (i1, i4)
- (i2, i3)
- (i2, i4)

There are therefore four tests to perform in order to cover all the paths from decision to decision. Some tools such as Logiscope from Verilog allow the verification of those paths that have been traversed in a piece of software after passing through a sequence of tests. By identifying the paths which have not been traversed, we can improve the test sequence until we cover the majority of paths through the software (it is not always possible to have total coverage.)

The test sequence which has allowed the validation of a software component must be stored with this complement so that it can be used to check the component after its extension.

Every sub-program of the components must be validated with the set of representative values. For example, if a sub-program waits for some numeric information whose value is between two limits, there are six tests to be performed:

- Value less than the possible minimum;
- Minimum value;
- Medium value (average);
- Maximum value;
- Value above possible maximum;
- Non-numeric value.

The test of all the inputs of the software must be systematic.

7.6.3 Poorly functioning code in some contexts

To avoid this problem, we can use the programming by contract technique which was described in the section on design components. We protect the different sub-programs by preconditions which verify that the use of the component is done to conform to that which was foreseen. Post-conditions ensure that after its execution, the sub-program has performed the processing that was expected. Invariants executed after execution of sub-programs verify that the context was not destroyed.

Post-conditions are devices for the self-protection of the component against bad use. They are an excellent means of implementing a policy of reuse. When you use a component improperly, you obtain incorrect results (possibly a crash). The temptation is strong, then, to think that there is an error in the components and never to use them again. With the system of preconditions, it is the component which tells you that you are using it incorrectly. The diagnostic is clear. You know that it is in your code that you have to search for the errors.

Post-conditions are self-protection of the component against errors during its maintenance. If during the correction of an error, we modify the behaviour of a sub-program, it can happen that it no longer works as intended. In this case, the post-conditions can detect the error.

Pre- and post-conditions consume time at execution. It is advisable to activate them only during the finalisation phase, and not to use them any more in the final product. This is foreseen in languages which offer, as standard, these assertions. If this is not possible, it is advisable that one uses a pre-processor to choose whether to use them or not.

Eiffel contains a standard for pre- and post-conditions as well as class invariants. To use them in this context thus poses no problem. For example, the square root method can be written

```
square_root (x : real) : real is
require
    x >= 0.0
do
ensure
        result * result - x > - EPSILON;
        result * result - x < EPSILON
end;
```

pre-conditions follow the `require` directive, post-conditions follow the `ensure` directive. result designates the return value of the methods and EPSILON is supposed to be a real constant denoting the precision of the calculations.

In the case of C or C++ code, there are macro definitions which allow us to write assertions. They can be found in *assert.h*.

For example, in C, the same example of the computation of square roots would be:

```
double square_root (x)
double x;
{
    double result;
    assert(x > 0.0);
    ... /* calculation */
    assert(result * result - x > -EPSILON);
    assert(result * result -x < EPSILON);
    return result;
}
```

In the case of a language which does not offer this possibility, it is enough to use a pre-processor to simulate this behaviour. We can write:

```
#ifdef debug
test the precondition and halt if error
#endif
```

7.6.4 Code that's too complex

To get well-behaved code, it is not enough for the code to be error-free, it is also necessary that it be maintainable. To verify that this is the case, we can measure its complexity and use tools to detect critical parts. A shuffling of these parts and of the code is too complex to be done.

7.7. Chapter Summary

To have components of quality is indispensable so as not to fail a policy of reuse. The quality is not just that of the code but also that of the documentation.

We have seen in this chapter a set of problems which can be found in different types of component. Some techniques allowing us to avoid them have been proposed.

There exist techniques for the systematic checking of software. They must be used for code components. For design and analysis components, switching readers is indispensable.

Chapter Eight
Component Storage

8.1 Introduction

In earlier chapters, we have seen how to identify reusable components, and how to construct and certify them. For these splendid components which are guaranteed fault-free (or almost) to be reusable, it is necessary to make them accessible to the maximum number of people. This is the role of two of the fundamental functions in the management of reusable components: storage and search.

In this chapter, we will consider everything concerning storage. The search functions, which must always be considered in conjunction with storage functions, will only be partially presented because they are discussed in detail in the next chapter.

8.2 What Must Be Stored?

The term storage of components covers the storage of a set of information which will subsequently allow the reuse of a component.

Let us take the example of a code component. We saw in an earlier chapter that such a component can be characterised by:

- A detailed design document;
- A source file;
- A user manual;
- A schedule of unit tests;
- A short description of the component;
- A description of the information manipulated by the component;
- A description of the functions to be handled;
- A document describing the overall design and in which the component figures.

Storing this component is not simply a matter of arranging for all relevant information to be in the same place, because it is very different to do, and their grouping represents nothing of any real interest.

What is useful is to store those items of information which allow one to know that the component exists and to retrieve it in certain kinds of search. Once the component is retrieved, the user can go and consult the associated information to really determine if the component is suitable. To visualise this information, it is enough to know where it is and to use the appropriate tools for manipulating it.

The role of the storage function is therefore principally to arrange descriptions of components in order to allow:

- Their retrieval in searches;
- The provision of information allowing one rapidly to know if it is necessary or not to examine them more closely;
- The storage location of the associated information to be indicated.

In order to allow the retrieval of a component during search, it must be classified. The usable techniques useful in such classificatiosn are described below.

The information which rapidly allows users to find out whether the component is perhaps suitable or not strongly depends on the type of component. We have seen in an earlier chapter what information is pertinent according to the different types of component.

References to the information associated with the component must be storable in a component base. It is not necessary to store the information itself.

8.3 Classification Techniques

In this chapter, we are going to study a set of techniques for classifying components. We do not pretend that this list is exhaustive. In particular, the use of artificial intelligence techniques is not considered here. With an eye on simplification, only the techniques which are simplest to use are considered. They are:

- Use of keywords;
- Use of characteristic words;
- Hierarchical classification;
- Facet-based classification.

8.3.1 Keywords

This technique is certainly the simplest technique to implement. It consists of doing nothing in particular. A component is the most frequently associated with several descriptions. We have seen that for code components, for example, we can find three types of description:

- A short, general description of the component;
- A description of the information it manipulates;
- A description of the functions handled.

These descriptions are used to characterise the component (possibly, we could add to the component lists of keywords if one judged that relevant words are not being used).

During the search for a component, the user provides a set of words which seem characteristic of what is sought. For each component, we count how many words in this set are cited in its characteristics and the user is presented with the list of components which contain the maximum number of indicated words.

This technique is very easy to implement since there is almost no work to be done. The tools associated with it are easy to implement; simple searches for words in texts. Its fault is that it gives very mediocre results. The reasons for this are numerous:

- Words have several spellings according to which are its singular, its plural, (masculine and feminine in languages like French, German and Italian you search for 'man' and there is only 'man' in the documents); in some languages, verbs have different endings ('take,' 'takes' and 'taken' in English);
- The spelling is not always well controlled and, in descriptions, perhaps, there are hidden errors in spelling which tends to imply that the component will never be found. (Ser woy carn we neva fin anyfin in dis bas?)
- There exist synonyms which mean that one must search for a component with one word while it is described with another (search for "remove" and it is "destroy" that has been used);
- The description of the components can be made in several languages and even a mixture of languages (Franglais, for example, which is so dear to some French computer scientists). We search for the French word and it is the English word that is in the text (or the other way round); you look for a command which manipulates directories and there are only commands which manipulate folders).

Certainly, one can try to correct these errors in different ways:

- By only giving the roots of the words that are sought, one has more chance of finding what one wants (and, quite often, we can get many more than we wanted);
- By using spelling checkers before storing the components, we can minimise the risk of error;

- By performing phonetic searches;
- By creating a lexicon of words to be used. Agreement can be achieved about the meaning of the different terms that are used and this increases the chances of finding what one is looking for;
- By creating a synonym dictionary. This also allows the performance of more complete searches based on the user's request. The implementation of this dictionary takes a long time.

From the moment at which one decides to implement everything as described above, the results are better, but this technique then becomes highly constraining (above all while it is being set up). It is necessary to evaluate whether the expected results justify all this work. If this is the case, it is necessary to standardise the vocabulary used in the company. The advantages are numerous and go beyond reuse by the fact that it helps create a real enterprise culture.

Using this technique, search time is proportional to the number of components and above all to the quantity of information associated with each component.

The larger the base of components, the longer the search time.

8.3.2 Characteristic words

The technique of characteristic words is an improvement over the keywords technique. It consists of associating a weight with each word likely to be used in a search.

If a word figures in the descriptions of all components, it is not useful to retain it during a search. For such a word, we associate a weight of zero (for example, the case for articles and auxiliary verbs like 'do'). In a search, zero-weight words are simply ignored. It is the same for a word which figures in the description of no components.

A word which appears in the descriptions of half of the components is less characteristic than a word which only figures in some. We will therefore associate a weight which is lower to the former word than to the latter.

Thus, when a query is analysed, we search in the words of the query for all those which do not have a zero weight (vocabulary reduction), then we perform a search in the component base using the resulting words. For each component thus identified, we can associate a weight which is the sum of the weights of the words in the query. The components are returned in order of their weights. This gives the better results than the simple keyword technique because we can take into account the relevance of the words rather than their number.

The major disadvantage of this technique is that it is necessary regularly to recalculate the weights of the words as and when the component base is expanded. This can take a significant time when the base is very large.

Certainly, to eliminate the risks mentioned in the keywords technique which are also applicable in this case also (spelling errors, synonyms, etc.), it is advisable that the words should not be worked upon, but on the roots of the words after removing all terms which are not significant (articles, auxiliaries, frequent adverbs, etc.).

Search time is proportional to the number of components and to the amount of information associated with each component. This technique requires the availability of a dictionary giving the weights of the different words. We can associate with each word the list of components which contain this word. We can therefore increase the space taken by the dictionary, but we make the search time dependent only on the number of words used which will reduce it in size in a spectacular way.

Using this technique, we could give an evaluation of the comprehension of queries which are performed by giving the weights of the words used.

For more information about this technique, [Helm 91] can be consulted as well as [Maarek 91].

8.3.3 Hierarchical classification

A major problem with the keyword classification technique is that this technique does not allow easy navigation through the component base. Words are cited which are more or less general, and components are retrieved as a result. The number of components can be high and there is no structure. If one does not already know exactly what one wants, one has little chance of finding it.

Hierarchical classification consists of structuring the base of reusable components. The entry point into the base is a set of themes. For example, we could have as themes:

- Data structures;
- Graphical components;
- Information storage components;
- Etc.

Each theme can be refined into sub-themes. For example, one can refine data structures into:

- Tables;
- Lists;
- Stacks;
- Etc.

And so on until a level is reached that one thinks of as useful.

To enter a component into the component base, one determines the theme to which it corresponds, then to which sub-theme, and so on until the place where it most naturally fits is reached.

This technique is the one used in libraries; books are arranged by genre, then, for each genre, there is a classification by author then for each author there is a classification by alphabetical order of the title, or by chronological order in a series. The first theme in the classification is the genre, and for each genre, there is a sub-theme which is the author.

The hierarchical classification technique seems *a priori* not to pose any particular difficulties. In fact, one is often confronted by a major problem: how to determine under which theme to store a component. For example, with the themes suggested above, if we have to store a component for storing data structures, it is unknown as to whether to store it under the data structures or under the storage theme. The same problem occurs during a search for this type of component: where should we look for it?

The way forward, in this case, is to store the component twice (once under each theme). Thus, one maximises the chances of finding it. It is still necessary to be able to imagine all the themes under which the user will be tempted to find a component. In the above example, if the data to be stored concerns graphics, the user will certainly search for it under the "graphics" theme (Murphy's law requires this).

Another problem with this type of classification is that of updating the structure. To have usable results, one should not have too many components for each final element in the classification. If, for example, we wish to store a hundred components under five terminal themes, but do not want to have more than ten components in each terminal theme, it is necessary to allow for at least two sub-themes per theme. When the component base is enriched and contains more than a thousand components, the initial hierarchy will no longer be applicable:

- During the introduction of some components, there will be difficulties in putting them in a given place in the hierarchy because they only have a few relationships with the proposed themes.
- If we have 10 terminal themes at the start, and this has not been expanded, we will have on average 100 components per location in the classification and this will make searching tedious.

It is therefore necessary regularly to add a place in the classification. This is very complex and time-consuming because it is necessary to review all the components already stored so as to determine whether it is necessary to modify their classification and to move them to different places.

Thus, even if the hierarchical classification of components seems relatively natural, it is very difficult to implement because it imposes many constraints at the level of maintenance of the classification.

From the moment when a component has not been found because it has not been known where to go to look for it in the hierarchy, there is only one possibility: sweep the entire component base to determine if there is a suitable one. This becomes impossible when the number of components is large.

Search time is difficult to evaluate. It depends on the number of themes and sub-themes and on the number of components in each sub-theme. It can be very different according to whether one immediately finds the good themes or not.

8.3.4 Facets

The facets technique is an improvement on hierarchical classification. It is described in [Prieto-Diaz90b] and [Prieto-Diaz91a].

We can imagine that each component in the base can be regarded according to different aspects. For example, under the aspects:

- What type of information does it manipulate?
- What type of function does it execute?

Each of these aspects is called a facet. Here, we have, for example, the two facets *data* and *functions*.

With each facet, we can associate a set of terms. For example, we can associate with the *data* facet the terms *file, integer, real, boolean, character, software*. We can associate with the facet functions the terms *create, destroy, copy,* and *modify*.

Data	Functions
file	create
integer	delete
real	copy
boolean	modify
characater	
software	

We can determine, for each component entered into the base, the terms which correspond to it on each of its facets. For example, if we store a component which deletes files, we can associate with it the term *file* for the facet *data* and the term *delete* with the facet functions.

In the base, each term on each facet is associated with components which refer to this term.

While searching for a component, we indicate the terms which correspond to what we want to find on each facet. The search consists then of identifying the list of components associated with the given terms, and to retrieve those which are associated with the maximum number of terms on the maximum number of facets. We have therefore the retrieval of components in the order determined by the probability with which they match the specification; the more the component has terms in common with the query, the higher its retrieval probability.

The search time for a component depends only on the number of facets and on the number of terms used in the query.

The interesting thing about this technique with respect to hierarchical classification is that one cannot know some information (for example cannot know with which terms to associate a component with a facet) and to be able all the same to search for it.

To improve the results of searches, we can establish connections between terms. We can specify, for example, that such a term on such a facet is close to some other term on some other facet. When one search fails, this allows one to try to extend it using near-by terms.

We can also improve the technique by accepting synonyms for facet terms.

We can also associate more general terms with facet terms. When a search fails, we can try another search using more general concepts.

The major problem with this technique is the difficulty of determining the facets and the terms in those facets.

The facets cited in examples: information manipulated and processing carried out are those which come to mind the most often. If we limit ourselves to just these two facets, it is necessary to find numerous terms to classify every component. If the number of terms is too small, too many components are found for a given set of terms and the search process becomes tiresome because it must analyse many propositions. One must not anyway have too many terms on each facet. If the number of terms is greater than the number of components, we can replace the search for components by a search for appropriate terms.

One must not, either, multiply the number of facets. It is, in general, very difficult to imagine which facets to use to classify a component base. To find other facets consists of trying to refine one or other of the basic facets which are about the information manipulated and the services provided. By having too many facets, we end up by having redundant terms and over-subtle nuances between facets. It then becomes very hard to see which is the best term to use for each facet, which will be as good in classification as in search.

We can control a part of the difficulty of the implementation of the classification by deciding not to use this technique for arrangement when we have an already large set of components to be stored. From the study of the components, we can imagine which points of view to use and which characteristics to employ for each of these viewpoints.

Another difficulty with the classification by facet system is the difficulty of extending the classification over time. We have seen that it is necessary to avoid having few facets associated with many terms. The greater the number of components grows in the component base, the more we need to increase the number of terms per facet to distinguish it. Each time that we add a term to a facet, it is necessary to review the set of stored components to determine whether they are or are not related to this term. When the number of terms becomes too high to be handle, it is necessary to decide:

- Either to create a new facet;
- Or to divide the component base into several bases.

In the two cases, it is necessary to redo the classification of every component in the base.

The solution of dividing a component base into several bases is preferable to the solution which consists of creating a facet which indicates the type of component. Moreover, if we continue in such a fashion, in order to avoid redundancy between facets, we end up by creating facets which group terms which only have meaning for certain types of components. For example, if in a component base, we add components to make graphical drawings, we will be tempted to add a facet *type of drawing* associated with the terms *bitmap, vectorial,* and *3d.* When we enter a component which has nothing to do with graphics, into this component base, we do not know what to put on this facet and we ignore it. Without this being declared, the base becomes a set of sub-base, each concerned with a subset of the facets. The search for components becomes increasingly difficult.

To multiply the number of component bases consists of reverting to a hierarchical classification with all the problems that it poses. In particular, in which base to search for a component?

8.3.5 The best classification technique

From the above, it can be deduced that each classification technique has advantages and also problems. There does not exist, sadly, any best technique.

It seems that to achieve good results, one should not shy away from mixing different techniques according to the type of component that we want to store.

We will see in the next chapter (which is about component search) that other criteria can enter into the choice of classification technique. We can cite, for example, the desire whether or not to automate the components processing.

8.3.6 Some words on databases

Databases are used to store information. They are therefore suited to storing components. A component can group together very different types of information (and which sometimes are not storable in a database), we can content ourselves, in general, with storing component descriptions.

Databases suit perfectly when it is a matter of performing searching over exact information:

- Search for a component constructed on such and such a project;
- Search for a component developed in such and such a year;
- Search for a component developed by Unitel;
- Etc.

They are ill-suited when we do not know which precise criteria to state in a query. This is often the case when we are looking for components such as those we will see in the next chapter.

Databases and their query languages offer, therefore, a technique complementary to those described above for component store.

8.4 Configuration Management

We will see in a later chapter that the peculiarity of a component is that it is not stable. Components evolve:

- Either because errors are corrected;
- Or because new facilities are added;
- Or because the environment in which it is used also develops (has new capabilities).

For different reasons, which we will consider below, the same component can be used in several different versions. It is therefore necessary for the component storage system to take into account the fact that they can have been in several available versions.

For physical storage of components (i.e., the files which comprise them), the use of a version or configuration management tool is essential. It is then a matter of making the component classification system coexist with this version or configuration management system.

The simplest technique for taking into account the different versions of a component consists of putting a component into the base as many times as there are versions by describing it each time with all its characteristics.

This technique has many problems associated with it:

- It requires the duplication of information and the component base ends up becoming very large;
- In the case of versions due to simple error corrections or to developments in the context of component use, the description is the same and it is up to the user to find the most current version;
- Search for components leads to the retrieval of several similar components. It is difficult to know which to use.

Another way of processing changes consists of only archiving the versions which correspond to developments in the component. The versions which are the result of error correction are simply known as implementations available at the component level. It is necessary to predict the possibility of indicating, for each implementation, what its characteristics are.

In this second way of doing things, we can distinguish between two different concepts:

- Development of a compatible version of a component;
- The variant which changes the classification of a component (because we have added, removed or modified the particulars of the component).

Tight discipline in the management of variants and of developments is necessary so that the component remains usable over time. For each development of a component, it is necessary to ask:

- If it is merely a development and in this case the description must always correspond;
- If it is a variant and in this case a large part of the description of the component must be accessible;
- If it is a new component because it has developed considerably.

To make things easier for future users, it is also necessary to update a history which explains the existence of different variants and versions.

8.5 Where to Store?

Having chosen a classification technique, when there is available a set of components to store, the question arises as to how one can know where to store the components.

We can choose to use centralised storage. The components are held in a space accessible by everyone. Each can store a component and each can search for components.

It is strongly ill-advised to leave everyone free to put components in the base. We run the risk of having components that are improperly validated, poorly document and/or mis-classified. Users falling upon this type of component ended up being discouraged about reuse. In the same way, users satisfied by a component can be quite upset by a new version of a component that is made available a little too soon. A component base administrator is indispensable.

On the other hand, it is interesting freely to give access to the component search mechanisms. To have a component base that is read-only to all provides this function.

A centralised component base is not always possible. For example, a company which has several geographically separated sites cannot use a centralised base with a single administrator. It is, therefore necessary to duplicate the component base and this poses a set of problems:

- How to ensure coherence between the sites?
- How to introduce new components?
- How to deal with inconsistencies?

Ensuring consistency between the sites means guaranteeing that on all the sites the same component base is always used. To be more precise, all the sites access the same set of components. They can, certainly, have a local component base (those which are only interested in their own site).

To do this, it is necessary to organise a regular update of the component bases at all sites. The propagation of a new version of the base (with new components and with the developments of existing components) must be done at the same time at all sites. This avoids disparities which complicate the localisation of errors. In the case of a problem with some components, it is necessary to provide a single point where users can get help. The people know all the known problems, in which state the components are, and know who can work on the correction of errors (component hot-line).

It is not enough for a site to modify the component base (even if it is to correct errors). If a component in the base is inappropriate, a new component must be created, in the local base, and developed from the unsuitable one and a description of the changes which have been made locally must be communicated to a central organ. If these changes are considered interesting enough by the set of sites, it will be propagated during a later issue of the base. One can, then, replace the use of the local component by the component in the base.

The introduction of new components in the base is first performed by the creation of these components in a local base. When they are judged satisfactory and fit to be communicated to a greater number of people, they are sent to the organ charged with handling the common component base. This organ then performs a general check of the component (general character, reliability, documentation, name) and communicate it to all divisions as part of an official issue.

Inconsistencies can appear between the local base and the common one. For example, during the issue of a new version of the component base, new components with the same name as components in the local base can be discovered (and, certainly, have no relationship to them). To avoid this, the simplest method is to admit naming rules for common components (for example, the first letter is reserved or a particular suffix is used). By requiring that components of the local base be un-named in the same way as a common component, we can avoid these problems. Another technique, one possible with some environments, consists of identifying the components as a function of the base in which they appear. There is thus no conflict between two components with the same name if they are in different bases. When a local component becomes common to all, it changes its name to respect the standard that applies to common names. It is necessary to wait until it disappears from the local base where it was created to avoid duplications which are always the source of problems.

Another type of incompatibility can appear when the central organ for handling components receives several proposals for new components for a single type of service, but which make different choices as far as their content is concerned. It is then necessary to choose a proposal which will become the official version (or create a synthesis of proposals). This requires modification of other forms of component which is not always easy to do.

8.6 Saving Components

It is not possible to force users to use components 'as is.' The temptation to adapt them to their particular needs is great. In this case, a common phenomenon is to create in the local base variants of the components which will become the official components at a site which no longer uses the common base.

To struggle against this tendency which loses some of the benefits of reuse, we can advise that the reader makes users aware of the need to warn the component handling organ of the existence of variants. These can then be later taken into account and possibly replace the existing components if they are more appropriate.

At the level of each local base, it is necessary regularly to take an inventory of the components to identify those which are the specialisations of common components and to determine whether their existence is justified.

8.7 Tools

The operation of storage of components presents a tedious side: components must be described. This operation can be simplified by requiring users to respect certain presentation rules for their work and using tools for extracting information.

We can, for example, standardise a header for software proposed as a component; this header contains all the information needed to store the component. The base administrator then only has to verify that the information is correct and make use of the software to extract this information and augment the base. The work of component description is thus distributed between all those who write the components. A part of this standard description can even be extended to the set of developments. This allows everyone better opportunities to find the information describing a piece of software.

In the case of analysis or design components, the use of a method and associated tools allows us to prefer the automatic extraction of information (to the extent that the tools are open).

Storage of components itself can be performed by using an appropriate tool or, perhaps a database and/or a configuration manager.

As we have seen in the different classification techniques, the work involved in storing a component is highly dependent upon the chosen classification system. If we decide to use the keyword technique, there is almost nothing to do (the more complex way is to build a library of synonyms if we want to improve the results obtained with this technique). If we decide to have a hierarchy of components, it is necessary to search all the places in the hierarchy where the component can be found, and, perhaps, reconstruct the hierarchy.

8.8 Chapter Summary

The storage of components consists of storing information which will allow the later retrieval of components and their evaluation.

Different classification techniques have been presented in this chapter:

- Keywords;
- Characteristic words;
- Hierarchical classification;
- Facets;

- Databases.

No technique is perfect. Each has its own advantages and disadvantages.
The problem of handling components in configuration has been discussed. The concepts of version and variant have been made clear.

Chapter Nine

Finding Components

9.1 Introduction

In this chapter we are going to examine the different techniques for searching for components. We will be interested in the context in which one is led to search for components, in the way in which we express a requirement, to that which allows us to make a good choice, and the way of retrieving a component. We also consider the possibilities of automating the search.

We will also study what sort of after sales care it is necessary to provide around a component base.

9.2 Expression of Need: When?

At what moment, one asks, do there exist components that are suitable for the software structure that we are currently constructing?

There is no general rule. Knowing the subject on which one is going to work, one can go and see if there is not something in a component base which allows the simplification of the task. If there exists an analysis of the same subject, it is enough to take it up again, to adapt to the new need and the job is finished. In this case, that which is being looked for is described by the requirements. The ideal reuse environment is then that to which we supply the requirements which replies by providing the analysis, the design and the corresponding code. At worst, it is necessary to make some local changes.

It can happen that we do not have the requirements for the problem to be handled. It is necessary to write it. In this case, we want to nose around, at random, in a set of components. This allows us to get ideas which help in making progress in the analysis of the problem.

In the case of a new problem, there is no choice: it is necessary to get stuck in. It is necessary to start the analysis of the problem (formally or not). Regularly, when we have progressed into this analysis, the component base is consulted when a part of what we have just done is not already handled.

At the end of an analysis, it is useful to go and look in the component base for what has been identified and what is already known. This allows the simplification of the transition to design.

In the design and coding phases, as in the analysis phase, we can, at any moment, ask if what we are considering has not already been handled and if it does not exist in some form as an unretrievable component.

In conclusion, there exists no general method allowing the determination of which moment to go and look for a reasonable component. This depends on the problem being handled, on one's knowledge and of the method one is using if for analysis, design and coding of the software.

On the other hand, according to the moment when one tries to find components, one will wish to make use of search functions using precise criteria or for search functions based on precise information.

9.3 Expression of Need: How?

We have seen that the search for components can be made any moment in the software development cycle. The question which arises then is: how should we search for components? How can we describe what we want?

There are several possibilities for this.

9.3.1 Reuse through habit

The first, the most simple, also the most used, consists of knowing which components exist. During a new development, there is no question to be asked: we know whether there exists a component for the item we are making. We know, therefore, whether we are going to engage in reuse.

This technique is the most common when we make reuse without knowing it. The users of an operating system, for example, know a set of commands, a set of functions and their uses. Their component base is formed from these commands, and augmented functions commands and functions which they have defined themselves, and which they know how to reuse in other developments.

Users of the C language know (and this has become a habit) that for I/O, it is necessary to use the *stdio.h* files; those in Eiffel know *std_files*.

The big problem with this technique is its fixed aspect. It happens that we develop functions when they exist and we do not realise it. From time to time, by consulting the documentation for the components in a fairly random fashion (because we do not remember the name of the function, for example) we discover new components. Other users can also discover new components for you which you do not know. To be persuaded of this, if you develop in C for example you make soundings in your company to find out how many people have implemented memory allocation functions which are protected against user errors (not freeing blocks, freeing of already freed blocks, etc.). You will be surprised at the results.

An advantage of this technique is that it costs nothing. There is no particular organisation. It is enough that each person has access to the component base and to its documentation.

9.3.2 Reuse by navigation in a component base

Another technique also allows one to avoid having to express a requirement which consists of running over the component base more or less randomly, searching for something which might be suitable. If we take the example of an operating system again, this consists of running randomly through the documentation of the commands. If we have an idea of what we are looking for, we can perform the search by isolating the commands and functions which have names close to what we are looking for.

This second technique requires, in order to be usable, a certain organisation in the component base, such as a hierarchical classification, can be appropriate. We are going to look for the components with a given theme, then the theme is refined, and so on. This is what we find in many on-line help systems.

While in operation, this navigation process leads us to discover components whose existence we did not even dream of. Later in other projects, we will know that there exists these type of component and we will go and search in the base.

The big problem with this technique is hierarchical classification. If we do not want to run over the entire component base, it is necessary to know when to search. It is not always clear how to identify the theme to which it relates and how that relates to what we want to do, especially if we have not started the analysis.

9.3.3 Search by requests

The third search technique consists of being a little more precise in the identification of what we are searching for; for example, searching for a component developed by someone last year in such a project. In this case, the request is clear; find all components for whom the author is someone, whose data storage is *XXXX* and which has been used for the project *PPPP*. This type of request is expressed completely by a query of a form suitable for the data base. In this case if the component base is a database, we have all the elements necessary to make the query.

The problem with this technique is that in order to be efficient, it is necessary to give lots of precise information. If we do not know any more who constructed the component, or if we do not know when, we take the risk of being provided with the complete works of someone, or all the implementations in that particular year. And in this case, since it depends upon memory, we can also remember the name of the component and then use the first technique.

9.3.4 Keyword search

A fourth technique consists of describing the characteristics of what we are looking for. We give a set of keywords and all the components associated with all the suggested keywords. If there are none, those associated with the greatest number of key words are suggested.

The problems with this technique are the same as those in classification by key words; attention must be paid to errors in spelling, and to synonyms.

The advantage of this technique is that it is usable for any type of component without any particular effort. If we take care to normalise the vocabulary used in the company we can even obtain good results.

9.3.5 Search by facets

The fifth technique is that of facets. We describe what we are looking for according to different points of view. The components which best correspond to that requested are suggested.

We have seen the limits of this technique. They are essentially due to the difficulty of keeping the different facets up to date.

9.3.6 Comparison

A common problem with the majority of the techniques cited above is that they require the user to characterise what they seek as a function of the way in which the components are stored. This requires an effort that is not always needed, particularly if the number of searches to be performed is large. If in some software, you have identified a hundred functions, you are not really going to have the courage to indicate for each of the hundred functions what their characteristics are when using a facet-based classification system.

So that the search is not overbearing, we wish to make use of a system that does not require us to abandon that which we have little intention of doing in order to express things just for a search phase. The ideal is to use automatic search systems which are integrated into the current work process.

We are going to take a closer look at this. According to the different types of component whose retrieval is desired, we are going to determine how to automate search.

9.4 Automatic Search for Components

9.4.1 Reusing while analysing

Whatever analysis, design or coding technique used, here is a proposition for starting a search for components which integrates it into the normal work process.

As a first attempt, we analyse the requirements of the problem to be handled and identify the major axes. This is expressed in the form of a set of simple phrases. When this is done, we start a first search in the component base. This search (which is still not the promised automatic search) can take the following forms:

- We search in the base for components which correspond well to what was described using search techniques based on keywords or on characteristic words;
- We perform a set of queries by taking, in order of importance, the elements that have been identified in the problem description (we search for components in such a domain, which treat certain aspects etc.);
- We navigate through the base among the domains which have been identified as characteristic of our problem.

The result of this first search can be a complete failure if we do not find anything at all corresponding to what we want. This is not too bad: we start the analysis task using the technique of our choice, just as we did when reuse was not possible.

The result of the search can, on the other hand, allow the identification of components which correspond to those which we want (even if it is not exactly what we desired).

The type of component found is going to orient the techniques used during the development of the software. If these are entity relation analyses, for example, all will continue along this way.

The most difficult part is stopping. The fact that we found components in the domain which are close to what we are looking for allows us to avoid having to start from scratch. We can look at what has been found for suggestions of ways to continue the work This suggest ways to continue the work. We do not necessarily retain everything that has been suggested, but we learn the lessons and the ideas necessary for knowing how to exploit them in the rest of the project.

At the start of this first phase we find ourselves with the problem of not finding satisfactory components amongst the first elements of the solution (see the complete solution if we have found ideal components).

The progress of the analysis is then a sequence of phases constituted from (Figure 9.1):

- An analysis of the problem being handled; we detail the elements that have been identified, introduce new elements and remove redundancies;
- Search for components;
- An alteration of the current analysis to take into account the components being reused.

The moment where we pass from analysis to a search for components is to be determined by each according to the problem which is being handled.

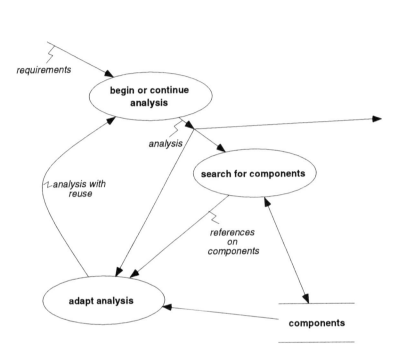

Figure 9.1 Analysis with reuse.

If we have introduced new information into the current analysis that we think is general, it is necessary to start a search in the component base. In the same way, if we think we have arrived at a stable state in the data analysis, it is also necessary to go and verify what we imagined as not already existing in the component base. We will indicate when this is possible and at which time to search for the components as a function of the technique being used.

The search for components can be performed automatically. In order to do this, it is necessary to make use of the tool capable of analysing the current project, to extract characteristic information from it and to go and search in the component base (which should contain descriptions of the majority of the characteristics).

9.4.2 Informal analysis components

In the case where we are making an analysis without using any particular formalism (or notation), the technique described above can be regularly used in the analysis. The different elements of the analysis are detailed and, when one believes that sufficient progress has been made, a search can be made in the component base (the search technique using characteristic words is, in this case, the least constraining). The analysis text being written is examined (preferably by a tool) in order to determine the characteristic words. The search can then be done to find components associated with these words. It can happen that if we find components realised using a particular formalism and it is necessary to keep them no matter what. These components contain a description which is more precise, more concise than the informal text that we have been able to put in its place.

We will see in the next chapter what to do with components which are retrieved but which do not correspond exactly to what we wanted.

9.4.3 Entity-relation components in an analysis

If we perform an analysis on the basis of entity relation modelling, we have a set of entities which are those of the problem which we are considering, and the relations between these entities. The entities and the relations can come from components which it has been decided to reuse following the first search described above, or entities which have been deduced from the requirements.

We continue the analysis cycles and search for components as we have just seen above.

The ideal for these phases in which components are searched for, is to make use of the tool capable of automatically extracting the characteristics of the model under construction.

For such a tool to extract the characteristic information, it is necessary to extract two sets of terms:

- A first set formed of the names of the entities and relations of the model:
- A second set formed from the characteristic words in the comments associated with the entities and the relations used to describe them.

With the first set we can look for components of a entity-relation type which have a great number of entity names and relations in common with a subset of what we are looking for (*common* signifies here identical or synonymous names).

Certainly there is no particular reason that what is proposed will correspond exactly to what we are looking for. Here are some examples of components that can be retrieved for one of the entities in the middle of its analysis.

Let an entity possess attributes *a1* and *a2* in relation *r1* with an entity *e1*, in relation *r2* with an entity *e2* and a relation *r3* with an entity *e3* (Figure 9.2).

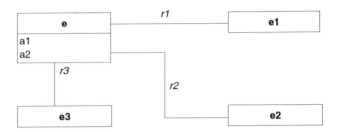

Figure 9.2 Analysed entity.

From this analysis entity, we can see ourselves composing components which have the following characteristics with respect to what we wanted:

- With the same name, with the same attributes but with different relations (that is to say with relations with names different or oriented towards different entities, or with different cardinalities, or even with more or fewer relations), (Figure 9.3);

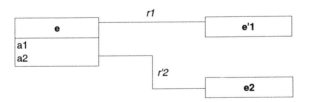

Figure 9.3 Suggested entity.

- With a name or different attributes (name of the attributes which are different or attributes in addition or fewer attributes) and with relations with the same name to identical entities (Figure 9.4.)

We can also find, certainly, all the combinations which have been presented here.

We will also see components suggested in which certain identified entities are modelled as relations and relations modelled as entities.

The probability that a retrieved component is acceptable is a function of a number of information items conforming to that which we wanted. In order to be more precise, it is necessary to weight these similarities; the presence of an entity is more important than the presence of a relation and is itself more important than the presence of an attribute.

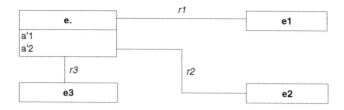

Figure 9.4 Another suggested entity.

Once we have decided to use a proposed component, it is necessary to adapt the analysis or adapt the component to the new need if it does not correspond exactly to what we wanted. The different possible adaptations are described in the next chapter.

This type of search risks, at first, yielding few results. This is due to several things:

- The component base contains few elements; at the time it is going to be enriched and this problem will be solved:
- The approach we are using to model the problem and the approach which is served to model the components are different. This will also be improved with time: by reusing components, we discover new techniques for modelling which we can use later, and certain components come from our implementations, a fact which allows others to discover the techniques which have been used: it also creates a culture in the company concerning components which helps to make reuse easier.

If we have not found components with the techniques which have just been outlined, then we can try to use the second set of characteristic words from the comments associated with the entities and relations. The search is performed over the set of components in the base, whatever the method used for modelling them is.

If we find entity-relation components, they are perhaps modelled from a point of view which is completely different from the one which we have used. It is necessary to take the time to examine these components. This is, perhaps, the better approach and in this case, one should not hesitate to overturn what has already been done.

We can, perhaps, also discover components modelled using a different approach to the one we wanted to use; we should not automatically reject these components. The best analysis technique for the problem currently being handled is, perhaps, the one used in the component, and not the one we expected to use, in which case it might be necessary to think again, and create a new analysis method, one better suited to the problems that are currently being tackled than to the methods that we are used to using.

9.4.4 Object-oriented analysis components

Everything said about entity-relation analysis is also valid for object-based analyses if we replace the word "entity" by the word "object."

We engage in the same analysis cycles followed by a search for components then a consideration of the components that have been suggested.

The essential differences between these two analysis modes come from:

- The presence of methods in objects;
- The possibility for inheritance between objects.

To determine the characteristics of an entity-relation model, it has been proposed that we take the set of entity and relation names. The attributes are only considered to determine whether the suggested entities are exactly suitable or not. The same approach can be adopted for object-based analysis by restricting one's view to the names of objects and relations.

The objects found by a search based on these characteristics can differ from what was wanted in the same way as has been indicated for entity-relation analyses. We can, furthermore, find objects which do not have the same methods as those that are wanted (different method names or different parameters or different numbers of parameters).

We can also use another search technique for objects: it consists of searching in the component base for objects which have the same structure. Having the same structure means having attributes of the same type and methods with the same parameters even if the names used are different. For example, if French words have been used to construct a model and in the components only English terms are used, it is necessary to be able to find the corresponding components to what would be sought even if the terms that were used are different (it is assumed that in the synonyms for terms for a search, English terms have not been used). Searches are made of the type "are there components containing an object with two integer attributes, a real attribute and three methods of which two have two integer parameters and which are in relation with objects having the following characteristics ...?" We save, as candidates, the components which have the most objects of the structure we are looking for.

If we used inheritance in the objects for which we searched in the components, to determine whether the suggested components are suitable, it is advised to make comparisons between the objects after resolution of inheritance. The component and the object for which it must suit are seen as if they had all the attributes and all the methods which they inherit.

For example, in Figure 9.5, component *Y* is considered as equivalent to *B*. It will be seen in the next chapter how to take into account this difference between the component and what was wanted.

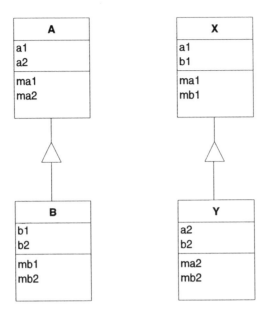

Figure 9.5 Equivalent components.

9.4.5 Components in a functional analysis

In the case of a data flow analysis, it is necessary to question the existence of reusable components for what has been identified each time a new level has been reached in the analysis.

After having detailed the high-level functions of the application that is being studied, a search is performed in the component base to see whether there are objects which cover these functions. The components corresponding to the functions for which candidates have been found can be reused, and the analysis continues by detailing the content of the other functions. When the decomposition of these other functions ends, we can go on to see if there are candidate components for what has just been identified. We proceed in this way until the analysis has been completed.

To search for functions which correspond to a sub-set of the functions that have been identified, we can use a tool which automatically determines the characteristics of what is sought and which performs a search in the component base.

To determine the characteristics of the set of functions in the model that is being constructed, a first technique consists of using the set of function names and the names of the data which they exchange. A search is performed in the component base for functions with the same names and which exchange the same data (using synonyms, as is usual). As for the case of entity-relation analysis and object-based analysis, this technique only gives good results when there is an enterprise culture about the way of reusing functional models and if the component base contains a large number of elements.

In fact, we can perform two types of search: one for functions which consists of searching for components which suggest functions that we had imagined, and one for the data which consists of looking to see if there are components manipulating the data that has been exchanged between the functions. This second approach can be surprising because it prefers data when a functional approach has been adopted. It allows the identification of other ways of manipulating the data than those that we wanted to use.

The other way to characterise the model under construction consists of taking characteristic words from the comments that have been included in the model (in particular in functions and in data). In this way, we can also find data components, that are built using an approach which can be different from the one being used. This is an opportunity for examining whether this new way of doing things is not better than the one that we wanted to use.

As in the previous cases, we can also find components which are suitable but which have not been made using a functional approach and again it is necessary to examine and perhaps question what has already been done.

The components that are going to be proposed can be different from what was wanted.

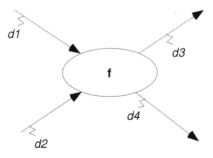

Figure 9.6 Analysed function.

For example in a function *f* that has been identified and which receives data *d1* and *d2* and which produces data *d3* and *d4* (Figure 9.6), we can find functions:

- Which do not have the same input data (different data or of a different number);
- Which do not produce the same output data;
- Which do not have the same behaviour (for example, the case in which the component that has been found corresponds to several functions that have been identified but not with the same exchanges).

We will see in the next chapter how to adapt these components to use them in the current analysis.

9.4.6 Components in an automata-based analysis

The way of handling reuse in an analysis in terms of automata is very close to that which was described for analysis in terms of data flows. If we perform the analysis by refinement of states into more detailed states, then each step in the refinement forms a stable point which is favourable to the search for components to be reused.

To perform an automatic search for components with this type of method, the first idea which comes to mind is to use, the names of the states and the names of the events accepted in this state as the characteristic of a model. This is, almost certainly, not the best way to do things. It can be seen that an automaton component was synthesised in the form of a macro-state in which a set of events is accepted. The names of the sub-states are not characteristics of such a component. What is characteristic are the accepted events and the associated actions. It is necessary to extract this information in order to characterise an automaton.

Extracting actions is not easy because they can be expressed in numerous different ways. We can only have as actions the names of the functions used, and the names of the variables that are manipulated. In the same way, to characterise a state, rather than use its name, we can also use the names of the variables which characterise this state because finally, in a given state, it is to have had an action on the variables which characterise the state.

To characterise an automaton in an automatic way, the names of the accepted events are kept, as are the variables used to characterise the states and the names of the functions and variables used by the actions.

This information being relatively general, we run the risk of making it difficult to find what is sought. This is why it is often preferable to perform a search by characteristic words using all the terms which appear in the automaton: names of events, descriptions of actions and associated comments.

The automata which are found to be candidates for reuse can differ from what was wanted:

- Not treating the same events;

- Treating them in different ways.

As for the other analysis modes, we will see in the next chapter how to adapt the suggested automata.

9.4.7 Components of a composite analysis

We have seen above that, no matter what the analysis method used, there are at least two techniques for automatically searching for components: one method connected to the formalism used which will tempt us to find components having a structure close to that which is wanted, and another, a more general one, which searches on the basis of the comments that are associated with the different items of information in the analysis which has been performed.

The last approach gives better results if we perform an analysis using a composite method. Indeed, if we express an aspect of the problem that is being tackled using one of the formalisms from the composite method, we can find components that are realised in one of the other formalisms. It is possible to use these components because the connections between the different formalisms are defined (in general).

If we have constructed an object model and we have found components using a functional approach, the data that was wanted will be retrieved in the form of information exchanged between functions. This makes clear the use of the data and allows the analysis to continue.

If we have constructed a functional model and we are looking for reused components in the form of object diagrams, some object methods proposed certainly correspond to the functions that are required. We can thus determine to which information items it is applied, and how these items of information are manipulated (and what are their other capacities).

If we have constructed an analysis with a composite method, we can use the techniques described above for all diagrams. The possibilities are thus multiplied for finding suitable components.

9.4.8 Design components

While we move to the software design phase, it is necessary to start by taking stock of the analysis which has been completed. A list is drawn up of the components which have been reused.

For each of these components, we look to see if there are associated design components. If there are, we can examine them and determine whether they are appropriate for the new software which is under construction.

These components can contain architectures that can be re-used. They can also correspond to services for which it is not yet known whether they will be used or not. In this case, they are kept for examination should the time come.

We have seen that it is possible, during general design, to use analysis methods. Reuse techniques that were suggested are thus usable.

During detailed design, we put together several services which have to work together. The use of object diagrams is useful here. We can then, during component search, use the techniques described for object-based analysis methods.

9.4.9 Code components

Is it useful to say that for coding, the first thing to do is to examine the code components associated with the design components that have been reused?

These code components are possible choices for implementation for some parts of the software that is being implemented.

If we use a base of reusable components, it is necessary to endeavour to use abstract representations of reusable code in order to make them easier to understand. This representation is in general useable during the design phase. It can therefore be thought, *a priori*, that in the coding phase reuse is limited to searching among the available design component implementations that have been reused.

If the effort has not been made to make reusable code accessible, during design, then it is necessary to look for code components.

At the start of detailed design, a set of operations are defined that must be coded. The description of an operation details the expected input parameters, the operations to be performed, the data to be provided as output, and the possible constraints that are to be respected (execution time, memory size, for example).

To look for candidates, the description of the operations to be implemented can be relied upon. The characteristic words of these descriptions are saved and the component base is searched for those components which have the best match. As far as choosing the order in which the suggested components are examined, the number of matches can be relied upon: higher priority is assigned to a component which provides more of the operations that we want. The final selection is performed by saving those which respect the constraints that have been fixed.

If an object-based approach has been used for detailed design, another technique for performing the search can be used which relies upon the data being manipulated. Components are sought which handle the analogous data types. By examining the operations suggested over these data, we look to see if there are equivalent operations to those we seek.

9.5 Finding Good Components

We saw above which components can be retrieved during a manual or automatic search. The problem to be dealt with, now, is to sort out which have some chance of being suitable.

If the search technique that you use relies on overly precise information and it responds in a systematic fashion that there are no components which correspond to what you want, you are rapidly going to have to give up all searches in order to save precious time.

Conversely, if the technique that you use is fuzzy, and it always finds you a hundred candidates for each of the searches that you perform, you will quickly decide not to waste any more time in finding out which component is suitable and you will give up reuse.

It is thus necessary to use a technique which suggests some components to you, but does so by suggesting a reasonable amount: less than ten for example. It is also necessary to be able quickly to identify which of the suggested components is suitable.

The ideal, for suggesting a reasonable number of components, is to use a technique which begins by doing a highly exact search: it only keeps the components which correspond exactly to what is sought. Certainly, the number of components retrieved depends, to a great extent, on the type of search that is performed. The more information is provided, the less the number of components which are going to be proposed. The less information is provided, the greater the number of satisfactory components. Techniques which start from a description of the problem under attack in a particular formalism, and which search in the component base if this problem has already been handled, gives results which are highly connected to the degree of development of the problem description: there are lots of candidates at the start because the characteristics are general, and fewer at the end because everything has become very exact.

If a search over exact criteria has succeeded, there is the possibility of having exactly the component that was wanted.

If the search does not succeed, we enter a cycle in which we will search for components which satisfy part of what is asked. The greater the importance of the satisfied part, the greater the chance that the component will be suitable. We must then be content with suggesting to the user the ten components which have the highest probability of being appropriate.

Remember that knowing how a component corresponds to a description, we can use a weighting system for the terms used in the search; they are weighted as a function of the frequency of their occurrence in the component base. This technique gives better results than simply counting the words found in the query and in the components.

It is necessary then to find out if, among the ten components, there is one which is particularly suitable. Two pieces of essential information provide the answer to this question. The first is the probability of being suitable; this is associated with the component by the search technique and guides the order in which the components are going to be examined. The second item of information which helps in making the choice is a succinct description of the component. This description can be formed from some phrases which characterise what the component does.

9.6 Component Retrieval

After finding a good component, it is necessary to move it into the development space so that it can be adapted to the new requirements. We will see in a later chapter, various different techniques for adaptation. Here, we are going to consider the problem of the physical transfer of the component from its storage environment to the place where it will be used.

The simplest case is that in which the reuse environment does not store components, but merely stores their location in the development space. In order to retrieve them, it is enough to note the component reference and to go in and look for it as is done with everything that has been used otherwise. Read access (without write permission) is indispensable if we do not want the components base to be destroyed. Access to components can even be automated if the reuse environment is capable of initiating commands in the development environment.

It is not advisable to have a reuse environment which also has control of component storage. If this is done, it is necessary to use a configuration manager for the component base. This makes the use of tools which themselves perform configuration management somewhat difficult. For performance reasons, sometimes we would like to use a particular parameterisation for configuration management. This is impossible if we are required to work with the component base's configuration manager.

It is preferable to have a component base which stores references to components in a unique fashion. It knows the version numbers of everything that needs to be handled in configurations in other spaces.

9.7 After Sales Service

A good component based system must help with an after-sales service (or rather an after-reuse service). Two major advantages of reuse are being able to make use of the correction of errors in the components which are reused and benefit from their extension. For this to be true, follow-up must be ensured after a component has been reused.

When a component has been reused, it is necessary to warn when an error is corrected or when a new version with extensions is available.

If we use a development environment with configuration management, it is enough to update all the components which have changed. All the users of these components will then know that a new version is available. It will remain to be determined whether this new version represents the correction of an error or an extension. To do this, several non-exclusive solutions can be suggested:

- The first consists of putting in place a news system for the components. All users can consult a file in which information classified by component name is located. For each component can be found a short description of its different versions with indications as to changes between versions. A user who discovers a new component version in their development space will consult this file to find out what this new version contains;
- The second solution consists of storing its own history inside the component, if possible. The reason for the new version is put into a note which is part of the component;
- The third solution consists of storing for each component, the list of the names of its users and telling them, by electronic mail, of the existence of new versions and giving them a description. This last solution is more costly in machine resources and not always easy to implement. It is necessary to know when a user stops using a component and when they are replaced by someone else as a user of the component.

Besides after-sales care, every operation aimed at making new components or extensions of existing ones known can only improve reuse.

9.8 Learning from Search

The point of component searching is to provide a user with the components they are looking for. This happens with the techniques mentioned above. Each search can also be used to improve the component base and lead to subsequent searches being more successful. To do this, it is necessary to handle a set of statistics at the level of the component base. We can, for example, assemble statistics about:

- Searches which fail;
- Components that are not used;
- Components that are unsuitable;
- Use of the base.

We are going to detail these statistical differences.

9.8.1 Searches which fail

Searches which fail must be recorded. By comparison with all the searches which have failed during a given period, the identikit picture of the components which are requested but unavailable can be established. This allows us to form a set of requirements and start their fabrication.

The analysis of the searches which fail can also help in revealing a poor component classification. The users make a certain type of query which does not succeed when the components exist and would have been found if the query had been differently formulated. It is necessary, in this case, to reconsider the component classification (and certainly, if it is not too late, to warn those who have performed searches for the existence of components which could be suitable).

9.8.2 Unused components

For each component, it is possible to store the date of the last time it was retrieved by a user. The analysis of this information allows the detection of components which have not been used for a long time (or even which have never been used): dead components. The reasons why they are no longer used can be that they are no longer fashionable, they are not up-to-date with respect to current techniques, they do not correspond to a requirement, or they are badly classified.

The result of this analysis must lead either to the removal of the component from the base if it really does uselessly clutter it, or to its modification (or the modification of its classification) so that it acquires a new existence.

9.8.3 Unsuitable components

To keep a component base at an adequate level, it is interesting to ask the users for their opinions about the components after use:

- Were they suitable?
- What changes needed to be made?
- Did they contain errors?
- Are there any precautions in use that need to be observed?

The answer to these questions must be the improvement of the components. If it is learned that all the users of a component have had to make the same change to use it, then the component is badly designed. It should be usable in its basic version. The description of the changes and errors allows us to make it better conform to the expectations of the users.

It is imperative that every error detected in a component in development spaces is returned to the component base so that the error is directly corrected at its source.

9.8.4 Use of the base

Usage statistics for the component base such as the number of consultations each day permit us to find out if reuse always works or if the users are engaged in re-writing everything themselves.

A modification in the rhythm of consultations of the component base must be analysed in order to react quickly if the users become dissatisfied with reuse is witnessed.

To succeed in reuse, the component base must always be of the highest quality.

9.9 Chapter Summary

We have seen, in this chapter, when and how to search for components. The quality of what is suggested depends on the quality of the component base and the level of accuracy of the queries which are performed.

Some statistics on the searches performed in the base allow the improvement of its quality and also form an identification technique for components which are to be implemented.

Chapter Ten
Adapting Components

We have seen in the last chapter how to find reusable components, wherever possible, in an automatic fashion. After the satisfaction which follows the discovery of these components, one is frequently confronted by a new problem: certain components differ considerably from what is wanted. How can they be used in the new development? We are going to answer this question in this chapter.

After a general recapitulation of what constitutes good reuse and on the goals sought, we are going to see, component type by component type, what differences there can be and how to remove them.

10.1 Reuse or Not?

When components have been found which are appropriate for the current construction, but of which some components are not completely suitable, it is quite tempting, particularly if it is the start of the implementation of a reuse policy, to copy components locally and to modify them so that they suit exactly.

This is a grave error!

We have seen, when we studied reuse techniques, that copying a component, then modifying it does not bring us the benefits afforded by reuse:

- There is no benefit from error correction;
- There is no benefit from development.

There is thus an imperative rule for when we engage in reuse:

LOCAL MODIFICATIONS OF COMPONENTS ARE BANNED!

Respecting this rule generally implies another behaviour which consists of considering the retrieved components which are not exactly suitable to what one wants. Here again, this reasoning shows an error. Reuse is difficult the first time. But, little by little, we acquire habits; the more components become available, the easier reuse becomes.

To succeed in a reuse policy, it is necessary to fix the following rule, at least in the early stages; it is necessary to try to reuse each time candidate components are found.

This general rule must not be transgressed except in a limited number of cases, amongst which the following can be cited:

- The software being constructed has size or performance constraints which mean that using a component does not allow the constructors to respect these constraints;
- The adaptation of a component requires more work than the benefit to be derived from reusing the component;
- The component is badly designed.

In the first case, it is often the same problem of reuse which cannot be retained because of the constraints which the software must respect. Rather than having found a component exactly corresponding to what is sought, and of a desired size and performance, it is preferable directly to develop specific software.

In the second case, it is necessary really to evaluate the benefit which reuse brings with respect to a new development effort. In this evaluation, it is necessary to take into account all the factors:

- Design time;
- Coding time;
- Testing time (unit and integration tests);
- Time to draft documentation;
- Predicted effort in maintenance as a function of the component's complexity;
- Predicted developments as a function of component type.

Above all, it is not necessary to reach a decision as just a function of coding time. If the component is complex, we can gain on validation time for it will be enough to validate the behaviour of the component in the new application.

The third case, where one can call a component into question, is the one in which the design of the component is poor. This means that to use it correctly, it must be modified. In this case, it is necessary to suggest a new version of the component to the manager of the component base. The manager will decide whether this new version becomes the official version of the component or if it should have the status of a variant.

Even in the case in which a component is full of bugs, it is necessary to try and preserve the component base. To suggest a new version of a component to the administrator of the component base is preferable by far than to let all the component users create their own variants. Otherwise we very quickly obtain a group of developers who do not use components anymore for they are no longer compatible with those they have created for themselves.

To warn the component base administrator of the existence of errors in some components must be considered a moral contact which all those who use the base must respect. By making corrections local to a component, by trying to remove an error which has been found, the error is left in the real component and there will remain other errors which are yet to be found and corrected (and this is a waste of project time and money). This runs the risk of having problems when the error is officially corrected (for example if the correction that has been made in the local component is a simple workaround which takes into account the fact there is an error).

Using components is a contract. To benefit from reuse, it is necessary to implement the components. All the local initiatives which are not profitable to all are to be proscribed.

In what follows, we are going to see how to adapt components to a new situation without modifying them. The circumstances in which it is necessary to demand alteration of the components will be highlighted and the way of making this change will be the subject of the next chapter.

This chapter does not pretend to be exhaustive and to present all cases of reuse. On the contrary, it is concerned above all with simple cases. For the different techniques of analysis, design and coding, only elementary information is given as examples of components. This does not mean that we assume that we only reuse elementary information, it means that we assume that complex components can be seen as assemblies of elementary ones to which the proposed principles can be applied. The combinations of the cases studied here are to be treated according to the context in which they are encountered.

10.2 General Rules for the Adaptation of Components

In what follows, we are going to detail a set of techniques which allow the reuse of a component which does not correspond exactly to what was wanted.

Before starting on these recipes relating to the way in which the analysis, design or coding is conducted, we are going to examine some reactions which it is good to have when a component has been found.

10.2.1 Don't say the component is bad

If there is a difference between what you imagined and what is to be found in the component that is offered to you, examine the component more closely. It deals, perhaps, with some things that you have forgotten. It has, perhaps, a parameterisation that you have not thought about.

A good way to reuse the component, in this case, consists of determining what has been done (analysis, design or code) and to take into account what has been learned with the component. Rather than following a path where it will be necessary to re-invent everything, asking questions can allow one to travel along a road where a large part of the work has already been done.

Reuse allows, in this case, an improvement in the quality of what has been done. The cases which have not been predicted at the start can be handled and parameterisation is better (if these reasons were those which were responsible for the components being kept).

10.2.2 Don't get a fixation about names

If the only differences which exist between the component that is suggested to you and the one you imagined derive from the use of different names, then it is necessary to examine if one of the following cases applies to you:

- The terms that you have used are too specific. Those which are used in the component are more general. In this case, it is necessary to replace the terms in your analysis that you have chosen by those which are found in the component;
- There are terms which are used in the component which are too specific. Yours are more general. This is an error in the component. It is necessary to ask the base administrator to correct it;
- The terms that you have used and those which are found in the component are all too specific. It is necessary to find more general terms which cover the cases. These new terms must be suggested to the component base administrator so that they can modify the component and you must modify your analysis;
- There is no relation between what is wanted and the corresponding information in the component. The information that was wanted does not therefore exist in the component and there is information in the component that is not wanted. The processing of these differences depends on the type of component. Descriptions will be found below about what can be done in this final case.

10.3 Adaptation of Analysis Components

10.3.1 Informal analysis components

Context

You have written down the principal ideas concerning the problem that you are in the middle of studying. You have looked to see if, in the component base, there are informal analyses relating to these different ideas. Some candidate components are suggested to you:

- Some perfectly suiting some of the ideas that you have had;

- Others corresponding to some ideas, but suggesting many more things than you wanted;
- Yet others corresponding to parts of ideas: they lack many things with respect to what you had imagined.

For the components which are perfectly suitable, no problem. Above all, do not duplicate them. Make reference to them in your new analysis and put some comments in if necessary. The majority of text processors will allow you to add an annexe in the specification document containing the text of the component without having to copy it (inclusion by reference).

For the other candidate components, here is how to adapt them to your new requirement.

Adaptation of overly rich components

You have analysed a part of the problem which you want to handle and a component has been suggested to you which analyses the same aspect. On the other hand, it also analyses other cases.

If you recall the general rules that were proposed, you know that the first thing to do is to ask whether the component has not brought the fact to light that this aspect of the problem has been badly analysed and that it is more complex than predicted. If this is the case, you can only thank the reuse policy of your company, take into account the case that you have omitted and verify the impact that it has on the rest of your analysis. After having updated your analysis, you will be able to go over the component base again. There is perhaps more important information to retrieve.

If your analysis is adequate, there could be a problem with the level of the component:

- It is perhaps too specialised, or;
- It mixes several problems.

If it is too specialised, it could well be that it deals with a specific problem whose general case corresponds to what you imagined. In this case it is necessary to verify that there is no component in the component base handling the general case.

If there is such a component, then there are two errors in the base:

- The component should be retrieved during the search. Perhaps it was and you rejected it. It is necessary to examine which is the case, and determine whether there is nothing to be changed among its characteristics. If it was not retrieved for you, it is without doubt improperly classified. It is necessary to ask the administrator to review its classification.
- The component which was retrieved must reference the component which you just found. There is duplication in information and it is necessary to communicate this fact to the base administrator.

If there is no component handling the general case, when you have terminated your analysis (without reuse, sadly), it will be necessary for you to suggest to the base administrator your analysis indicating that it is more general than the component which was retrieved. Be careful yourself not to propose a special case. The base administrator will have to verify that what you propose is really a generalisation of the existing component. If this is not the case, and if what you propose is also something specific, he must try to construct a component which generalises the existing component and the one that you have made. If the more general case does not exist, it will be necessary, then, to record your analysis as a variant of the existing component.

If the retrieved component is a mixture of several problems, it is necessary first also to verify that it is not the same mix as yours. If this is the case, the component covers several aspects of your problem. If it is not the case, it is necessary to communicate the problem to the base administrator. If you are the only one who needs the corrected component, he will doubtless suggest to you that you make the division yourself to isolate the part of the component which suits, and after your project he will make official the division of the component into several parts on the basis of your work.

Adaptation of very poor components
A component has been retrieved, which handles aspects of your problem but this component takes into account only some of your ideas.

The first check to be made is to look to see whether what has been studied is not a particular case of what is handled by the component. If this is the case, the analysis containing the aspect covered by the component can be decomposed into two parts: a general part which refers to the description given in the components and a specific part which describes the particularities of the case being considered. At the end of the project, the analysis will be suggested to the administrator of the component base as an example of a use of the component.

If the study that has been done is correct, there is perhaps a problem at the level of the component: it is incomplete. In this case, it is necessary to advise the component base administrator and complete the component. The final version will become the official version of the component at the end of the project and after verification by the base administrator.

It can also be the case that there is no problem at the component level; but that in the analysis several issues have been confused. It is then necessary to know how to distance oneself with respect to what has been done, in order to see if it is not possible to separate more cleanly the different parts of the analysis and, from this, reuse the proposed component and, perhaps, others, once the reorganisation has been completed.

Other adaptation cases
It can also be the case that the component is unsuitable, even though it is close to what is wanted. In this case, it is not necessary to try at all costs to reuse it by means of expensive and dangerous alterations.

A possible technique for reuse consists of citing (or inserting) the proposed component and giving the description of the differences found in the work. This is, certainly, possible if the differences are few in number or highly localised. If it is not the case, it is preferable to retake all of the description without reusing it.

10.3.2 Entity-relation analysis components

Context
You have studied the data relating to the problem you have to solve. You have to construct an entity-relation model showing the different entities in the problem and the relationships which connect them. In general, an entity in your analysis corresponds to the description in figure 10.1.

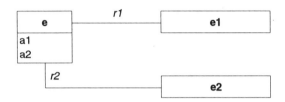

Figure 10.1 Desired component.

An entity *e*, with attributes *a1* and *a2*, is associated via relations *r1* and *r2*, to entities *e1* and *e2*.

You search in the base of reusable components to see if there are entities that match the ones that you have identified. Components corresponding to sub-sets of entities in your analysis are retrieved. For an element such as e, several candidates are retrieved:

- Some agree exactly to what you have identified;
- Others are similar (same name, same attributes), but do not have the same relations;
- Others have the same relations but have a different name or different attributes.

Perfectly agreeing components
For entities which correspond perfectly to the entities that you have identified, there is no problem. In your analysis, you are going to replace the entities which correspond to the reused ones by references to the latter.

It is imperative to use references and not copy the reused·component. This allows one to benefit from later developments of the component. In the case where we use a modelling tool, it is necessary for this tool to allow the referencing of common information. This information must be visible in the new diagrams that we construct, but it must not be possible to modify it. It is necessary to be able to indicate that this is previously defined information. Every modification of this referenced information must always be suitable for communication with those who use it without requiring complicated manipulation. Respect for these criteria is important when one chooses a tool to simplify the use of a method and that one wishes to reuse.

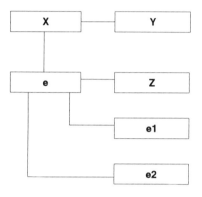

Figure 10.2 Without reuse.

The fact that a component is being reused allows the simplification of the task that one is engaged in performing. If, for example, the analysis in Figure 10.2 has been performed, and a reusable component has been found that corresponds to entities *e*, *e1* and *e2*, the analysis can be simplified as in Figure 10.3.

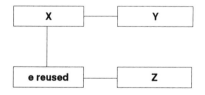

Figure 10.3 With reuse.

Different relations
The differences (apart from differences in name) between relations which are found in the retrieved component and the relations that you have imagined for a particular entity can be of several orders:

- The cardinality of the relations are different;

- The entities with which the proposed entity is in relation are different;
- There are more relations;
- There are fewer relations.

Here are some possible adaptation techniques for each of these cases.

Different cardinalities
For an entity such as that described in Figure 10.1, the entity in Figure 10.4 is suggested to you.

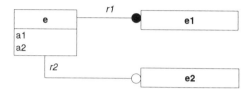

Figure 10.4 Different cardinalities.

You certainly retrieve your entity e, it is certainly in relation with entities *e1* and *e2*, but the relations have cardinalities different from what was wanted.

Several cases are possible (in addition to errors in analysis or in the component):

- The cardinalities are different because the point of view that has been taken in doing the modelling is not the same as that used during component modelling;

Figure 10.5 General view of marriage.

- For example, let us assume that the couple component is described as indicated in Figure 10.5. The point of view used to model this component is that every man is associated with one or zero women by the relation of marriage and that every woman is associated with at most one man by this same relation. This is the general case which has been taken into account;

Figure 10.6 Machine view of marriage.

- Marriage could also be modelled as indicated in Figure 10.6. In this viewpoint, the case of a particular man is considered. He is associated with at most one woman by the marriage relation. The cardinality of 0 or 1 is no longer represented with the man because it would have no meaning; if the man is married to a woman, this woman is married to him.

The differences in cardinality are therefore to be studied with care. A component can be kept if the differences are only due to the use of different viewpoints during analysis. It is necessary to explain this difference if the component is used. We need to be watchful during design to make the right choice.

- If the cardinalities are really different between the analysis that has been made and the component. There is no identity between the relations; there are additional relations in the component and there can be fewer than what was wanted (see below).

Different associated entities
For an entity such as that described in Figure 10.1, the entity in Figure 10.7 is suggested.

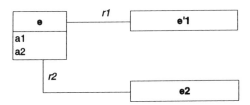

Figure 10.7 Different associated entity.

You will certainly retrieve your entity *e* and there are the same relations from *e* to other entities. These relations have identical cardinalities and neighbouring meanings.

On the other hand, some of the entities with which *e* is related does not correspond to what was wanted (here, for example, it is associated with *e'* in place of *e1*). It is considered that an entity does not suit if the entity retrieved from the component is not appropriate (by one of the techniques that we are currently examining, for example) to correspond with what was wanted. In this case, the relation *r1* does not fit; it is unnecessary in the component, and the relation that was wanted does not exist in the component. We are going to deal with these two cases.

Additional relation
For an entity such as the one described in Figure 10.1, the entity in Figure 10.8 is retrieved.

There are clearly relations *r1* and *r2* to *e1* and *e2*, but there is an additional relation between *r3* to an entity *e3*.

If the difference is not due to an error in the analysis or in the component, it is necessary to verify whether the additional relation is indispensable for the component, but useless to the current analysis. Depending upon the case, it is possible to decide whether the component is appropriate or not. For example, if the relation is simply one whose usage is known, it is perfectly possible to decide to use the component. During the design phase, this relation will be ignored. On the other hand, if it is fundamental to the component, it is not necessary to reuse it: it will certainly not be appropriate.

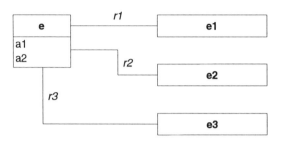

Figure 10.8 Additional relations.

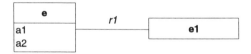

Figure 10.9 Missing relation.

Missing relations

For an entity such as that shown in Figure 10.1, the entity in Figure 10.9 is suggested to you.

It lacks the relation *r2* to entity *e2*.

Two cases must be considered:

- The relation is something that has been forgotten in the component: it is necessary to ask the administrator of the component base to add it;
- The relation is specific to the new analysis; this is the normal case during reuse. The general component is referenced and what is specific is added by associating with it the desired relation (Figure 10.10).

Figure 10.10 Addition of missing relation.

For this to have a meaning, it is necessary for the relation to be a use of the component (relation oriented towards the relation). If this is not the case, it is because a variant of the component is needed.

Different entities
The retrieved entity can have the desired relations with the desired entities, but not be exactly suitable because:

- It does not have the same name, or
- It does not have the same attributes.

We are not going to revisit the case of name difference. Adaptation is always of the same type. It is necessary to change the name in the component, in the analysis, or in both.

The attributes can be different for several reasons (different from difference of names):

- There are additional attributes;
- There are fewer attributes.

In the case of too many attributes, it is necessary to determine the role that they play in the component. If they can be ignored during design, or if it is possible to assign them a value by default, then the component is useable, otherwise it is inappropriate. It is possible in this last case to construct what is wanted by copying components and by removing of what is extra (a solution to be avoided whenever possible).

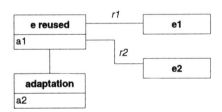

Figure 10.11 Addition of an attribute.

If there are fewer attributes in the component than it is suitable. It is enough, when it is retrieved, to put it in relation with the entity which contains the missing attribute (Figure 10.11).

This set corresponds to what was wanted.

10.3.3. Object-based component analysis

Context
You have drawn the object diagram in Figure 10.12. You are looking to see if there are any components for object *B*. In order better to determine if what is suggested to you is adequate, it is necessary to proceed in two steps.

In the chapter on component search, it was seen that the first thing to do is to flatten inheritance. This consists of seeing object *B* as shown in Figure 10.13. It has attributes, methods and relations that it has inherited from its ancestors.

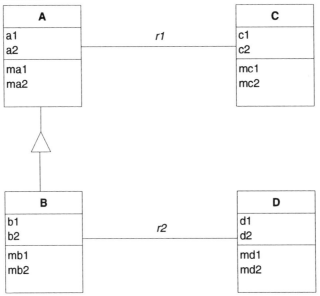

Figure 10.12 Original model.

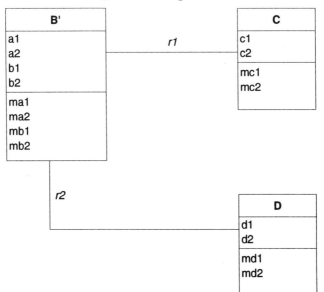

Figure 110.13 Flat model.

We then look for those objects which are closely similar to *B*. Candidate objects are also those with flattened inheritance in order better to determine the differences and the changes to make.

When some objects that can be reused have been found, we can look again at the initial inheritance diagram so as to situate oneself in the real context.

After the phase during which the search is performed for components corresponding to object B with flattened inheritance, it is possible to find different types of candidate (we do not speak of possible naming differences because we know how to handle them):

- Some correspond exactly to B: same attributes, methods and relations;
- Some do not have the same attributes or the same methods;
- Some do not have the same relations.

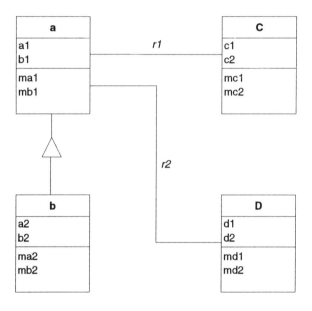

Figure 10.14 Different decomposition.

Objects that fit perfectly

You have found the object B of your dreams: same name, same attributes, same methods, same relations pointing to the same objects. Before reusing this fabulous object, it is necessary to look at how it is formed. If it looks like the description in figure 10.12, it is wonderful. Sadly, you can also have the composition in figure 10.14 where, a priori, nothing corresponds.

Do not despair, look calmly at the situation. If the component is designed in this way, there are certainly reasons for it. The object a in the components has certainly many more possibilities than the object A that you want. Look at your analysis from this new viewpoint. You are going, perhaps, to find that this suits you better, and that a part of what you have done is going to earn the privilege of being used again.

If the architecture of the component really does not suit you, it is necessary to indicate this to the component base administrator. If there are already complaints along the same lines, the component then is badly designed and it is necessary to redo it.

Different attributes or methods

Different attributes

The difference between the attributes of the object that is suggested and the attributes that you have identified can be of different orders:

- One or more attributes have different names;
- One or more attributes have different types;
- The object suggested to you has more attributes than you want;
- The object suggested to you has fewer attributes than you want.

We know how to handle different names, but it is not always simple to determine whether the different names are acceptable or not. In some cases, it is necessary to see some objects that have been identified by someone else in order to be ready to accept reuse.

Figure 10.15 Different objects.

For example (Figure 10.15), if we have the two objects book and person characterised by title and date of publication for one, and name and date of birth for the other, it is necessary to be ready, if one is only interested in these items of information, to consider them as identical objects: objects with names and dates. The object in Figure 10.16 can be used for both.

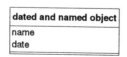

Figure 10.16 Common object.

Be careful, for this is not really appropriate unless, in every analysis that has been made, we only take into account name and date of the information items book and person. It is necessary to pay attention to everything which is not mentioned in the analysis. We could very well have shown only the attribute's *name* and *date*, and have half understood that person knows how to walk and think. In this case, it is clear that the object *named and dated* object is not appropriate.

If one or more attributes have different types from what was required, it is necessary to look for a more general type. Precision at the level of attribute types will be discussed below, during design and coding. If there really is no possible correspondence between types, it is preferable to name the attributes differently, and to consider that one has one of the cases of difference described above (more or fewer attributes).

If the component object has more attributes than desired, it is necessary to see whether this is an oversight in the analysis currently underway that must be repaired, or whether it is an error in the component which is too specialised. In this last case, it is certainly preferable to reuse an ancestor of the suggested object. It is therefore necessary to examine all its ancestors. If one is not found that is suitable, it is necessary to ask the component base administrator for components to examine if it is not possible to construct one. Otherwise, if one can attribute a default value to the attributes then the component is useable. It will be necessary to think of removing the attribute in the chosen implementation.

If the component object has fewer attributes than desired, we have the usual case of specialisation. We reuse the suggested object by creating a subclass which adds the missing attributes (perhaps under renaming). This subclass can be used even if it is not predicted that it will be encoded with an object-oriented language. It will be enough, at the moment of coding, to replace inheritance by the contents of what is inherited (if possible by reference).

Different methods

The differences between the methods in the retrieved object and the methods that you have identified can be of different kinds:

- One or more methods have parameters or a return type different from what is sought;
- The suggested object has more methods than desired;
- The suggested object has fewer methods than desired.

If a method has parameters or return types that are different, it is necessary to examine the differences more closely. They can come from:

- Parameters which do not have the same name;
- Parameters which do not have the same type;
- A different number of parameters;
- A different return type.

Since the names of the method's parameters have no importance to the analysis, the first case is done with and the method is suitable.

If the types of the parameters have no relation to what was predicted, then it is necessary to consider that the method is not what is wanted.

If the types of the parameters are of ancestor or descendant types of the types that we want, the method is appropriate. Eventually, if it is envisaged that the coding will be in Smalltalk or in Eiffel, a redefinition of the component method will be possible. In other cases (C++ or Ada, for example), it will be necessary to create a new method which calls for the one in the component.

If the number of parameters is different, the method is not the one we want (unless some parameters can take default values).

If the return type is different and has no connection with the type we are looking for, then the method is different.

If the return type is an ancestor of the type we wanted, then the method is suitable. In the other case, the method is not suitable.

If the component object has more methods than is wanted, it is necessary to see whether this is a mistake in the analysis which is being undertaken which needs to be repaired, or if it is an error in the overly specialised component. In the latter case, it is certainly preferable to reuse an ancestor of the component by ignoring the extra method (this is a very frequent case with data structure components). In this case, in the coding phase, it will be necessary to use an implementation of the component which does not contain the unused methods or to use an optimiser that deletes dead code.

If the component object has fewer methods than wanted, we have the normal case of specialisation. The proposed object is reused by creating a subclass which adds the missing methods (after possible renaming).

Different relations

What was said for entity-relation components on this subject is appropriate here also. In the case in which there lack relations with respect to what is wanted, it is possible to add them in a subclass.

The concept of relation connected with a different entity needs to be examined in detail. A relation can be found in the component which relates to an ancestor of the class that was wanted. If what is contained in this class is enough for the problem under attack, then the relation which is in the component is better than the one that was imagined. If the relation in the component goes towards a descendant class of the wanted one, then it is perhaps an error in the component (to be told to the administrator) or an omission in the current analysis. If it is neither of these two cases, we are really in the presence of a different relation to be handled as we have already seen.

Particular case

It can happen that we find not one but several components each of which correspond to a part of what is wanted. For example, for the object *A* in Figure 10.12, we can find objects *A1*, *A2* and *A3* in Figure 10.17.

In this case, we can use multiple inheritance to construct the object that we want from the components that have been found (Figure 10.18).

If the language that is being used later for coding does not support this technique, it is necessary to simulate it (if possible by code generation) by creating an object A which takes all the characteristics of the objects which it should inherit from.

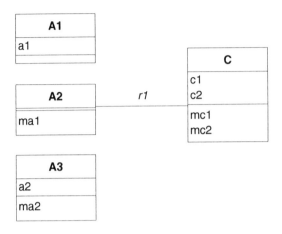

Figure 10.17 Several candidates.

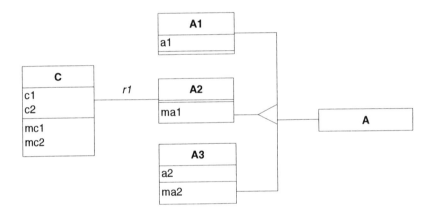

Figure 10.18 Composition of the candidates.

10.3.4 Data flow analysis components

Context

A sub-set of the functions that you have thought up can be synthesised by the diagram in Figure 10.19.

The components retrieved for this sub-set can belong to one of the following categories:

- They correspond exactly to what was wanted;
- They do not have the same input and output data;

- They do not have the same decomposition into sub-function.

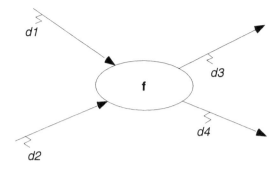

Figure 10.19 Desired component.

Here is how to adapt these different components.

Suitable component
If you have found a component which perfectly suits, then it is necessary, in your analysis, to replace all the functions which become useless, by means of a reference to the component and of connecting the inputs and outputs of the components to the proper places. It goes without saying that the component should not be copied.

Different data being output or input

The different cases of different data (not with different names) are:

- One or more data in input to or output from the function do not appear in the component;
- One or more additional data items appear in the component.

Additional data
For a function such as the one shown in Figure 10.19, the function in figure 10.20 is suggested.

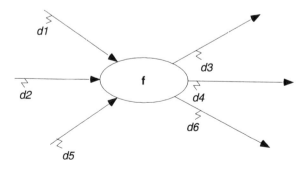

Figure 10.20 Additional data.

There are certainly the data *d1*, *d2*, *d3* and *d4*, but the function also uses data *d5* and *d6*.

If this is not an error in either the analysis currently in hand, nor in the component, then we have one of the following cases.

In the case of an additional input datum, the cause can be a matter of the parameterisation that we have not adopted. We can then certainly determine a value by default for this datum. We can reuse the component by making clear that during design, it will be necessary to see how to simplify the function so that it does not use this useless parameter, or see how to provide it with a default value (for example in another function). Possibly, we will be able to find a design component which has already foreseen the case.

If the datum is mandatory for the proper functioning of the component, the analysis that has been undertaken must really be re-examined to be sure that there is no omission. If the analysis is correct, then it is necessary to abandon use of the component.

In the case of a datum that is produced in addition, there is no problem. The component can be reused. It is enough, quite simply, to forget the extra datum. In the design and implementation phases, it will be necessary to try to neutralise the part of the component which produces the datum so as to avoid having useless code.

If the surplus datum in the component is an error (the component is too specific), it is necessary to signal this error to the base administrator. We will see how to correct the component in the next chapter.

Missing data
For an entity such as that shown in Figure 10.19, the entity in Figure 10.21 is suggested.

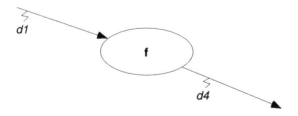

Figure 10.21 Missing data.

It lacks the data *d2* and *d3*.

If there is no error in the component, then the missing data are specific to the new analysis that you are currently undertaking. The desired function can be constructed using the proposed function and by adding a function which handles the two missing data.

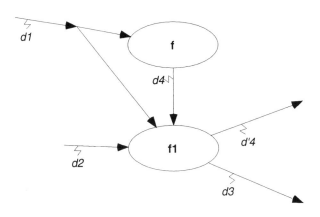

Figure 10.22 Addition of missing data.

An example of the decomposition of this function is given in Figure 10.22. The component receives the datum *d1* and produces datum *d4*. A new function *f1* receives *d1*, *d2* and *d4* and produces *d3* and *d4*. If the datum *d4* produced by the component conforms to what is wanted, it is not necessary to have it produced by *f1* again. According to context, we can determine which input data are needed by *f1*. In this example, we have taken an extreme case.

Different decomposition

Different decompositions in the component and in the analysis that you are undertaking can come from the fact that a different viewpoint was taken for the analysis. To the extent that the retrieved component performs the functions desired of it on the basis of correct input data and that it produces the expected data, there is no problem: it is necessary to use it.

If the retrieved decomposition is very complex and if that of the component is very simple, it is necessary to verify whether all the required processing is ensured by the component. If this is not the case, it is necessary to abandon what has been done in order to isolate that which is found in the component from that which is not.

10.3.5 Automata analysis components

Context

You have constructed an automaton which describes the problem that you have to attack. The component which you want for a sub-set of the automaton must have the form shown in Figure 10.23.

Figure 10.23 Desired component.

In this sub-automaton, events *ev1* and *ev2* must cause actions *a1* and *a2* and the event *ev3* allows the sub-automaton to exit.

After a search in the reusable component base, you find different candidates for this sub-set.

Among the components that have been retrieved, you can find the ideal candidate corresponding to this description. You can also find candidates which differ from it because:

- They do not handle the same transitions, or
- They do not have the same decomposition.

We are going to study these different cases and see if the components are useable and how.

Case of the perfectly suitable component

If you have found a component which corresponds to what you want, then it is necessary to replace the corresponding states in your model by a reference to a global state representing the reused automaton. It is then necessary to determine which transitions lead to one of the sub-states of this automaton. These transitions can be ones you have identified which lead to states that you replace, or new transitions that you introduce into the model by taking account of the reused automaton.

It is then necessary to determine to which state to go after output from the automaton.

Different transitions

The reasons for which transitions can be different are:

- Events do not cause the expected actions;

- One or more events, whose processing had not been predicted, are accepted by the component;
- Events that had been foreseen are not handled by the component.

Here is how to adapt these different cases.

Events with different associated actions

In an automaton, the arrival of an event causes the firing of a transition. This transition is the execution of a set of actions and is also the passage to another state of the automaton (it can equally remain in the same state). A state is characterised by a set of values of variables. It can be deduced from all this that the result of a transition, from a macroscopic viewpoint, is the result of the execution of the actions associated with the transition plus the modifications to the variables which characterise the current state.

During the analysis phase, what is produced by a transition must be capable of being summarised in one or two phrases. During detailed design, a list of the processing performed, and the changes to variable values, is compiled.

It is considered that the actions associated with the processing of an event are different if the results are different. The order in which the actions are performed is immaterial.

For each event in the automaton that has been suggested for reuse which is not associated with desired actions, it is necessary to determine from the description of the effects of these actions whether the difference is real. If the differences concern variables that have been predicted as being used, then we can possibly consider that the automaton is suitable.

If the actions in the component are more specific than what was wanted, then there is perhaps an error in the component that must be reported to the base administrator.

Actions can be described in a general form which is the call of a sub-program. During design, the contents of the sub-program are made more precise as a function of the context in which it occurs.

If there is really a difference in the actions, the it is doubtless preferable to give up reuse of the automaton.

Unhandled event

If the automaton that is suggested for reuse does not handle an event that has been identified, and if this is not an error, then there is no general rule. It is necessary to look at what is produced, when the event arrives, by examining all the sub-states of the automaton. If it is possible to determine a global behaviour, then the component can be reused, otherwise, it will be necessary to consider the implementation of a variant.

Extra event

If the automaton handles more events than is wanted, there is no problem. We have to examine whether these events are of no interest to the analysis that has been done, and if they are not used, it is necessary to show that their omission does not lead to a sub-state from which it is impossible to exit. If all is correct, the automaton can be reused. We indicate that during the design phase, it will be necessary to try to find a component which does not handle the useless events.

Different decomposition
As for the analysis in terms of data flow, a different decomposition of the component is not problematic if it handles all desired events with the desired actions. If this is not the case, we have a case of difference that we saw above.

10.3.6 Composite analysis components

An analysis by composite methods uses the different techniques studied above. While we find components for an object diagram or a data flow diagram or for an automaton, we can refer to what has been seen to determine how to adapt it to a new requirement.

It must not be forgotten to update all the diagrams if there are changes to be made.

10.4 Adaptation of Design Components

To adapt design components, we can refer to everything that has already been said about analysis and to what will be said about code. According to whether one is engaged in general or detailed design, one or the other of these approaches is suitable.

In the general case, a design component can be compared to an object in relation with other objects. Everything that has been said on this subject is also appropriate.

10.5 Adaptation of Code Components

According to the type of code, we are going to identify what it means to adapt a component which contains an unsuitable action.

For each of the types of code, it can be assumed that there is the need for some processing whose algorithms contain parts {P1, P'2, P3}. In the component that it is desired to implement, the corresponding processing contains parts {P1, P2, P3}.

10.5.1 Code that is not object-oriented

It is necessary to ask the component base administrator to modify the component in order to a test what will give the old or the new behaviour. For example, using the C pre-processor, the component can be re-written in the form:

```
/* P1: */
instruction
```

```
      . . .
instruction
#ifdef witness

/* P'2 */
instruction
. . .
instruction
#else

/* P2 */
instruction
. . .
instruction
#endif

/* P3 */
instruction
. . .
instruction
```

The users of the component will not have anything to change and for the new use, it is necessary to compile the component with witness = true.

This technique is only useful a limited number of times, otherwise there will be too many conditional compilation variables and the components will become very difficult to handle.

It is also possible to proceed in an identical fashion by adding a test in the coding language. The value of a datum positioned by a particular function allows it to have the behaviour *P2* or behaviour *P'2*.

10.5.2 Object-oriented code

With object-oriented code, it is also necessary to modify the component by transforming into a method. Let us assume that the processing *{P1, P2, P3}* was the content of a method m. For example in Eiffel syntax:

```
m() is do
      instruction1
      . . .
      instruction1a
      instruction2
      . . .
      instruction2a
      instruction3
      . . .
      instruction3a
end
```

where the instruction1 and instruction1a are the first and last statements of *P1*, instruction2 and instruction2a are the first and last statements of *P2*, and the pair `instruction3` and `instruction3a` delimit *P3*

It is enough to create a new method `m2` which has the following content:

```
m2() is do
     instruction-2
     ...
     instruction-2a
end
```

and modify m in the following way:

```
m() is do
     instruction1
     ...
     instruction1a
     m2()
     instruction3
     ...
     instruction3a
end
```

(where the interpretation of the pairs of statements is as above).

The class containing m continues to work in the same way. To obtain a new component, it is enough to inherit from the class and to redefine m2 as:

```
m2 () is do
     instruction
     ...
     instruction
end
```

where the entire body implements .

Other examples of the adaptation of components can be found in [Gamma 94].

10.6 Optimising Reuse

Reuse of components is seductive because it improves productivity. However, it can lead to the constructions of executables that are too large if, each time that a component is reused, on the way, we pick up a set of unused processes and unused data.

As far as possible, it is necessary always to reuse components which correspond most exactly to the required. It is not necessary, through laziness, to be content with the first component that is found, above all if it is rich in properties.

The ideal is to use tools which can discover what is used in the code and what is not (this is not always a simple task in object-oriented code that uses polymorphism) and eliminate the useless code.

A good reaction in object orientation consists of verifying, if it is wished to use a class and if this class has ancestors, whether one of the ancestors is unsuitable.

10.7 Inheritance and Reuse

Inheritance is a valuable technique for adapting components. It has limits which must be taken into account particularly if reuse is undertaken during analysis or design. Not knowing the limits of inheritance can lead to the production of a design that cannot be coded.

10.7.1 Single inheritance

Single inheritance poses few problems. The only limit to consider in C++ is the impossibility of changing the interfaces of the methods being redefined.

For example, if you create a class called fruit with a method called copy whose goal is to provide you with a copy of the fruit, this method will have fruit as its return type.

If you create a class apple, you will naturally make it a subclass of fruit and certainly, it will have a copy method. On the other hand, the copy of an apple does not give an apple; it will give a fruit by the fact that it is impossible to change the return type of copy.

From this example, it can be seen that during analysis, it is possible to imagine general objects, foresee lines of inheritance which seem natural, but unfortunately, sometimes the language used does not allow it to be coded.

This type of problem does not occur in Eiffel and Smalltalk.

With Eiffel, for example, the copy method would be described as:

```
copy () : like current is
```

`like current` means that the return type of copy is that of the class which contains the method. Copying a fruit yields a fruit, and copying an apple gives an apple without its being necessary to state at which point inheritance occurs. This considerably simplifies the process of coding.

10.7.2 Multiple inheritance

Multiple inheritance poses numerous problems. For example, it is possible to inherit from classes which possess methods with the same name. If the language being used does not include facilities for renaming, it is necessary, in order to distinguish the methods, to indicate the name of the class which contains them. This requires writing code in which the ancestors of the classes that are being handled must be known. Later, it becomes very difficult to change the classes because the inheritance hierarchies are known for too many classes and their update is then too messy.

In Eiffel, this problem does not occur because it is possible to rename inherited information. In C++, it is necessary to encapsulate the redundant functions using inline functions.

The major problems with multiple inheritance are connected to the existence of repeated inheritance.

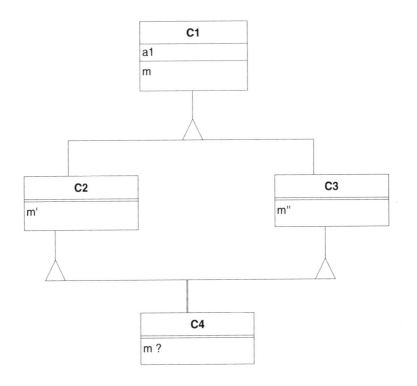

Figure 10.24 Repeated inheritance.

10.7.3 Repeated inheritance

We say that there is repeated inheritance if one class inherits several times from a single class. For example, in Figure 10.24, there is repeated inheritance of class *C1* by class *C4*. It is inherited once via *C2* and once via *C3*.

If class *C1* has an attribute *a1*, the *C2* and *C3* have an attribute *a1*. What happens with *C4*? Does it have one or two attributes *a1*?

If it has two attributes *a1*, this causes problems. Indeed, if in existing code, objects *C1* are manipulated and if the attribute *a1* of these objects is modified, it can easily happen that objects *C4* are used in place of *C1* (polymorphism). If there are two instances of *a1* in the object, it is not known which has been modified and the software can exhibit random behaviour. To avoid this problem, it is necessary to have only a single attribute in $C4$ which corresponds to the attribute $a1$ in $C1$.

If class $C1$ has a method m, and if this method is redefined in $C2$ and in $C3$, it is necessary, as for attributes, to have only a single method playing the role of m in the object $C4$ in order to be polymorphic. One can hope that this method has:

- The content it had in $C1$, or
- The content it had in $C2$, or
- The content it had in $C3$, or
- A new content (which possibly appeals the content that the method had in $C2$ and $C3$).

Few languages allow this precision in the resolution of repeated inheritance conflicts. This must be taken into account if one wants to do lots of reuse.

10.8 Chapter Summary

This chapter has attempted to given a set of paths for a domain which is not in general treated in studies of reuse: the adaptation of components so that they are suitable to new requirements.

The object-oriented techniques used in a language supporting repeated inheritance are the best for adapting components in a great many cases.

We have seen that often enough, it is necessary to ask the base administrator to extend components because they are not suitable. This process must only be undertaken in exceptional circumstances. For the component base to survive, it is essential for the users to ask for extensions each time that the components are not suitable for their needs.

We are going to see, in the next chapter, how the administrator can extend the components without affecting the uses to which they have already been put.

Chapter Eleven

Maintenance and Evolution of Components

11.1 Introduction

Having seen how to identify components, how to fabricate them, how to verify if they are of good quality, how to find them and how to adapt them, it is time to take a look into their daily life.

An important observation justifies the existence of this chapter: the components are never fixed!

At the start of their existence, components evolve a lot because it is necessary to correct their errors. The more they are used, the more errors are discovered. It is also necessary to add new possibilities to them because those originally designed into them are always inadequate.

Then, when we encounter a certain stability, fewer and fewer errors are discovered and the components deliver all the services required of them.

The third phase of their existence is that of the evolution of technologies. The components have been designed on the basis of certain habits and a certain know-how and the techniques have evolved. The components are outdated. The question arises as to their further extension or their replacement by components more in keeping with the times.

All these modifications must be made without disturbing the applications which use the components.

How can we make these corrections and extensions? This is what we will consider in this chapter.

11.2 Identification of Extensions

How does one go about finding out whether it is necessary to correct an error in a component or let it evolve?

For the correction of errors, it would seem simple. It is enough that the users indicate the errors that they have found and that there are people responsible for the correction of them.

In fact, it is far from being as simple as this for several reasons:

- Some component users look for the source of the error which is stopping them and make a local copy of the component in which they then correct the errors. They do not warn the base administrator. There is no error correction within the component and it is even unknown that it contains faults. To avoid this, it is necessary to put in place access rights which prevent users from copying components in order to modify them (for example in C++ by giving read access only to header files and binaries, not to class sources). Users must be required to go through the people in charge of component maintenance. In an emergency, it is possible temporarily to give modification rights on condition that a list of problems encountered and modifications made is produced.

- Other users do not search and immediately accuse the components of being faulty. This leads those in charge of the components to spend a considerable part of their time in correcting errors in applications which use the components rather than actually working on the components. To reduce this load (it cannot be totally eased), it is absolutely necessary that the components are protected against harmful use (using preconditions, for example) and that they are properly validated. It is then necessary to ask the users to produce evidence that the error they have found really does originate in the component and to refrain from intervening in this case.

- In the case in which object-oriented techniques are used, some users correct the error by creating a sub-class of the problematic component, and by redefining what does not work properly. This cannot be prevented. On the contrary, it is necessary to regularly perform checks in the development environments to find subclasses of components and to identify why they exist (specialisation, correction of errors or addition of functions). In this case, attention should be paid to those people who copy an entire class and use inheritance specifically to correct only one or two operations. This is not further use of the component, but duplication camouflaged as inheritance.

- We have seen in the last chapter a set of cases where it is necessary to indicate to the component base administrator that there are errors in some components. In general, they are errors in the design of the component which should be corrected while correcting errors in code.

A good relation between component users and those who maintain components is indispensable. There must be a true client-provider relationship. In cases of urgent problems, there should be no hesitation in entrusting the component to the user for repair. The official correction can be made later.

The identification of extensions of a component can also have several sources:

- We have seen in the last chapter a set of cases where it is necessary to ask the component base administrator to evolve some components.
- Awareness of the technology can show up the existence of new technologies which call into question existing components.
- An analysis of the current one can help one in discovering whether there are many variants of a given component.. This means that the component is badly designed and that those who use it are required to modify it. It is doubtless necessary to evolve it by taking into account the content of all of its variants. If the component base allows users to give opinions on the components they use, we can find suggestions for evolutions.
- The number of users of a component also gives indications. If a component is no longer used, this is perhaps because it is no longer up-to-date (technology has changed) or that it is poorly designed. It is necessary in this case to take the decision to remove it from the base or to redesign it. It is perhaps also quite possible that it has been incorrectly classified. It is necessary to verify if certain requests which have failed might not be about this component.

11.3 Versions and Configurations

We have seen a set of methods that allow the determination that there are is an error to be corrected in a component or that it must be developed. The question which is then asked is: when to make the modification?

There too, the answer is not always simple. By definition, a reusable component is reused and, when it is necessary to modify it, it is currently being used by several projects (Murphy's law). Some of these projects are at an early stage and definitely need modification. Others are reaching their end and require no extension at all. Still others are in the middle of development and, for them, we are in the middle of making another modification to the component.

Problems never come singly. In general these components themselves use other components for which a modification is to be made with the same constraints. Some projects do not want this modification (let us bet that they are people who want the development of the other component) and others cannot continue until it has been done.

There is a technique for solving these problems: configuration management. If we have a reuse policy, it is inconceivable not to have one for configuration.

Each component must be handled in versions. In the above case, the projects which do not want modification of the component use a version n, those who have a modification underway, use version $n+1$ and the others use version $n+2$.

A project works on a configuration of components, that is, a set of components each of which has a version.

Every evolution of a component does not give a new version of the component. Some extensions lead to the construction of a new component which is not compatible with the earlier one. In this case, it is preferable to not create a new version of the component but to make a new component. Other extensions are variants on the component: it only has a different behaviour on a restricted number of aspects (or better, it has a behaviour that is identical on all known aspects and adds new possibilities).

In the case of the use of object-oriented techniques, we can use version management to correct errors in a component and use inheritance to make extensions with the intention of creating variants.

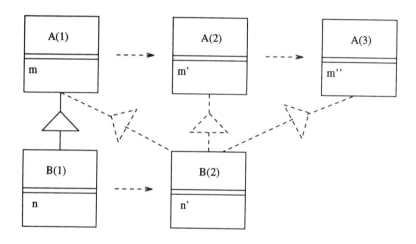

Figure 11.1 Developments and variants.

For example, in Figure 11.1, we show a class *A* which has three versions: *A(1)*, *A(2)* and *A(3)*. This class has a method *m* of which the errors are corrected in the different versions of *A*.

Class *B* inherits from *A*. It is a variant of this class. It adds method *n*. There are two versions of *B*: *B(1)* and *B(2)*. Version *B(2)* corrects errors in *n*.

This way of proceeding allows benefits to be gained from the extension of *A* in the form of class *B* without disturbing the users of *A* and by profiting from the correction of errors in *A*.

If, for example, we create *B* based on version *A(1)* when an error is corrected in *A* which gives version *A(2)*, it is enough to change the configuration used in order now to inherit from *A(2)* and thus profit from the correction of the error. This way of doing things is not always possible. Let, for example, there be two classes *A* and *B* as in Figure 11.2. *B* is a variant of *A* obtained by inheritance.

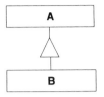

Figure 11.2 Nominal case.

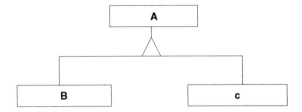

Figure 11.3 Development.

We make an extension *C* of *A* (Figure 11.3).

We wish to create a class which conforms to *B* by completely benefiting from the development of *C*. The solution is the inheritance graph in Figure 11.4.

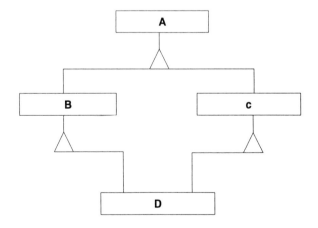

Figure 11.4 A variant.

There is multiple inheritance from *A* by *D*. We have seen that this was not supported by all languages.

The coexistence of version and configuration management, and of variants and coexistence with the inheritance technique is not always trivial. Before launching into highly practical but tricky constructions, it is necessary to verify that the language used supports them.

11.4 Processes

Here is one of the processes possible for maintaining components.

All the information concerning the components (errors or request for extensions) goes to one (or several) people who are responsible for components. This must be mentioned in the procedures describing how the software development process unfolds.

Each information item is examined as soon as possible within its degree of urgency (an error that blocks things waits much less than a demand for development).

If we have to deal with an error, it is necessary to determine its severity. We can use the following criteria:

- A blocking error without a bypassing solution has considerable importance;
- All the other errors are of average importance (blocking errors with bypassing solutions and non-blocking errors).

If we have the list of the applications which use the components, we can send them a message signalling that there is an error in one of the components which they use and by describing the error.

In a component development space, we can look for the source of the error and the corrections to be made. This is done as a priority for high-severity errors.

Whatever the severity of the error, a new version of the component must not be published immediately after the correction.

After correction of the error, in the case of a high-severity error, we can suggest to the projects waiting for the correction that they get a new version of the component. The other projects must continue to use the old version if the error does not block them.

The new version of the component is only made official at a date which allows it to be completely revalidated. To the extent that this is possible (that is, if few projects are victims of the error in the component), we can expect this official issue to have corrected all the known errors in the component (or, at least, those errors that block projects) and to have performed the developments which seemed necessary.

It is necessary to try to minimise the number of releases of new versions of a component and to take many precautions during releases because there are always risks of disturbances to the projects using the component.

If the component of which we want to release a new version is a much used component, one should not hesitate to validate it on several applications which include it, before making the release official. Every release of a new version of a component which introduces errors is a catastrophe. It can lead to delays in several projects (maybe even in all the projects for some data structure components) for it invalidates all the tests which have already been performed as part of these projects.

When the new version of the component is ready, all users of the component are notified of the existence of this new version.

The notification must give the list of corrected errors, the list of developments and the precautions to take when using the new version of the component (recompilations, for example).

11.5 How do You Make Extensions?

We are going to reply to this question by taking up again the case alluded to in the last chapter for which it was necessary to evolve components.

Be careful, because when we modify a component, it is necessary to examine the components with which it is associated in the life cycle. If we change a specification component, it is necessary to verify that the change does not impact upon the associated specification components, and if a design document is changed, it is necessary to see whether the code associated with it is not also to be modified.

11.5.1 Name change

We have seen in the previous chapter that it can happen that the names used in a component are too specific. It is then necessary to change them.

If we use tools which take into account the effects of changing names in performing analysis and design, then there is no problem. We can change the name used in the component and this change will be valid for every user of the component (at least in the nearest versions of their application). This change is made in a new version of the component in order not to disturb the users of the current version.

In the case of code components, we can change a name by using a pre-processor. The old name will thus remain useable.

If we cannot propagate name changes, then it is preferable to avoid the modification (which is a pity). It is then necessary to add a comment in the component noting the name which it would be preferable to use.

If the name to be changed is used for classifying the component, then it is necessary to review the classification. Perhaps, if the change has not been possible to do, it is necessary to classify the components in places corresponding to the previous and to the new name.

11.5.2 Informal analysis components

We are going to assume in this chapter that we have an informal analysis component *COMP* which contains the chapters (or paragraphs according to the level of detail with which it is done) *C1*, *C2*, *C3* (Figure 11.5 using an entity-relation notation).

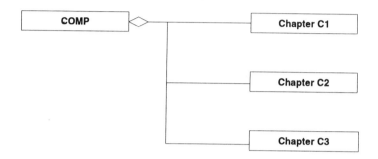

Figure 11.5 Component to be extended.

Information to remove

A first possible type of evolution consists of removing one of the chapters which is too specific (for example chapter *C2*).

It is not a question, certainly, of simply deleting the chapter. Every application which uses the component will become incorrect.

We can create a new component *COMP0* containing chapters *C1* and *C3*. We can rewrite component *COMP* by replacing chapters *C1* and *C3* by references to chapters *C1* and *C3* in *COMP0*. Chapter *C2* is unchanged (Figure 11.6).

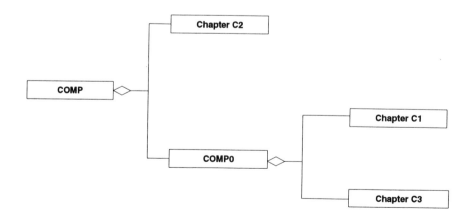

Figure 11.6 Removal of a chapter.

Information to add

We wish to add a chapter *C4* to the component.

If this chapter is really something we forgot, then we can modify the *COMP* component and add the chapter (Figure 11.7).

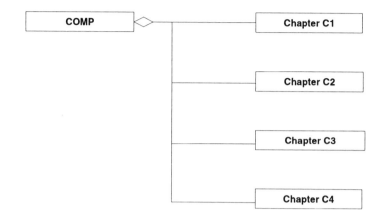

Figure 11.7 Addition of a chapter.

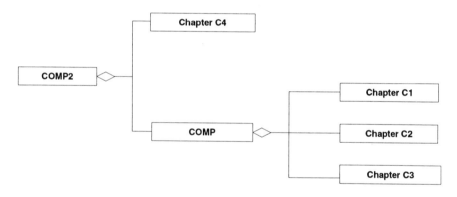

Figure 11.8 Restructuring.

It is imperative to warn all users of the component.

If it is an addition, we can create a new component *COMP2* which refers to *COMP* and adds chapter *C4* as in Figure 11.8, (We can also decide whether it is a variant of the *COMP* component).

Components to be restructured

We wish to change the contents of a component completely.

If the component is referred to by other components, it is preferable to create a new component with the new structure.

If the component is not referenced, it is necessary to search for the applications which use the component and to determine whether this change is possible or not. According to the outcome, we modify the component or create another.

11.5.3 Entity-relation analysis components

We assume that the *COMP* component corresponds to the entities in Figure 11.9.

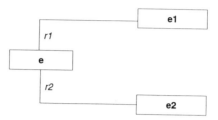

Figure 11.9 Component to be extended.

Relation to remove

We can assume that relation *r1* is irrelevant to the component.

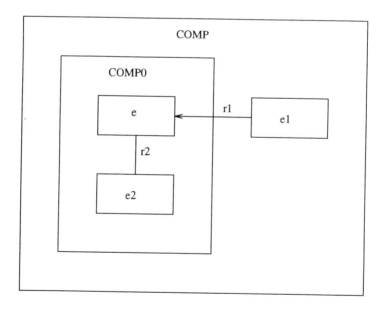

Figure 11.10 Removal of a relation.

If relation *r1* is oriented from *e1* to *e*, then we can create a new component *COMP0* which only contains the entity *e* and relation *r2*.

We rewrite the component *COMP* by using component *COMP0* and adding the relation *r1* (cf. Figure 11.10).

The new component that we wanted is *COMP0* and the component *COMP* is identical for those who use it.

If the relation is oriented from e to e1 then, we cannot modify the component. It is necessary to create a variant.

Relation to add

We want to add a relation *r3* that points to an entity *e3* in the *COMP* component.

If there is an error in the *COMP* component, we add the relation and we warn all the application project managers which use this component of this error. This is the case if the relation goes from *e* to *e3*, in particular.

Otherwise, we create a new component which references *COMP* and add the relation *r3* to entity *e3*.

Different attributes

The change of an entity's attributes cannot be done without affecting the users of the component. To perform this type of change (addition or removal of an attribute), it is advisable to create a new component that conforms to what we want to obtain and to warn the users of the component that we wanted to modify the content of this new component and explaining to them the reasons for its presence.

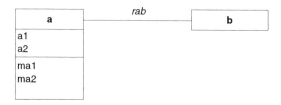

Figure 11.11 Component to be extended.

11.5.4 Analysis component by objects

It is assumed that the component to be evolved is formed of a class *a* containing the attributes *a1* and *a2* and methods *m1* and *m2*. It is in relation with the class *b* by a relation *rab* (Figure 11.11).

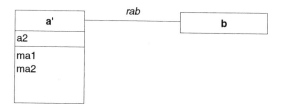

Figure 11.12 Removal of an attribute.

Attribute, method or relation to be removed

We assume that attribute *a1* is irrelevant for the component. We create a new component which contains the class such as we want (Figure 11.12, class). We modify the original component by representing it in the form of a class *a* which inherits from class *a'* and adds attribute *a1* (Figure 11.13). It thus remains compatible with its old version.

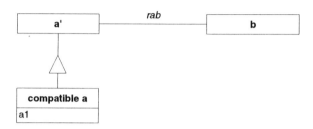

Figure 11.13 Re-establishment of consistency.

We can be led to not putting all the methods of in class . If some methods use the attribute a1, they are not put in . We proceed in the same way in the case of a method and of a relation.

Attribute, method or relation to add.

To add an attribute is performed by creating a new component which is a subclass adding the attribute (Figure 11.14).

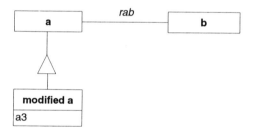

Figure 11.14 Addition of an attribute.

We proceed in the same way for a method or for a relation.

Attribute to be modified

To modify an attribute is to change its name or type. We have already seen the name change.

Let a class *X* possess an attribute *X1* of type *t1*. We want to change this type to *t2*. It is necessary to redo the code components which are associated with it as implementations. According to the language used for the latter, the change will be more or less awkward.

In the case of C++, we create a new component which is based on a class which does not contain attribute *X1* and the methods associated with this attribute. We recreate the original class *X* by sub-classing and adding an attribute *x1*. We create class *Y* which corresponds to what we wanted to obtain by creating a new subclass of which adds the attribute x1 of the type that we wanted (Figure 11.15).

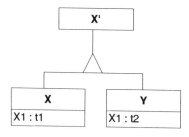

Figure 11.15 Change of a method.

This problem with types does not arise in Smalltalk.

In the case of Eiffel, if the type *t2* is a subclass of *t1*, then we create the new component in the form of a subclass of *X* which redefines the type of *X1* as *t2*. If the type *t2* is an ancestor of *t1*, then we create a new class which corresponds to what we want and we recreate *X* in the form of a subclass of this class which redefines the type of *X1* as *t1*.

Method to modify
Besides the modification of the name that we have already seen, possible changes to a method are the change of its return type, change of the number of its parameters or the change of one or more of its parameters.

Here also, the implementation of the code components associated with it depends upon the language being used. In the case of C++, it is necessary to use the method which is described below for attributes.

In the case of Eiffel and Smalltalk, we can change, in a subclass, the signature of a method (return type and type of parameters) provided that one does not change the number of its parameters nor change their type or the return type except to compatible types (this is not required in Smalltalk, but is advised).

For the return type, a compatible type is a subtype. For a parameter, a compatible type is an ancestor type. This restriction being too strong, we can change the type of a parameter into a subclass provided that we protect the method with a precondition verifying that the type actually passed is at least the expected type.

Starting with these possibilities, we can see that in a certain number of cases, the change can be made using inheritance. The modified component is a subclass of the component which was to have been modified.

Relation to modify
The possible changes to a relation are:

- Change of name of the relation or change of name of its roles;

- Change of cardinality;
- Removal of a relation;
- Addition of a relation.

Change of cardinality

The change requires that the users of the component are warned as well as the verification of whether if it has an impact on the design and code components which is derived from it.

Removal of a relation

We want to remove the relation *rab* from the component in Figure 11.11.

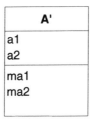

Figure 11.16 Removal of a relation.

We create a new component which does not have the relation (Figure 11.16).

We reconstruct the component which existed by inheriting from the new component and add the relation to it (Figure 11.17).

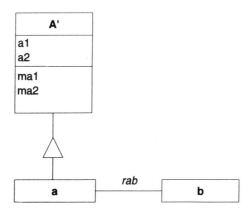

Figure 11.17 Re-establishment of consistency.

Relation to add

We want to add to the component in Figure 11.11 a relation pointing to a class c.

To do this, we create a new component which inherits from the component to be modified and which adds the relation (Figure 11.18).

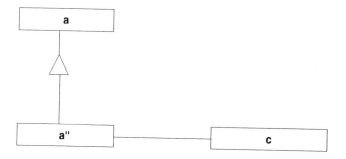

Figure 11.18 Addition of a relation.

11.5.5 Analysis components by data flow

Modifications of analysis components using data flow diagrams are awkward. We will find below some indications on the restructuring of components. It is necessary to examine the design and implementation of the components associated with it in order to change each of them.

Data to be removed
We assume that the component in Figure 11.19 must be modified. The datum d2 is to be removed.

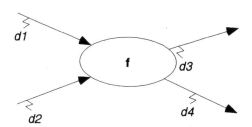

Figure 11.19 Component to be extended.

We create the new component as in Figure 11.20.

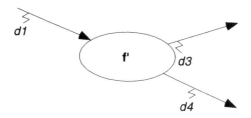

Figure 11.20 Removal of a datum.

This component conforms to what we wanted to obtain. We reconstruct the component which existed by giving the function *f* the decomposition in Figure 11.21.

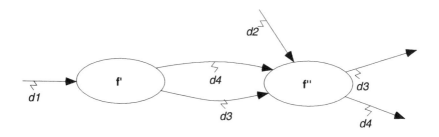

Figure 11.21 Restoration of the original component.

This decomposition uses the new component which has been created. A function is created to process the datum *d2* and, perhaps, to adapt the data produced by in order to produce the expected data *d3* and *d4*.

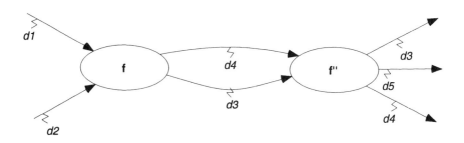

Figure 11.22 Addition of a datum.

Data to add

We assume that we want to add a datum *d5* to the component in Figure 11.19.

This is performed in a new component which has the content shown in Figure 11.22.

It uses the function f of the component that has been evolved and a complementary function aimed at providing the expected data.

11.5.6 Component design using automata

The modification of an automaton, leaving it completely compatible for those who use it, is very difficult. We cannot give general rules for the addition or removal of transitions. It is necessary to examine the components on a case by case basis and carefully evaluate the impact of the changes that we want to make:

- If we add an event, it is necessary to determine the impact of the occurrence of this event in all automaton states;
- If we remove an event, it is necessary to verify that we do not introduce any well states into the automaton.

11.5.7 Design component

As in the chapter on the adaptation of components, we are going to denote a design component by an object containing data and processing. The cases of evolution for design components are:

- Change of type of data;
- Addition of a datum;
- Removal of a datum;
- Change of an process interface;
- Removal of a process;
- Addition of a process;
- Change of data type.

We certainly find ourselves in the case where there was an error in the component. We perform the change and we emphatically warn all the applications which use this component of the change. It is preferable, certainly, to use a tool which propagates the change to the relevant applications.

Removal of data

We create a new component which neither contains data nor processes which use the data. The component to be modified is recreated with reference to the new component and by adding the data and processes which are lacking.

Addition of data

It is made in a new component which references the component to be modified and adds the data.

Change to a process' interface

We write a new process with a new name and the new interface. It uses, as far as possible, the old process.

Process added or removed

We proceed as for added or removed data.

11.5.8 Code components

There are few things to add with respect to what has been said about design components.

In the case in which we use a pre-processor, we can handle name changes using a directive of the type:

```
#ifdel old_version
define new_name old_name
#endif
```

which allows us to save an old name leaving new users free to make use of the new one.

For the change of behaviour of a method, we use the techniques described in the chapter about adaptation of components.

11.6 How to Keep Components Reliable

The technique of programming by contract of which we have already talked in an earlier chapter is an excellent aid in avoiding numerous errors in the maintenance of code components (even, indeed, of design).

A post-condition is a condition which must be true when the execution of a method terminates.

A simple example of post-condition is that which we must systematically put in every method intended to modify the contents of an attribute. Here is an example in Eiffel:

```
set_attribute(v : type) is
-- implementation of "attribute with v"
do
     attribute := v;
ensure
     attribute = v;
end;
```

And the same example in C++:

```
set_attribute(type v){attribute = v;
assert(attribute == v)}
```

The post-condition verifies that after the execution of the method, the attribute certainly has the value that we wanted it to have.

In a maintenance phase, we are going to discover that, when we modify an attribute, it is also necessary to activate the method z and change the value of the attribute *a2*. Thanks to encapsulation, this is done by changing the contents of `set_attribute`. For example, in Eiffel:

```
set_attribute(v : type) is
-- implementation of "attribute with v"
do
    attribute := v;
    z();
    set_a2(v+3);
ensure
    attribute = v;
end;
```

During the course of the modifications, we add some code. One day, following from an error, we remove the command `attribute := v` (this happens more often that might be imagined). At the first test of the modified component, we can see that it no longer respects the contract and that the modification is no good.

The systematic use of post-conditions makes component maintenance more reliable. It is the same for invariants. If in a component list, we indicate that the number of elements is positive or zero, we can remove lots of maintenance errors which consist of forgetting to implement the counter of the number of elements.

11.7 Chapter Summary

We have seen in this chapter how to know that it is necessary to make components evolve (evolutionary and corrective maintenance) and how to make these extensions. The extensions of a component must not call into question all the applications which use this component. Using appropriate tools simplifies this component maintenance.

Post-conditions and invariants are a good way of making maintenance of code components more reliable.

Chapter Twelve

Organisation for Reuse

The previous chapters have helped us to identify a set of procedures which allow us to implement reuse. To use these techniques is not unfortunately sufficient to engage in reuse. There remains an enormous hurdle to be surmounted: to convince information processing people that it is necessary to reuse things which they have not written. This is far from being simple as you are going to see.

12.1 New State of Mind

In the software industry, if you suggest to someone that they are going to reuse what has been done by another, you will almost certainly get the following replies:

- I can't reuse this component because it does not correspond exactly to my needs and if I adapt it that would take me much more time than completely rewriting it;
- I can't reuse this, it was made by somebody who is reputed for making programs that contain lots of errors;
- I can't reuse that because it is not stable and the extensions which have to made don't suit me in the slightest;
- I prefer to rewrite the software, it will be more compact and it will be much more efficient;
- I have implemented a whole development environment and what you are proposing is not compatible with that;
- I have no interest in reuse because I look at the number of lines of code I have written;
- This component was written by Untel which has gone bust: who will support the maintenance of the system if I have any problems.

In fact one could write an entire book about the reasons which are given for not engaging in reuse.

When we succeed in convincing someone to engage in reuse we also get the following reactions:

- I have tried reuse but I have found an error; I think there are others and that's going to cost me in time, I am going to build the whole lot from scratch;
- I have tried reuse but there is an important function missing; if I add it to what I am constructing it's going to cost me a lot of time, more than if I were going to reconstruct the whole lot;
- There are also reasons for not pushing further at a first or somewhat limited attempt at reuse and these reasons are too numerous to list.

To start reuse in a company, you need to first of all convince people that there is much to be gained by engaging in it.

We have seen in the above chapters the advantages brought by reuse. This needs to be communicated.

Here are some arguments which can then perhaps be used to help people accept reuse:

- By not reusing, we are always condemned to putting in a maintenance effort which becomes more and more onerous. This strongly resists creativity. At the limit, we might be reduced to doing nothing other than maintenance and not making any progress. By reusing, maintenance is shared and thus takes less time.
- By engaging in reuse, we know what others have done. We discover the techniques that we haven't already thought of using ourselves.
- By making things that are reusable, we can intervene in several projects and standardise the techniques up to the level of the entire company.
- By engaging in reuse, we share a single culture in the company and we have greater performance.

Many information technology people completely resist all the arguments that we can find. To make them accept the idea of reuse, it is sometimes useful to confront them with the evidence: somebody demonstrates a finished implementation of which they are proud. We can show that by engaging in reuse, we can do the same thing (even better perhaps) in less time and with the time that we have saved, we can add to what was the difference between us and the competition. For the moment we make use of a component base, this type of demonstration is relatively easy to make.

There are always people who refuse, under any circumstances to reuse, and demonstrate that to construct specific software is always more rapid than reuse. It is a good idea to show them that they reuse more quickly, without wanting to admit it. For example compilers, libraries, graphic libraries and so on. Once the first step has been taken why not go further?

Even when a large part of the company is convinced, victory is still not assured. If the components do not extend correctly, if the new components which are necessary do not arrive, the old demons of the do-it-yourself school will reappear.

Construction is the pleasure of the IT person. Not reusing is therefore written in their genes.

12.2 New Organisation

How to reorganise so that reuse becomes reality in a company?

There are several possible organisations which all have advantages and disadvantages. We are going to look in detail at six. The reader wishing to have more information on this subject can consult an article by Danielle Fafchamp (Fafchamp 94) which examines in detail four of the organisations proposed here.

12.2.1 "Isolated manufacture" organisation

In this type of organisation, one person in the company is charged with the implementation of reusable components for its projects. This person does not belong to the teams which work on the projects, they report directly to the person in charge of all project teams (Figure 12.1).

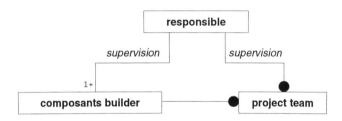

Figure 12.1 Isolated manufacturer.

The advantages of this organisation are:

- The components are well suited to the needs, because they are only implemented for identified projects;
- One and the same person knows what is done to be reusable and can indicate it to the different projects.

The disadvantages are:

- The position held by the implementer of the components is not easy; they belong to no team and depend upon the good will of the teams in order to engage in reuse;
- There are risks of overload if numerous teams make claims upon the component implementer;

- The component implementer must take into account several people (their boss and the project managers for whom they work);
- It is difficult to determine how to manage priorities (one project demands a change in specification which another project does not want. What should be done?);
- Maintenance runs the risk of posing numerous problems if it is performed by a single person for several projects; for example, when this person leaves the company what happens?

The risks connected with these problems are also more constraining than the advantages that can be obtained. This type of organisation is not advisable.

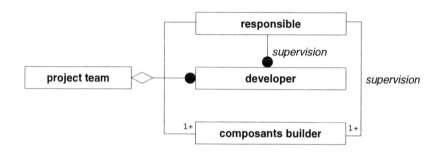

Figure 12.2 One constructor per team.

12.2.2 "One constructor per team" organisation

In this type of organisation, each development team has at least one person who is responsible for the implementation of reusable components for the project teams. These different people are in regular contact in order to exchange information (Figure 12.2).

The advantages of this type of organisation are:

- The people responsible for the implementation of reusable components belong to a team for which the components are to be made;
- The components are made by a given project and thus suit that project.

The disadvantages of this organisation are:

- The person who constructs the components cannot be competent in all the domains and therefore there is nothing to guarantee that all the components that they implement are effective in the projects which use them, and that they are reusable;
- The contracts between the different persons and persons in charge of reuse can only be infrequent because nothing *a priori*

requires that they are going to work on the same type of components;

- The temptation to use these people on specific developments is quite high when there is a high demand for resources;
- There is the same potential problem for maintenance as in the case of the isolated producers.

This organisation is not to be recommended either.

12.2.3 " Common provider group" organisation

In this organisation, several teams decide to develop common reusable components. To do this, a new team is created. It is composed of people coming from the different teams who want to make use of the components. These people are chosen from those who have a good knowledge of the domains in which it is desired to develop the components. The team is disbanded as soon as the components are completed (Figure 12.3).

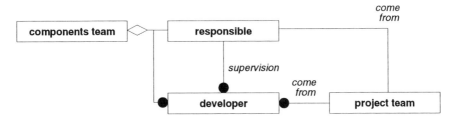

Figure 12.3 Common provider group.

The advantages of this organisation are:

- There is no change in the organisation of the company choosing this solution. The component team is created when there is a need for it and disappears immediately after;
- The components are designed by several projects. They, therefore, have a high probability of being appropriate and of being reusable.

The disadvantages are:

- The new team depends on different entities;
- There is the risk of conflicts which are difficult to resolve because different interests are at play between the clients of the producer group;
- It is difficult to solve the problems priorities within the various teams;
- There is no longer anyone who will engage in maintenance of the components when the team has been dissolved.

This organisation is only suitable when we put into place a component policy because the conflicts which come from the different interest groups imply a high risk of failure. On the other hand, when the components are available and reuse is accepted in the company, this organisation is appropriate. It is indispensable, before starting a project, to be clear about the objectives of the project (contents, dates).The resources allocated to the reuse team are only recoverable by the teams from which they come at the end of the project. One or more people must then be nominated to engage in the maintenance of the components which have been constructed.

12.2.4 "Component fabrication centre" organisation

The organisation of the company has changed. A special group is formed which is in charge of the fabrication of reusable components. This group supervises the work of the other teams (specification and design phases) and identifies the common needs. It implements components to satisfy these common needs either during the implementation of the projects which are going to use them, or without reference to any project (Figure 12.4).

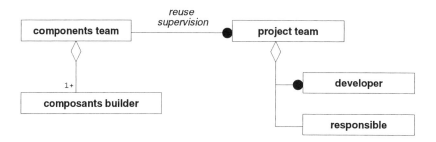

Figure 12.4 Component fabrication centre.

The advantages of this organisation are:

- The materialisation of the desire to construct components; there is a team dedicated to this work;
- The fact that the implementers of the components are no longer isolated;
- The recognition of the component construction job;
- The optimisation of developments in the company;
- The team has charge of the maintenance of components.

The disadvantages are:

- The component makers are isolated from the projects, there is the risk that components will lack credibility. They are constructed by people who do not know the needs of the projects because they are not in the projects;

- There is the risk of constructing components just for pleasure. These components are technological marvels that are useless as far as any project is concerned;
- There is the risk of lack of satisfaction on the part of the component manufacturers. They only perform part of the job. They do not work on projects that complete the stock. Their work is not seen in the final realisation.

Users are tempted to rely on the component group. They confer the implementation of specific tasks, or attribute to them the responsibility for problems and delays in the project.

This type of organisation is appropriate when reuse is instituted in a company. Some people become specialists in reuse. To avoid their isolation it is necessary, for example, to make them work within projects and to implement components which they have realised and to adapt them to the real needs of the projects. In such a case, it is necessary to foresee rotations. The passage through the component groups is formative. It allows people to assimilate the techniques used in the company.

When we have a sufficient component base, it is no longer necessary to use a specialised centre in the fabrication of components. We can then pass through another kind of organisation (a common providing group for example).

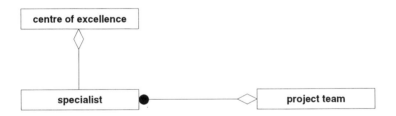

Figure 12.5 Centre of excellence.

12.2.5 "Centre of excellence" organisation

In this organisation (Figure 12.5) there exists groups specialised in the implementation of components. They are organised by domains. The embers of the different teams know the components available for their domain and how to adapt them or to extend them. The purely application-specific teams are also constituted along these lines. Their speciality is formed from their knowledge of the specific software available in the company. When a new project is started, a project team is created by taking the specialists from the different teams. Each is going to participate in the development from the viewpoint that they know best. After the development each specialist has a relationship with other member of the team on the basis of the way in which his work has developed. In particular they make a list of the use of components, the problems encountered, the extensions to be made, or new components to be developed.

Free time between two projects is given over to performing a technology watch. The advantages of this solution are:

- An effective use of components because they are precisely the people who were in charge of those who used them in projects;
- The components closely follow the needs of the applications;
- There are competent people who can maintain them.

The disadvantages are:

- The risks of poor use of resources if some domains have too many specialists;
- The risk of lack of resources if a single specialist is necessary to too many projects at the same time;
- A risk of tiredness in the specialist teams as they are always working on the same subjects;
- The risk can be minimised by allowing mobility between the different specialists. In the case of lack of resources in a particular domain, someone can be found from another team who has worked previously in the domain. Mobility prevents tedium.

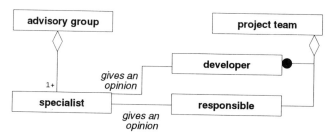

Figure 12.6 Advisory group.

12.2.6 "Advisory group" organisation

In this organisation, there are not just a few people dedicated to component reuse. They can be used by anybody or any team or project. There are, for example, a team of specialists in reusing components which already exist or are under construction (Figure 12.6).

The members of the team participate in the start of projects. They show what has already been done on identical subjects, introducing projects which have similar needs.

They also participate in design reviews and give an opinion on the solutions adopted (always pro reuse)

They take reusable components and make them available for other projects in the company.

The advantages of this organisation are:

- Better sharing of knowledge between projects;
- Better control of reuse;
- Components adapted to the user's needs because they are realised by the project teams which are to use them.

The disadvantages are:

- It is uncertain who will maintain the components at the end of the project;
- The group of specialists risk being rejected by the project teams because they do not have the same constraints (they should try to improve sharing of resources between projects, while the projects seek to complete without time over-runs and to achieve the desired quality.)

This type of organisation depends a great deal on individuals.

12.2.7 Conclusions about organisation

There is no ideal organisation. It is necessary to search for the organisation which is best suited to the personalities of the developers.

It is also necessary to think of developing the organisation so that the company progresses towards reuse.

12.3 New Methods

We have seen in the above chapters that it is possible to reuse in many contexts. Object-based approaches give best the results and informal approaches are those which give poorest results.

Reuse is inconceivable without a minimum of organisation. A set of measures must be taken if you want to succeed in performing reuse well.

The first thing to do is to use methods for the analysis and design of software. It is easier to process analysis and design documents than pieces of code, particularly if they are not commented. Analysis and design documents are more abstract and thus easier to understand than code which is full of implementation details.

Reuse is a new way of approaching these problems: instead of diving into code, we begin by reflecting. We state the problem (analysis) and we look through what has already been done for anything that might be of use. When the problem is posed we search for how to solve it using software (design). Again some solutions can be made available and then reused.

Certainly one can be an information society and process software manually: specification documents are informal documents which are stored in files. Reusable components are also stored in the form of files.

We can also see that the software used to solve these problems could also be reused. It is then necessary to see the use of tools for software engineering. We will revisit this point in a later section.

An important point in order to ensure that reuse works well is to have an enterprise culture: everyone uses the same words to denote the same thing. A good start for beginning reuse is to define a common vocabulary. We can define each word in the subject that we practice, and rule on the convention for writing them. The extraction of information from one person to another is therefore simplified and all the techniques for searching for components based on the vocabulary thus used will function better.

The conventions for writing can include, for example:

- The presentation of information (what sorts of comments, what order of chapters);
- Methods used (conventions for the use of notation if there are several possibilities);
- How to name the identifiers in software.

The sharing of these directives reinforces the feeling of belonging to a single group.

12.4 New Tools

Reuse is to automate some of the tasks which previously have been have done manually. It is hard to conceive of the implementation of reuse without the use of tools. Amongst the indispensable tools are:

- Editors for the formalisms used in analysis and design which allow referencing of reusable components and exploitation of their extensions. They allow the avoidance of personal changes to common notations for personal needs, and allow much time to be saved in the development and maintenance phases of the software by allowing us to avoid a great many errors;
- Through code generators for all the repetitive parts of the software (data encapsulation, for example);
- Configuration managers without which it is impossible to envisage reuse—that is, documentation tools able to extract information from different places and form coherent documents;
- Tools for storing components in libraries;
- Tools for searching for components in libraries;
- Tools for the identification of components in existing code (in general we have thousands or millions of lines of code which we do not suddenly want to re-write).

The choice of these tools is important. The principle criteria for the choice are:

- They must support a reuse policy, that is to say, they must be capable of performing operations such as extraction, storage, search and maintenance of components;
- They must be open, that is to say, present an interface which allows one to access the information, then manipulate and use it in a new context.

We should pay attention, for numerous analysis and design tools which only serve to produce documents in a particular format. What we want to reuse has a meaning. Tools which are not semantic (drawing tools) cannot help in understanding this meaning, and are difficult to use as part of a reuse policy.

12.5 New Skills

Reuse requires the creation of new techniques. We discover many new jobs in enterprises which want to reuse:

- Librarian;
- Component constructor;
- Component certifier;
- Component consultant.

This list is not exhaustive.

12.5.1 Librarian

The librarian plays a key role in the organisation of reuse. It is this position which is responsible for the processing of a component library. In the activities associated with this job, we can give a description of the tasks which can be consigned to it:

- Archiving of components. The librarian receives candidate components. The librarian must determine, helped by the component certifier, whether they have the statutory right of components (generality perameterisation), and if they are acceptable (reliability, performance, documentation). The librarian collects the information characterising the components and archives them in the component library;
- Component maintainers. They receive error reports and requests for extensions to components. They organise the correction of errors and the implementation of extensions. They verify that the components are acceptable after maintenance and make them available in their new versions;
- Helping the user to find components.

12.5.2 Component maker

Component construction is a profession. It requires someone able to imagine all the possible uses that can be made and to be able to anticipate certain developments.

The choice made by the component implementers are used in numerous projects. They can strongly influence the implementations in a company for several years.

12.5.3 Component "certifier"

A component which contains errors can lead to problems in many projects if it is a component used by many applications. For a new component which is required by several projects, errors, as in the case of specific development, are equally the cause of very important problems. To know how to verify that a component is correct and will not cause problems in use is a profession. Validation must use rigorous techniques.

12.5.4 Component consultant

In the first years of the implementation of a reuse policy, few components are actually available. Techniques for component search yield few results. It is advised therefore to rely on specialists in components to help the teams who are developing software to perform their analysis and designs, to find components which can exist and to identify those which it is necessary to construct.

This type of profession is learned on the job. After some experience with reusable components which are not reused, we learn better to decide, in a given context, what is reusable and what is not.

12.6 New Motivations

The importance accorded to reuse must be revealed in incentives to reuse. These take different forms:

- Regular publication of the component hit-parade: a list of components which are most often reused in the company with indications of the names of the authors and the projects which reuse them;
- Bonuses for the authors of the components which are most reused or which save the most time during development;
- Regular publication of the hit-parade of reusers. A list of the applications which most reuse components the most (of which the percentage of lines reused is the most important);
- Judgement about productivity based on apparent productivity and not on real productivity; apparent productivity is the number of lines per application divided by the time (in hours) required for its implementation; real productivity is the number of lines

not reused in the application divided by the number of man hours required for its implementation.

It requires a certain liveliness in interpreting the theme of reuse, particularly at the start, so that reuse becomes a success.

12.7 Starting to Reuse

To start a policy of reuse is a problem as insoluble as that which consists of determining whether it is the egg or the chicken which comes first.

When we decide to start to reuse, there are no components, and, thus, there is nothing to reuse. It is necessary to start by constructing the components. These are hardly used at the start and clearly cost a lot therefore. As we have not achieved a useful number of components, reuse remains a frustrating process and the majority of searches fail.

Furthermore, at the start we often make errors in fabricating in what we think to be reusable components and what, with use, turn out to be unsuitable implementations:

- They are not suited to what we want to do (too generalised);
- They are not sufficiently paramaterised;
- Their performance is inadequate.

All of this leads to a lot of discouragement.

It is necessary to be able to wait for the moment where we use a component base which is adequate for supplying a large part of the application. From this moment on, the phenomenon of standardisation occurs, as if dictated by nature; this means that we can very easily find the required component. When you reuse a component, you adapt what you do in order to use the component. It then becomes consistent with what there is in the component base and it is even easier to find other components.

For example, you have imagined the model in Figure 12.7.

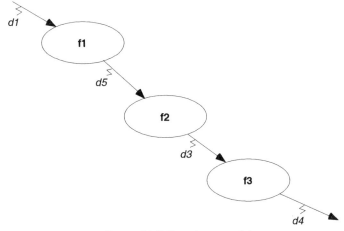

Figure 12.7 Imaginary model.

You find a function in the component base which is suitable for *f1*. The problem is that it produces data *d5* in place of data *d2*.

You modify your analysis in order to be able to reuse the component. You redesign function *f2* as the function *f'2* which consumes data *d5* as an input.

The new function now uses a data type which is already available in the component base. There are greater chances of finding a component corresponding to this, and if later on we put this function into the base, it is consistent with the existing component.

12.8 How to Launch Reuse

You are almost ready to launch a reuse policy. A question still remaining is: will it going to be necessary to redo everything that we have already done in terms of software or can we recover something?

It is certainly not a question of stopping all the activities of a company and giving people the time to reconstruct all the software using reusable components. It is necessary to allow several years before being able to make reuse a habit and to make use of a component base.

It is advisable to start archiving some components. We can start with the data structures, mathematical libraries and graphical interfaces. If these components are available in the company, it is necessary to validate them and to describe them unless they have been bought or constructed from scratch.

These components are then used in one or more pilot projects. We can profit in these projects by identifying new components that are extracted from the projects or that are constructed.

Learning errors concerning reuse are also localised in a restricted number of projects.

Watch out for being discouraged! During the first years, the components will be accused of everything bad. They will be blamed as the origin of all the errors discovered in the software which uses them. It is therefore imperative to validate the components to as high a standard as possible in order not rapidly to discourage the use of them, should the users' suspicions of them be well-founded.

12.9 Chapter Summary

In this chapter we have seen different organisations which allow the implementation of a reuse policy. The organisation can change in the course of time as a function of maturity.

There is no miraculous way for a company to adopt reuse. It requires great dedication from everyone; from managers, as well as from developers. Everyone must be convinced that it is in their best interests to reuse and together to seek the best results.

It is necessary to put in place an organisation which makes reuse as easy as possible by automating everything which can be automated. Some reflections on the organisation of the company and the methods and tools to be used must be performed.

Chapter Thirteen

Possible Profit

13.1 Myth

Reuse, as we have seen, brings many advantages:

- Increased productivity;
- Increased maintenance;
- Increased extensibility.

We have also seen in previous chapters that reuse is not as easy as all that. It requires new techniques, new habits, and, possibly a suitable organisation of technical teams. This is acceptable if the benefits are really great.

For the predictable benefits, in general, the calculations are simple: if we assume that in your new software you will use 50% of the components:

- You will develop software at twice the speed (there is only half the code to write);
- It will cost you half (there is half the work);
- Their maintenance is half as expensive (the components are maintained elsewhere);
- Their development is free (it is done by other people).

Given such evidence, one can only be convinced to move rapidly to a reuse policy.

And then, given such predicted gains, we can even dream of pushing reuse even further: we only need to develop software by assembling components. And given this hypothesis:

- Development time is zero (there is nothing to develop);
- Development cost is zero (for the same reason);
- Maintenance and extension are free (there are only components).

Having reached this point, it is important to note that there must be a mistake in the hypotheses we have made:

- Assembling components takes time: it is necessary to know what we want to produce, how to find the components, how to put them together, and how to validate the assembly;
- If we spend time, the cost is not zero; moreover, documentation for the software level must be provided, and this is certainly not done uniquely by the assembly of document components.
- Some components are certainly internal developments and even if their maintenance is not the responsibility of the project which uses them, this cost is paid by the company;
- Extensions are made at the request of some projects and thus are not free as we had assumed.
- In conclusion, reuse has a cost (in time and in money). This is the cost that we will determine below.

13.2 In Reality

The development of software is a sequence of tasks each of which has a cost. The costs are:

The establishment of the requirements:

- Specification;
- General design;
- Detailed design;
- Coding;
- Unit testing;
- Integration;
- Validation;
- Writing documentation;
- Extensional and corrective maintenance.

In the case of commercial software, it is necessary to add the manufacture of sales material.

The implementation of a reuse policy does not have the same impact on all of these tasks. It can strongly diminish some such as:

- Detailed design;
- Coding;
- Unit testing;
- Corrective maintenance and changes.

And diminish some of the others a little less, such as:

- Specification;
- General design;
- Integration;

- Writing of documentation.

It does not affect others such as:

- Requirements;
- Validation.

Reuse can create new tasks such as:

- Construction of components;
- Search for components;
- Modification of components.

To evaluate the benefits of a reuse policy, it is necessary to take all the factors into account. This is the objective of this chapter.

13.3 The Price of Components

The development of components has a cost. This is in general larger than that of the development of specific software. A component requires, in addition to analysis and solution of a specific problem, the analysis of all the variants of this problem and the implementation of solutions which will be useable in many cases.

Experience shows that making a reusable component costs two to four times the price of the corresponding specific software.

If the realisation of a component has cost CDC (Cost of the Development of a Component) and if this component is used in n items of software, it is natural to consider that its implementation costs $CDC \div n$ to each of the items of software that use it.

If the maintenance of this component costs CMC (Cost of the Maintenance of a Component), then each of the software components using the component must allow a maintenance cost of $CMC \div n$.

These observations lead to several remarks of which some, however obvious, are not always taken into account.

If a specific development costs on average CDS (Cost of Development of Specific item) and its maintenance costs on average CMS (Cost of Maintenance of Specific item), if the corresponding component costs $CDC = k_d$ (CDS, and its maintenance is $CMC = k_m \times CMS$, then, in order for the component to be profitable, it must be used in n items of software with:

$$n \times (CDS + CMS) > k_d \times CDS + k_m \times CMS$$

We do not, in general, ask this type of question when we start the implementation of a library of reusable components. The first components are often relatively simple and are reusable by the majority of software. On the other hand, when we have a component library of some size, it is always necessary to ask if we must construct new components.

Another comment is that to determine the cost of a component's use, it is necessary to know how much software is going to use it. To do this, we must make assumptions (and use them in determining whether it is profitable to develop the component). After the library has been available for some time, three cases can be identified:

- The component is used by exactly the predicted number of items: this rare case does not interest us;
- The component is used by more software than predicted; in this case, we can decide to make the new software pay only for maintenance or that the component remains at the same price and that the obtained benefit extends to the following case;
- The component is not used by the predicted number of software items; this case corresponds to a badly identified need, or to a badly designed or classified component. If it is badly designed, either deleting the component (for its rare users, it will become a specific development), or simplifying it by reducing to the identified cases of use, must be contemplated. Its maintenance will then be less expensive and it can remain a component. If it is badly conceived or classified, it is necessary to settle the issue.

The last case poses problems of failures. Not every component construction yields something that is useful. In particular, when a reuse policy has just been adopted, errors occur. The cost of these mistakes must be somehow covered. It is taken as part of the self financing of the company or distributed across all the projects under the heading of contribution to the construction of the component base. This component tax cannot be to everyone's taste.

13.4 Cost of Components to a Project

A project which reuses components must then pay for part of the cost of their fabrication and maintenance. This is not the only predictable cost.

The search for components takes time; this must be included in the cost of the project. The cost of this search (CR) is not proportional to the number of reused components. It is proportional to the number of searches performed: searches having succeeded in yielding for reuse of components + failed searches. We can consider that this cost is proportional to the size of the software (TL) which is being produced:

$$CR = k_r \times TL$$

(k_r is strongly dependent on the number of components in the base and on the type of reused component).

The other cost to be taken into consideration concerns adaptation of components so that they are appropriate in the new context. We can consider that this cost (CA) is proportional to the cost of the reused components:

$$CA = k_a \times CDC$$

These costs are to be taken into account when we examine the requirements of a project engaging in reuse.

13.5 Cost of a Project with Reuse

From what we have just seen, we can infer that the cost of a project in which there is reuse is:

$$CPR = CS + CC + CR + CA$$

With:

- CS: cost of everything specific;
- CS: cost of reusable components;
- CR: cost of component search;
- CA: cost of component adaptation.

Certainly, the word component used here covers all the phases of the life cycle: we can reuse analysis components, design components, code components as well as their associated tests.

The problem with this formula is that we are unable to determine the value of most of the parameters. We can determine the cost of the specific software and the cost of reused components only when we know what is reusable. It is difficult to determine, moreover, how much the adaptation of components will cost.

To determine the advantages that we can gain from a reuse policy, it is necessary to collect a set of hypotheses and to do some simulation.

13.6 Hypotheses

We are going to assume that we have the information relating to companies which engage in reuse and to others which are not. We thus assume that we are able to enumerate the reused components and to know what part they represent in applications. To simplify the calculations, we will assume that the components have been implemented in the first year and that for the following years, there is only maintenance (corrective but also extensive for these components). The number of components does not grow over the years. This hypothesis is partially verified by the real experiences of reuse (see Chapter 15).

13.7 First Simulation

A first simple hypothesis consists of imagining that we are to develop the components which are present in every application. It is assumed that these components represent (in size and cost) $x\%$ of the average application. Their construction cost is n times the cost of the corresponding specific software (with, in general, n taking values between 1 and 4). When we reuse these components, there is an overhead due to search and adaptation. We are going to make the assumption that this overhead is a fraction p of the cost of the components that are reused.

If the overhead on an application developed without components is C and if the number of applications which reuse the components is m, we obtain the following values:

$$CS = ((100\ \text{-}x) \times C) / 100$$

$$CC = (n \times x \times C)/(100 \times m)$$

$$CR + CA = (x \times C)/ (p \times 100)$$

From this, we can infer that the cost of an application developed with these components:

$$CPR = C \times ((100 - x) + (x / p) + (nx/m))/100$$

For the fabrication of the components to be profitable, it is necessary for CPR to be less than C.

If we consider that reuse of a component costs a quarter of that of the development of the corresponding specific software ($p = 4$), and that its development costs twice as much as the cost of the corresponding specific code ($n = 2$), then it is necessary to develop at least 2.6 applications to make the components profitable.

The maximum gain that can be hoped for depends in part on reusable components. When the components are profitable, it is directly proportional to p and to x. If we keep $p = 4$ with $x = 5\%$, the maximum gain is 3.75% per application. With $x = 10$, it becomes 7.5% and with $x = 50\%$, it is 37.5%.

We can, by taking $p = 4$, and $n = 2$, compare two companies: one which reuses and the other which does not. We assume that these companies produce ten products each year at a unit cost of 100. The production of the company which does not engage in reuse is 50 products at the end of 5 years. A company which reuses 20% in all its software spends 40 units in its first year for the production of components. It only produces, therefore, 9.6 products in this year. In the following years, a product only costs it 85 units. It therefore constructs 11.8 products per year. Its total production at the end of 5 years is 56.8 which is 13.6% better than the other company.

With reuse at 5%, a gain of 3% is obtained.

With reuse at 50%, a gain of 46% is obtained.

13.8 Improving the Simulation

The fundamental hypothesis for the above must not be forgotten: we assumed that the components that are constructed are present in all the applications that we construct. In general, it is rare in a company for components common in all application to represent a significant part of the software. If this is the case, the company is already organised for reuse and these studies are of no interest.

We are now going to study the case of companies where the common part of all applications does not represent an important percentage of the applications (less than 5% in general). The gains that we can hope for are slight: 3% as we have seen. To obtain better results, two solutions can be proposed:

- The first consists of not taking into account every application, but to organise them in terms of resemblance. We have seen above that at least 2.6 applications are required to justify the construction of components. If we find groups of at least 4 applications with significant percentages of their parts in common, we can develop the components which will be profitable from the fourth application (and which will reduce the maintenance costs as we are going to see).
- The second solution consists of making components which will not be part of all applications but only in the majority of them. It is this hypothesis that we are going to study now.

If x represents that part of an application constructed using components which appear in q% of applications, then the set of the necessary components represents:

$$100 \, x \, / \, q$$

as a percentage of the size of an application. Their development cost is thus:

$$Cnx \, / \, q$$

If we again take up the formula given above, the cost of the development of software involving reuse is therefore:

$$CPR = C \times ((100 - x) + (x/p) + ((100 \, m \, x)/mq)) \, / \, 100$$

With the above hypotheses ($p = 4$ and $n = 2$), we find that to get a cost less than the cost of specific software, we need:

$$mq < 266$$

For $m = 100$, we regain the profit threshold at 2.66 applications. If the reuse policy applies to components present in half of the applications, the profit threshold goes to 5.32 applications.

As in the previous case, the gain depends upon x; that is, the fraction of the applications that is represented in applications.

13.9 Impact of Maintenance

In the above paragraphs, we have imagined an ideal world where software is perfect and does not change. Reality is completely different; there are errors which must be corrected and developments which are necessary so that the software remains up to date.

Let us first look at the impact of maintenance on a company which does not reuse software. We again take the previous example of a company which produces 10 software items per year. Each piece of software costs 100 units. The novelty is that this time we consider that the company must maintain its software for 5 years and that the cost of software maintenance is, each year, 10% of its development cost.

The first year, the company produces 10 items of software.

The second year, a part of the production staff (10%) is used to maintain these 10 items of software that were produced in the previous year; production is thus 9 items. The total production in these two years is therefore 19 items and it is necessary to provide for a maintenance cost of 190 units for the third year.

The third year, production is 8.1 items because the remainder of the effort is devoted to maintenance.

And so on, with the relations conforming to the values shown in the table facing.

The average production ends at around 6.6 units per year.

The reduction in maintenance cost in the seventh year is due to the fact that the software finished 5 years earlier and is no longer maintained.

13.10 Impact of Reuse

We are going to assume that the company described above decides to construct and maintain components. We assume that the components are constructed in the first year and are only useable from the second year onward. The maintenance cost is 10% of their development cost.

The development cost of the components is:

Year	CM	SM	CC	NSI	TOT
1	0	1000	1000	10	10
2	10	900	1900	9	19
3	190	810	2710	8	27
4	271	729	3439	7	34
5	344	656	4095	6	41
6	410	590	3686	6	47
7	369	631	3417	6	53
8	342	658	3265	7	60
9	327	673	3210	6	v
10	321	679	3233	7	73
11	323	677	3319	7	80
12	332	668	3356	7	87
13	336	664	3362	6	93
14	336	664	3352	7	100
15	335	665	3338	7	107

SM: cost of software maintenance.
SC: annual cost of software construction.
M: cost of software to be maintained in the following year.
N: number of software items produced in the year.
TOT: total production.

Cnx/q

The development cost of an application (ignoring component cost) is:

$$CPR = C \times ((100\text{-}x) + (x/p)) / 100$$

We are going to assume that:

- The cost of reuse is a quarter of the cost of the development of the corresponding specific software ($p = 4$);
- The development cost of a component is twice the cost of the development of the corresponding specific software ($n = 2$);
- Maintenance of components never stops (they always evolve).

If we consider the case in which components represent 10% of applications ($x = 10$), and that the are present in 80% ($q = 80$) of applications, we obtain the results shown in the next table (overleaf).

The total production is 114.06 at the end of 15 years while it was 106.66 without reuse. The gain is therefore 6.94% which is low with respect to the expectations that have been generally expressed for reuse.

Year	CM	SM	CC	ACC	YSN	NSI	TOT
1	0.0	0	25	975	975	9.75	9.75
2	2.5	97.5	0	900	1875	9.73	19.48
3	2.5	187.5	0	810	2685	8.76	28.24
4	2.5	268.5	0	729	3414	7.88	36.12
5	2.5	341.4	0	656	4070	7.09	43.21
6	2.5	407.0	0	590	3686	6.38	49.59
7	2.5	368.6	0	629	3415	6.80	56.39
8	2.5	341.4	0	656	3261	7.09	63.49
9	2.5	326.1	0	671	3203	7.26	70.74
10	2.	320.3	0	677	3224	7.32	78.07
11	2.5	322.4	0	675	3309	7.30	85.36
12	2.5	330.9	0	667	3346	7.21	92.57
13	2.5	334.6	0	663	3353	7.17	99.74
14	2.5	335.3	0	662	3344	7.16	106.90
15	2.5	334.4	0	663	3330	7.17	114.06

CM: cost of component maintenance.

SM: cost of software maintenance.

CC: cost of component construction.

ACC: annual cost of component construction.

YSN: cost of software to be maintained during the year.

NSI: number of software items produced in the year.

TOT: total production.

Here is a table giving the percentage gains with respect to a policy of non-reuse with values of q (ordinate) plotted against values of x (given as the abscissa):

	x = 2-	x = 40	x = 60	x = 80	x = 100
q = 20	13	32	62	116	238
q = 40	14	35	68	126	255
q = 60	15	36	70	129	260
q = 80	15	37	71	131	263
q = 100	15	37	72	132	265

The assumptions that have been made lead to better results as x increases. In the ideal case in which applications are only assemblies of components, we triple production. Doubling of production is obtained with components representing 80% of applications.

The conclusion is asollows it is necessary to look for subsets of software which have strong common points and to construct components for these subsets. The results will be better than when we try to reuse policy applicable to all applications.

13.11 Purchase of Components

We are allowed to assume that, in the near future, the purchase of already developed components will be possible. We will have libraries of components available whose maintenance can be assumed. A project which reuses these components will have purchase costs for its components, as well as costs for search and adaptation. It will no longer be necessary to monopolise efforts for component maintenance (we will pay for the maintenance to be done).

If we use the previous calculations again, now with a reuse cost of 1/4 ($p = 4$), the gains obtained with respect to non-reuse using values for x (q has no influence in this case) are:

x	20	40	60	80	100
profit	18	43	82	145	300

To operate in the same way as electronic engineers and assemble purchased components to construct software allows the production level to be multiplied by 4.

To decide today to invest in a reuse policy is a preparation for confronting in the future companies which will buy the components that comprise their products.

13.12 Resistance to Evolution

To be complete, we still have to analyse the impact of reuse on a last case: technological developments.

Recent progress has, in recent years, rapidly brought to the fore technologies which it is impossible to ignore; examples are:

- X windows on workstations;
- Windows on the PC;
- CORBA, OLE and Active X;
- Multimedia.

Taking these new technologies into account has an impact on existing software: it is necessary to adapt them, which can be very expensive. New, unforeseen, developments will not stop in the coming years.

We are going to redo the above simulations by assuming that, in the fifth year, there is a change in technology which forces us to modify all the software. The cost of this modification represents 20% of the development cost of the software being maintained.

In the case of a company which does not reuse, production at the end of 15 years has reduced by 4%. Production falls away completely in the 5th year.

In the case of a company which engages in reuse, the diminution in production with respect to that which is created when there is no change in technology can be seen in the following table:

	x = 20	x = 40	x = 60	x = 80	x = 100
y = 20	3	3	3	3	3
y = 40	0	0	1	1	1
y = 60	0	0	0	0	0
y = 80	0	0	0	0	0
y = 100	0	0	0	0	0

Starting with the case of reuse involving only a few applications, there is no visible impact on the company's production. In particular, the drop in production in the 5th year is slight.

Another advantage of reuse is a greater resistance to technological change and thus a better control of software development.

13.13 Conclusion

What we can infer is that it is necessary to look for common points between software (part of the domain analysis) and to have reuse policies that relate to groups of software items.

An idea for finding these software groups is to use on a set of existing software that the company has, a set of techniques for the identification of components that was proposed in the last chapter, and to try to evaluate the cost of analogous components. We can thus determine the values of the different parameters x and q which allow us to get an idea of what a reuse policy can bring (it is sufficient to use a table like the ones above to make such an evaluation). For values of n and p, it is necessary to be prudent at the start and to predict, for example $n = 3$ and $p = 3$. Then, values can be arrived at which are more classical: $n = 2$ and $p = 4$ (indeed, more for p when the components are well-known).

In domains subject to technological developments, it can be useful to reuse, even if this does not bring much in the way of a reward, in order to prepare to confront the changes without damage.

13.14 Chapter Summary

This chapter has proposed a number of simulations to evaluate the gains which can be hoped for from a policy of reuse.

The gains we can hope for depend on many factors and can vary from 3% to 300% in the cases that have been examined.

One observation is that it is right to be careful and not look to construct the maximum number of components. It is preferable to spend time in carefully determining which components are necessary.

There are thresholds concerning the number of reuses of a component outside of which component construction fails to be profitable.

Chapter Fourteen

Buying and Selling Components

One of the conclusions of the last chapter on the gains of a reuse policy is that one can obtain the most important benefits by buying components. Why not start these purchases now?

You can also decide to commercialise the components that you use internally. What can be done to sell components?

This is what we will study in this chapter.

14.1 Buying Components

14.1.1 Which components to choose?

If you are used to developing in C, you will have never asked yourself the question about how one knows which component library to use when one manipulates, files or processes. You will use the libraries available as standard with the C that you have. A character is a type *char*, a string of characters is an object of type *char**. To copy one string to another, the *strcpy* function from the standard C library is used.

If you decide to move on to C++ because this language is object-oriented and must make reuse easier for you, you will find that you now have choices.

There are numerous libraries of reusable C++ components. We find, for example, in [Harmon, 93] the description of thirty C++ libraries. In many of these libraries, you will find character string objects much more sophisticated than the simple *char** in C. The quantity of functions applicable to character strings is impressive. You will not regret moving to C++!

After a comparison of some libraries, you will decide to use one of them. Generally, you are going to find in this library a whole range of objects offering lots of possibilities:

- Character strings, of course;
- Files;
- Data structures (lists, stacks, etc.);
- Etc.

You will thus rapidly get a taste for reuse.

One day, used as you are to digging in your component library to find the objects which you need, you will discover that you need a particular object which seems elementary (to you). Your efforts are in vain; it does not exist in this library.

This is not the kind of thing that stops you. You look to see if there is a library which offers the service you are looking for. You find one and decide therefore to buy it and use it to complement your usual library.

This is where the trouble begins!

The new library also contains character strings, files, lists, etc. Some have different names, but others have the same name. On the other hand, the descriptions of the objects are different: the string class in your former library has no resemblance to the string class in your new one. Of course (always bearing in mind Murphy's law), the object that you want to use needs the new character strings and your application needs the old ones. It is impossible to use the two libraries at the same time.

Conclusion: you are tied to a component provider. If they do not provide the components you want, you cannot go elsewhere to find them.

14.1.2 When will components be standardised?

The standardisation of C++ is in progress. On the other hand, there is nothing underway on the standardisation of basic components needed to build applications. There are as many character string objects as there are component libraries.

This lack of standardisation creates noticeable incompatibilities between libraries.

Standardisation will eventually come:

- Either because the majority of users will make the choice of a single component library;
- Or because a standards organisation will propose basic components which are accepted by everyone;
- Or because a market-dominating computer manufacturer will impose *de facto* their basic libraries.

Standardisation of components begins for certain languages. For example, Java has a set of standard components.

Today, numerous users of C++ use public domain libraries because they are free. The main interest in these libraries is that they cost nothing. They do, though, have major faults:

- They cannot, in general, be used to implement commercial software and cannot, thus, become standards for commercial software;
- Nothing guarantees their users upwards compatibility (it has often been noted that public domain products have an anarchic development);

- There is no support for getting bugs fixed in a reasonable time;
- There is no chance of the release of higher-level commercialised components using these libraries because it is not permitted.

Being free could be a mechanism for more rapid standardisation [Cox 90], but it does not seem to be the best way.

The standards organisations are concerned with languages. There is nothing in their priorities about treating the problem of standardising of libraries. The work on OMG (Object Management Group) around CORBA (Common Object Request Broker Architecture [OMG 91]) are to be closely followed. They might be at the beginning of the first important componnent standards.

Compiler manufacturers are much more active in this domain. Standardisation can come very quickly from a Microsoft or a Borland (are Microsoft Foundation Classes this standard?).

If a standardisation of components exists, interface standards will be defined for the basic objects in applications. Every library will have to offer objects conforming to these interfaces. The difference between the two libraries will be:

- In terms of chosen implementation and its performance;
- Of the additional components (compatible with the basic components);
- The capability for extension.

A standard is not therefore an obstacle to a market in components. On the contrary, it can only increase it.

14.1.3 What to do while waiting for standardisation?

While waiting for standards to arrive, it is preferable to choose libraries that are delivered along with their sources.

If the source of a library is available, it becomes possible to rename objects and thus avoid naming conflicts between libraries (component x of library *lib1* is renamed *lib1_x* and the one in library *lib2* is renamed *lib2_x*) or extract the components from one library to introduce them, after modification, into another library.

This means that one is condemned to making sure that all the maintenance is done oneself.

It is not surprising after all these observations that experiences with reuse which we hear about deal with libraries that are local to companies.

14.1.4 Standards and extensions

Standardisation of components can be scary because it leads one to assume that components are fixed. This is untrue. One can decide to introduce new components on a regular basis. This can be in completely new domains or can be extensions of existing components. Object-oriented techniques, and particularly inheritance, facilitate this.

We have seen in the chapter on component maintenance that components are always being extended. This is certainly true for components that have been purchased. A library must always be kept up to date.

14.2 Sale of Components

14.2.1 In what form to sell components?

If one wishes to sell components, one immediately hits on the following question: must I sell my components in the form of source or as binaries?

The sale of components in binary form is the simplest solution. The components keep their secrets. Only interfaces can be seen, the implementations remain the know-how of the company which makes the components. For the client, this form is not very practical. If the component is not suitable for him, he must adapt it to his needs by creating a subclass which will redefine what is unsuitable. With C++, this is not possible in a number of cases because:

- The methods that one wants to redefine are not declared virtual;
- The limits of multiple inheritance not handled by C++ are reached;
- One wants to change the types of parameters to a method.

The sale of components together with their source gives the user more freedom. The disadvantages of providing them are more numerous, on the other hand.

- It is difficult when the users signal errors to decide between real errors in the components and errors introduced by modifications to components; the simplest is not to ensure maintenance of modified components.
- It is difficult to control the use which is made of components. If they are efficient, we run the risk of finding them disseminated along parallel paths. All the know-how of the company which made the components is diffused at the same time from the component sources.

14.2.2 Must components be paid for?

A company which uses components belonging to it to construct software for another company's use must rigorously verify the contract which is signed with the client.

There are two possibilities to choose from:

- Paying for the components from the client. It then seems reasonable that the latter will acquire the rights to reproduce them, to extend and distribute them. They can, for example, pass them on to other companies in new projects. These companies can be the rivals of the one that constructed the components. It thus loses a little of their know-how;

- The company only pays a licence for the components. The contract states that the client does not have the right to copy the components (only for legally sanctioned backups) and has no rights to distribute them. The company's know-how is thus protected. The second possibility seems better:

- For those who make the components, there is preservation of know-how and profitability of the components which can therefore be used in different projects. It is just a matter of watching that the components are not under-priced;

- For the client, the cost of construction is less because they pay less for the components; they retain (by law) the right to adapt the software (and therefore the components it contains) for their own purposes; they are thus not subject to the good will of the provider.

14.2.3 To whom do modified components belong?

Another problem which can arise with reusable components is the following. A company has bought the rights to use some components. The company modifies some of them to suit their needs better.

Is the modifier the owner of the software?

The law says that there is new software (and therefore property) if it has been created. The concept of creation is not clearly defined. How many lines must be altered before a component is no longer the same? From which momemnt is there an original work when software is modified? Reuse must bring much work to jurors.

Another important question concerns the interfaces of components. To find good objects is a fundamental problem in object-oriented development. To find good objects which, moreover, have the property of being reusable by other applications is yet more difficult. In these conditions, imagining the interface of a component is more complex than coding its implementation. We can therefore realise two components whose code almost always differs but which have the same interface (with similar names). How does one distinguish between the copies?

14.2.4 Component purchase and dependence

The last barrier that must be broken down if one wants to buy components is accepting that one must be highly dependent on another company's implementations. When there is a standardisation of basic components which when there exist libraries of high-level components built on these basic components and are thus compatible, one will be able to construct applications by mixing components from several libraries. One will become dependent, therefore, on the companies which build these libraries. If there are not several interchangeable offerings, it will be necessary again to take precautions by asking for the sources.

14.3 Chapter Summary

This chapter has described the problems of component trade (sale and purchase). Numerous questions remain to be asked.

There still remains much progress to be made before a healthy market in reusable components exists:

- Standardisation of basic components;
- Identification and establishment of rules for the legal problems.

While waiting for this time, it is necessary to be very careful when one uses libraries of components and if possible, one must ask for their sources.

Chapter Fifteen

Experience with Reuse

15.1 History

Verilog is a French company which specialises in the fabrication of tools for software engineering. It produces tools covering all phases of the development of software (analysis, design, code generation, tests, simulation, documentation). These tools are available on different types of computers and different operating systems.

As with many manufacturers of software products, it handles several products. Each of them:

- Has at least one new version each year;
- Runs on several versions of operating systems on several machines;
- Must be up-to-date with respect to the current standards (MOTIF Tool Talk etc.);
- Must be coupled with other products (other tools for PAO, development environments, version and configuration managers, etc.) which themselves are released regularly in new versions and which provide new facilities which have to be taken into account.

These projects must, of course, be open to enable it to allow to be adapted to the clients' particular needs.

We arrive thus at a combination of the form:

$$P \times OS \times STD \times CT \times SA \times V$$

P: products
OS: operating systems
STD: standards
CT: coupled tools
SA: specific adaptations
V: versions

which quickly become impossible to handle

In 1988, Verilog decided to implement a reuse policy in order to manage this combination.

The goal aimed at by the introduction of reuse was to pass to a combination of the type:

$$(P + OS + STD + CT + SA) \times V$$

which is much simpler to manage. A product then became an assembly of components amongst which are found components for standard items, couplings with other tools and handles allowing specific modifications.

In 1988 the object oriented techniques were less developed than today. The analysis and design methods for object orientation were at am early stage. The principle languages which were available were:

- Smalltalk, only in interpreted mode;
- C++ at that time only with single inheritance;
- Eiffel 1.0;
- Objective C;
- Simula;
- Ada.

A comparison of these different languages highlighted Eiffel for several reasons:

- The compiled mode was more efficient than Smalltalk;
- Language typing which made it more reliable than Smalltalk;
- Multiple inheritance was considered important for less restricted reuse (single inheritance in Smalltalk and C++);
- The existence of generics (absent in C++ at that time);
- The simplicity, the clarity and power of the language;
- The concept of programming by contract.

A Pilot Project, realised by a single person in 1987, with the Eiffel compiler had allowed us to verify the qualities of language.

15.2 First Experience with Object Orientation

Starting in 1988, a new pilot project employing two persons was started. It was immediately necessary to face up to a set of problems due to the absence of configuration management. The two developers shared the same classes. While one of them made changes, there was recompilation for the other because the Eiffel compiler controls consistency between classes. To avoid this problem it was necessary to duplicate the classes for each user. The solution was judged insufficient because with 100 developers, there was no question of copying all sources 100 times. The use of a version manger such as SCCS also appeared to be proscribed because, before compilation, it was necessary to remove all sources which also used a lot of space.

The providers of the Eiffel compiler did not provide their compiler with a management or configuration manager. Verilog then decided to develop its own Eiffel compiler, one which was strongly coupled to a configuration manager. This was done and the first version of the Verilog development environment was available in September 1988.

15.3 First Version of the Verilog Environment

The language processed at that time was Eiffel 1.0 with several extensions and variants:

- An obligatory use clause placed at the start of the class which was used for documenting the class. This clause was decomposed into three subclasses:
- Keys: a set of characteristic key words for the class;
- Summary: a short summary of the role of the class;
- Description: a complete description of the way the class is used;
- The requirement in an import clause to declare the set of classes which are used (this allows us to omit a pass of the compiler that is expensive in terms of time);
- The possibility of writing method bodies using either Eiffel or C syntax (the key word *do* introducing Eiffel syntax and the keyword *cdo* introducing C syntax-the C syntax had the no-pointers restriction that is found in Java);
- The automatic extraction of all character strings from classes and their storage in a file to facilitate the translation of applications.

The compilation of a class, and all classes used by it, was performed by a command which had, as its single parameter the name of the principal class of the application to be compiled. This command was responsible for:

- Finding the physical place of the current version of the named class;
- Finding the set of the classes used by the named class (at all levels and all current versions);
- Determining what was not up to date and to recompile it;
- Linking.

The philosophy was to automate the following tasks as far as possible:

- No writing of files describing what was to be done (*makefile* or system files);
- Automatic location of files;
- Transparent management of configurations.

Configuration management in the environment was based on classical and elementary principles.

The reference versions of classes were stored in a reference space. Each user found themselves in a workspace which allowed them:

- To have access to particular versions of classes in the reference environment;
- To update new classes or new versions of classes.

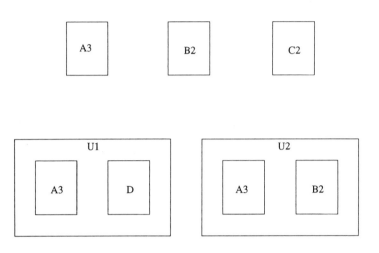

Figure 15.1 First shot at configuration management.

For example (Figure 15.1), if the three classes *A*, *B*, *C*, have respectively 3, 2, 2 versions available in the reference space, we can have the following configuration:

- User *U1* used class *A* in its last available version (3) and was in the middle of modifying this class; they were also in the middle of creating class *D*;
- User *U2* was also using class *A* in its version 3 and class *B* in its version 2.

When *U1* decided that the new version of *A* was up to date, they put it in the reference space by creating a new version (4). *U2* was also warned that the new version of *A* was available and was free to choose between:

- Continuing to use version 3 of *A* to update its class *D* and subsequently to pass to the new version *A*, or:
- Immediately use the new version of *A*.

An implementation of the development environment in a pilot project (8 people for one year) showed three types of problem:

- The limits of the language;
- Problems with configuration management;
- Difficulties for sharing tasks in the project.

15.3.1 Language limits

The limits of the language came essentially from problems related to repeated inheritance. No construction in Eiffel 1.0 permits the handling of the problems such as those described in Figure 15.2.

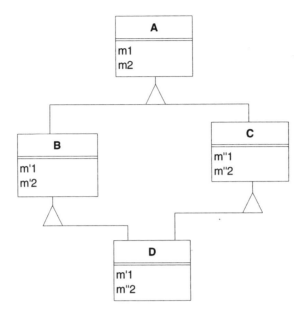

Figure 15.2 Repeated inheritance.

Class *A* possesses methods *m1* and *m2*. Class *B* inherits from *A* and redefines the content of *m1* and *m2*. Class *C* inherits from *A* and also redefines content of *m1* and *m2* but in a different fashion. Class *D* inherits from *B* and from *C* and want for this class, the behaviour of *m1* from Class *B* and that of *m2* from Class *C*.

To handle this problem the keep directive was added later to the language in order to allow us to make clear which definitions to save. These additions have also been made in Eiffel in 3.0 (with a slightly different approach and syntax).

Another need which was felt was that of constrained genericity. That is to say the capacity to say that the generic type is at least a descendent of a given task.

Apart from these problems the language was judged to be pleasant to use. The techniques of pre- and post-conditions allowed the elimination of numerous errors from the first attempts at software.

The assimilation of object concepts, (particularly dynamic binding) took between two and six months depending on the person.

15.3.2 Configuration management problems

The problems with configuration management came from the existence of a single reference space and from the difficulty of distinguishing between what must be saved and what must be destroyed.

The presence of a single reference space meant that once the developer wanted to make available a new version of a class to another developer, this version became available for every group in the company. People did not know if they had to use the new version or not. This led to two kinds of behaviour:

- Some systematically used the new version, with all the problems that it entailed if it was not sufficiently up to date;
- Others systematically decided not to change the version which rendered their work spaces inconsistent with respect to others.

15.3.3 Task sharing problems

A significant difficulty with the first project, using the object oriented approach, was the organisation of work and sharing of tasks.

Before, using Pascal or C for software development, the teams shared the different functions in the software: one person was in charge of the implementation of function A, another had the implementation of function B.

With object orientation it is necessary to share objects which are generally much more highly inter-connected. One person was then charged with the implementation of functions A and B over a set of object and another with the implementation of the same function over other objects.

During a long period, it was difficult to find the frontier between object and function.

It was necessary to arrive at a sharing of tasks by objects which does not correspond at all to the specialisations required by developers in the past.

15.4 Second Version of the Environment

After the first uses, it was therefore decided to bring out a new version of the environment to handle the problems that had been encountered. The development principally concerns the language and configuration management.

15.4.1 Language

As far as the compiler is concerned, the major language developments were those mentioned above, that is the introduction of repeated inheritance processing and constrained genericity.

15.4.2 Configuration management

As far as configuration management is concerned, the new version had the following characteristics:

- There was a hierarchy of reference spaces;
- Each reference space had access to the classes of the space above it;
- Each user had a workspace located under a reference space which afforded access to all versions of classes available in the latter space.

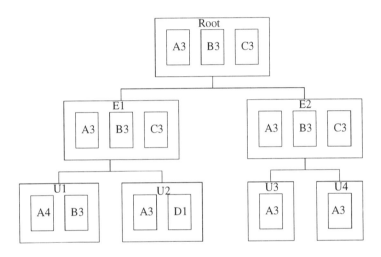

Figure 15.3 New configuration management approach.

In the example of Figure 15.3 there exists a root reference space, called root. This space contains three classes:

- *A* in three versions;
- *B* in three versions;
- *C* in three versions.

Under root are two other reference spaces: *E1* and *E2*. These two spaces have access to the three classes *A*, *B* and *C* in versions which are known to root.

Under space *E1* there are two user workspaces: *U1* and *U2*. User *U1* is in the process of creating a new version of *A* and uses *B* in version 3. *U2* uses *A* in version 3 and is in the course of updating a new class D.

In *E2* there are two user workspaces: *U3* and *U4*. These spaces use class *A* in version 3.

After a while, *U1* has stopped updating the new version of *A*. He must make it accessible to *U2* who has need of it in order to finish the update of their new class *D*. *U1* then references *A*. As shown in Figure 15.4, a fourth version of *A* becomes available to *E1*. *U1* and *U2* then have access to this new version.

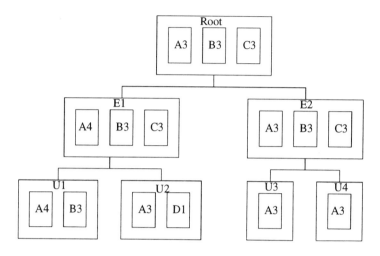

Figure 15.4 New version of A in E1.

U3 and *U4* are not altered by this appearance of a new version of A. For them, there only exists three versions of *A*.

During the update of *D*, *U2* finds errors in *A*. They then require *U1* to correct them. *U1* constructs a new version of *A* (Figure 15.5).

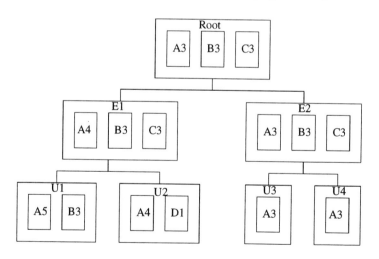

Figure 15.5 New versions in E1.

U1 corrects the errors and then references the new version of *A* in *E1*. *U2* can thus finish *D* and refer to the first version of *D* in *E1* (Figure 15.6).

U1 and *U2* work on the same sub-project. *U3* and *U4* work for another sub-project. The work of *U1* and *U2* being finished, they want to make classes *A* and *D* in their new versions available for other sub-project. To do this, the project manager asks for references in root space to classes *A* and *D*. We obtain the result in Figure 15.7.

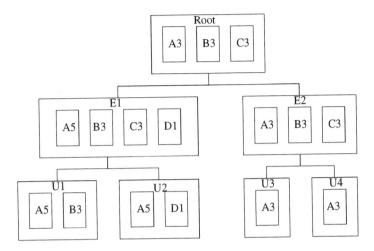

Figure 15.6 New versions in E1.

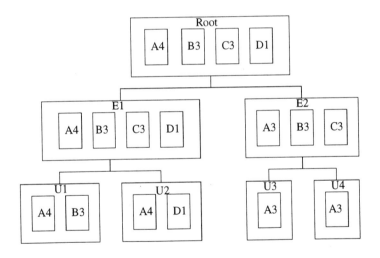

Figure 15.7 Promoted to the root node.

It will be observed that only the last version of *A* is transferred into root. There is, therefore, automatic deletion of all intermediate versions of classes. All versions referenced by the sub-spaces of *E1* are up-to-date. Space *E2* continues to be unaware of the new version of *A* and *D*. While its administrator decides if the *U3* and *U4* can access these new classes, then the update of *E1* with respect to root. *U3* and *U4* are then warned that there exists a new version of *A* and can, if they so desire, make use of it (Figure 15.8).

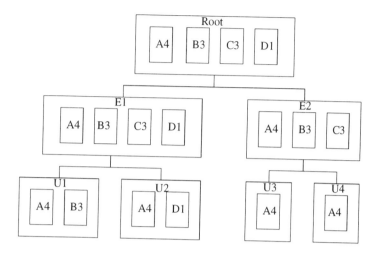

Figure 15.8 General movement of classes.

This new configuration management therefore controls the two problems encountered in the proceeding version:

- Users can be organised into teams;
- The destruction of all intermediate versions of classes was automatic.

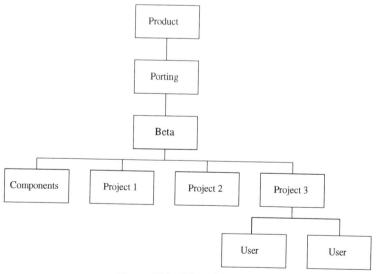

Figure 15.9 Adopted hierarchy.

Little by little, it was necessary to find the best environment hierarchy. The one that seemed the best is shown in Figure 15.9.

The root references a space (*product*) which only contains classes which constitute software to be delivered to clients. These classes are never destroyed.

Immediately under product is the *porting* space. It contains the sub-spaces for working which allow the porting of products onto different machines.

Under *products* is the *beta* space which contains the reference versions for everything used by the company.

Under *beta*, we find spaces for the components used in the various projects. Under these spaces are workspaces used by the development teams.

When a new project is started, reference and workspaces are created for it, and workspaces are created under the spaces containing the components that are to be adapted. The project update is performed in a project space on the basis of the availability of suitable components in the *beta* space. At the end of the implementation, all project classes are transferred into the *beta* space (in fact, uniquely in their last valid versions). Transfer to the *porting* space allows adaptation of the classes to the specifics of the machines on which they are to run, and the final product is transferred into the *product* space prior to delivery.

This organisation has allowed better correspondence between a great deal of sharing among components by allowing better separation. We do not want constantly to be bothered by reusing many components.

Users have demanded an evolution. The possibility of seeing one or more classes in a space which is not directly available via the hierarchy; it has become possible subsequently.

We end with configuration management. This is a major problem for object-oriented development which engage in much reuse, it is necessary to signal another problem with the configuration management mechanisms which was chosen.

The configuration management was active configuration management. This means that a user had the right to chose any version of a set of classes and to require the construction of an executable. The compiler then tried to verify whether the co-existence of these classes was possible possibly by recreating all the necessary files. It is very soon clear that the notion of class is too fine for effective configuration management. A class rarely exists on its own. It depends upon other classes (by inheritance or by use). We use, in fact, a set of classes. It seems that it is preferable to manage configurations of coherent subsets of classes rather than isolated classes. This simplifies configuration management and is more suitable for our needs.

15.5 Organisation

At first, the work consisted of putting into place a language and development environment. As far as reuse is concerned, the results were somewhat deceptive at the start.

After a year of using the environment, a sounding among the classes which had been developed, allowed us to determine that the users did not reuse, but created lots of variants. For example, we counted more than 20 variants of the class list. The reaction was the following: I am looking for a class that implements lists; the official list class does not suit me exactly so I'll create a sub-class of it which adds or modifies the operations I want. I will not bother to find out whether such a sub class exists already.

The observation that this copying was happening made us realise the fact that a component is never fixed. Base classes seem solid, intended to be suitable for all needs, yet, in fact, all the variants showed they were far from being perfect.

When we examined the class variants, we were led to create new versions of the base classes. Some were even completely redesigned better to cover the requirements.

Later on we counted fewer specialisations of new base classes. They continued to develop less each year.

It is necessary to know what is happening in terms of what is being reused, and to know which components are exactly suitable to their various uses. For efficiency, it seems necessary to take these facts into account, together with available human resources.

To take into account the reuse aspect, the organisation of the technical division of the company was modified. A new centre was created: the Technology Centre. Its mission was to favour reuse in the company. The centre was composed of three groups of people:

- The Production Environment group which was in charge of maintenance and development of the object-oriented development environment (compiler, configuration manager and associated tools);
- The Components group in charge of the development of reusable components on behalf of the other teams in the company;
- The O-O Experts group in charge of following the implementations of the other group and advising them on the components to be used.

The experts suggested architectures for the software in the company. They had to intervene during design reviews on the projects in order to:

- Identify the predicted implementations which could be engaged in reusing existing components;

- Identify the needs common to several projects and also write the requirements documentation for the components which have to be constructed by the Components group.

At the start of the Components group, after considering the architectures of the tools, component development was started without regard to any project.

The Components group existed for two years. The lessons learned from this existence were the following:

- The majority of project-independent component developments were a mistake. At the end of implementation, it was noted that the components which had been constructed did not suit the specific needs for which they had been designed. Later, the only component developments in the company were those generalising specific developments.
- Some projects were behind because of a delay in the fabrication of components which they needed to use.
- Many components were too general, and had too poor a performance. Simplified versions of these components has to be constructed, and great efforts at optimisation of the code generated by the compiler in the environment were undertaken.
- The Components team had to deal with very difficult clients: internal developers. They were accused of all the problems encountered in development. There was a lot of argument about the components. It was necessary to organise campaigns of counter-information in order to re-establish reality.
- Resistance to novelty never diminished. New components were never accepted immediately. There was always a period of lack of faith, of attempts not to use the new components. After a period of acclimatisation, the components were used. Resistance occurred at all levels of the hierarchy.
- There were not always new components to be developed. After two years in existence, the components available permitted a reuse level of the order of 50% per application to be attained. There appeared no ideas for new components which allowed further increase of the reuse rate. The Components group was then reduced to just a few persons who were charged with extension and corrective maintenance of the existing components.
- The great majority of reused components were made by the Components group. There were few components made by the application teams, and these components were not widely reused.

Today there is no Technology Centre at Verilog. A very small group in Technical Direction has been charged with component maintenance. This is essentially a matter of development. Errors in components are, for the majority of cases, detected in the first months which follow their entry into service. There are always developments of new components even if they are less numerous than at the start of the reuse policy. These developments are performed by project teams which are specially constituted for the occasion by mixing members of several teams. The development of components is always performed on the basis of a first attempt being made inside a project.

Beside this official reuse which is the same throughout the company, there exists reuse inside the product teams. For example, for the range of projects ObjectPARTNER/OMT, the reuse rate for software is 70%.

15.6 Statistics

A set of measurements on Verilog components was performed by the Tools Europe 1993 workshop [Coulange '93].

Here is a summary of the information. They relate only to Verilog. One should not rush to draw too rapid a generalisation from the information. They give a good idea of what use of the object-oriented technique can be.

It is useful to recall that the language used for the development is a derivative of Eiffel. Everything is an object in the software. This explains certain figures (on inheritance in particular), which are impossible to attain with a language of a hybrid nature like C++.

The measures were performed on a set of 4494 classes.

15.6.1 Class size

The average size of a class of 250 lines (including comments). The number of lines in a class ranges from several dozens to ten thousand (the classes of 10,000 lines being produced using a code generator). Two-thirds of the classes have less than 200 lines. Inheritance has no impact on the size of classes.

It seems that without particular instruction, the developers have in their head an idea of what the complexity of a class must be. This is shown by a number of lines which is of the same order in the majority of classes. Inheritance is not felt as additional complexity: classes which inherit from other classes have the same number of lines as the average.

15.6.2 Number of attributes

It is necessary to distinguish own and inherited attributes. Own attributes are those which are declared in a class and which exist in this class and its descendants. Inherited attributes are those which compose part of the class because they have been inherited from one or more ancestors.

On average, a class has two own attributes. Half of the classes have no own attributes.

The total number of class attributes (own plus inherited attributes) is on average eight.

We note that this average is important when half the classes have no own attributes. This is a perverse effect of inheritance. It is necessary particularly to look at the number of attributes in reusable components classes. This attribute represents the consumed memory. For an object which has millions of instances, we save megabytes by deleting an attribute. Numerous optimisation tasks have been undertaken in order to reduce the number of component attributes. Tools which allow, for a given class, to find out its exact content after inheritance resolution are very useful in doing this.

15.6.3 Number of methods

By making, as for attributes, the distinction between own and inherited methods, we arrive at an average of five methods as the own methods of the class. 50% of the classes have less than three methods and 20% of the classes have no proper methods (they redefine methods which they inherit from their ancestors).

The total number of methods (own and inherited) is 148. This is a considerable number, particularly if we take into account the fact that, in the count of inherited methods, we have not taken into account the 24 methods which come from the class any (the ancestor of all classes). This large number is principally due to considerable use of inheritance which means that we have, particularly with classes of components providing many services, many methods which are not always of use.

A particular command in the Verilog environment (available in the Eiffel environment) allows the optimisation of the code generated by suppressing objects whose methods are not used. We can see the merit of such a command.

15.6.4 Inheritance

All classes inherit from the class any. This is not taken into account in the measures.

We are going to distinguish between direct and indirect inheritance. Direct inheritance is that which are declared in a class. Indirect inheritance is that which comes from the classes which are inherited. The father is the direct ancestor and the grandfather is an indirect ancestor.

On average a class has one direct ancestor. 89% of classes inherit directly from one other class. 49% of the classes inherit directly from more than one class.

This use of inheritance is characteristic of completely object-oriented languages (like Smalltalk in the case of simple inheritance). We rarely find such a use of inheritance in C++.

Nine times out of ten, a designer imagines one class as a specialisation of another. Inheritance is therefore a useful concept (to the extent that the language that we are using supports it correctly).

The total number of ancestors of a class (the sum of the direct and indirect inheritors) is on average eight.

24% of classes have to handle inheritance conflicts due to repeated inheritance (happily, a mechanism for processing such conflicts was introduced into the language!).

On average, classes have a depth of three in the inheritance lineage (this means that they are granddaughters of the class any).

These results on use of inheritance are fairly impressive. They completely falsify all the statements that we hear saying that inheritance is a concept which does not function, that there is no point in using multiple inheritance, and there is not point having classes with more than two levels of inheritance.

As far as inheritance is concerned, it is necessary to base oneself on the capacities of the language being used. In the case of Eiffel, there is everything that is necessary in the language to allow us to have problem-free multiple inheritance:

- Redefinition of signatures;
- Resolution of conflicts under repeated inheritance;
- Renaming;
- Friend types;
- Constrained genericity.

The problems that we cite as due to multiple inheritance are predominantly problems with C++. The limits are known and it is necessary to take this into account when we use this language in order to produce code.

It is important for object orientation not to confuse the basic concepts and languages which permit partial implementation of these concepts.

15.6.5 Used classes

Here too we are going to distinguish between direct and indirect use. Direct use concerns classes which are directly used by a given class and indirect use concerns classes used by those used directly or indirectly (as well as all the ancestors of these classes).

On average, a class directly uses nine classes. 47% of the classes use less than six classes.

On average, one class uses indirectly 226 classes.

This result can seem enormous. Again, it is necessary to recall that the language used is completely object-oriented: the principal class for applications indirectly uses all the other classes in the application. The average size of applications is around 600 classes, so we can understand why the number representing the average for indirect dependence is high.

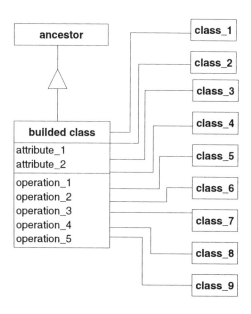

Figure 15.10 A class as seen by its creator.

15.6.6 Class complexity

From these measures we infer that the class has two very different sides. For its creator, it is a source of 250 lines composed on average of two attributes and five methods which inherits from one class and uses nine others (Figure 15.10). Reality is completely different: a class is a set formed of eight attributes and 148 methods which had eight ancestors and uses 226 other classes. Object orientation (and principally inheritance) allows us really to mask the complexity of these objects. This is an advantage because we can manipulate information of low complexity, but it is also a danger because we end up by forgetting that the amount of information we are manipulating is large and the applications are becoming huge.

The observation for Verilog is that the use of inheritance is delicate but it enormously simplifies the complexity of classes and assists the development of applications.

15.7 Examples of Components

Here is a short description of part of the components implemented by Verilog.

A component is a set of classes treating a single subject.

15.7.1 Base class: kernel_sys

This component contains nine classes:

- *Any*: ancestor of all classes which introduces the methods to copy objects, to save and restore them, etc.;
- *Comparable*: comparisons;
- *File*: file management;
- *Hashable*: calculation of hash codes;
- *Internal*: access to object descriptions;
- *Math*: mathematical functions;
- *String*: character strings;
- *To_ special*: communication with the structures in C.

15.7.2 structure_sys: data structures

This component contains 80 classes. We find all the data structures (lists, stacks, tables, sets, trees, hash tables etc.) in many different forms.

15.7.3 tool_sys: utilities

This component contains 20 classes. We find there are classes for handling dates, for handling interrupts, call-backs, locks etc.

15.7.4 file_sys: files

This component contains 7 classes for handling different types of files and stores.

15.7.5 reference_sys: referencing objects

This component contains 11 classes for the unique identification of objects and the handling of inter-object references between different models. It supports the implementation of tools for the consistent processing of models which can be divided into several parts and manipulated by different users.

15.7.6 ero_sys: entity-relation systems

This component contains 39 classes. It provides standard services to classes automatically generated from entity relation models (traversal of relations, backup, restore). These parts of an application concerning the structure of the data to be supplied to tools, as well as the operations for their manipulation, is generated automatically by this component. The entity relation model used today is that of OMT.

15.7.7 asn1_sys: backup and restore asn1

This component contains 32 classes. It allows the automatic backup and restoration of information using a format compatible with the standard ASN1. Backup is upward and downward compatible. An example of the use of the component is seen in ObjectPARTNER: any version of the tool is capable of reading a model generated by any other version. Teams can work without problems and can share models with different versions of the tool.

15.7.8 p_base_sys: graphic base

This component contains 14 classes. It provides objects which are basic to graphics (positions, polylines, etc.).

15.7.9 g_graphic_sys: encapsulation of MOTIF objects

This component contains 156 classes. It provides all the objects needed to construct a Motif application:

- Resources;
- Windows;
- Containers;
- Labels;
- Buttons;
- Complex objects;
- Menus;
- Graphics.

The encapsulation goes beyond the simple encapsulation of Motif entities. It also encapsulates the style guides. To create a window with its menu is done by performing several calls. There are components which afford a power comparable for those provided by rapid prototyping tools.

15.7.10 editor_sys: multiview kernel

This component contains 110 classes. It supports the implementation of applications for visualising information using a number of windows in various formats and guaranteeing consistency. It has the functionality of the system model/view/controller of Smalltalk.

It simplifies the work of developers who can work on the independent views without permanently having to deal with problems of consistency.

15.7.11 Drawing

To be complete it is also necessary to mention all the components for drawing, such as graph drawing, tree drawings or organigrams.

All these drawings contain all necessary algorithms:

- Determination of position of entities;

- Incremental drawing (only re-drawing things which change).

To use such a component, we inherit some classes in order to define how the entities in the drawing representation are represented and we do not need to know about how the drawing is performed.

15.8 Results Obtained

15.8.1 Re-use global to the company

Here are some measures performed in 1993 (also published during TOOLS Europe) which give information on the obtained re-use rate.

We have analysed 32 applications which were in a stable state of development. These have been realised by using the development environment described above.

The result of these analyses are as follows.

The applications are formed of 100-1,090 classes with an average of 600 classes.

They use a total of 3,606 classes. Amongst these, 16 classes are present in all applications. These are the base cases (string, file, data structures).

We have examined each one of these applications and seen what percentage of their classes are present in other applications. This gives the following table.

	1-7	8-15	16-24	25-32
% classes	47	7	14	32
% lines	43	6	15	36

This table is read in the following way: on average, for an application, 47% of its classes (which represents 43% of its lines of codes) are present in 1-7 of the 32 applications analysed. The other columns give the percentage of classes and lines present in 8-15, 16-24 and 25-32 applications.

From this measure, it turns out that on average, an application shares half of its code with at least half the other applications.

The part of the components which are present in more than 3/4 of the applications was 90% realised by the Components Group. There were very few components realised by the application teams.

15.8.2 Re-use by domain

Beside this re-use of the components common to all the projects in the company, there was a reuse along product lines.

Here, to illustrate this reuse are the measures made for the product line ObjectPARTNER (OP). This is composed of three editors, one for each of the types of formalisms in the OMT method:

- OP/Object Editor (OP/OE) supports the editing of class diagrams and instance diagrams;
- OP/Function Editor (OP/FE) supports the editing of data flow diagrams;
- OP/Behaviour Editor (OP/BE) supports the editing of automata.

These editors were realised in the following order:

- OP/OE;
- OP/BE.

The following table gives the size in number of classes and lines in each of these editors.

Product	Classes	Lines
LOV/OW	437	146970
LOV/FE	376	121233
LOV/BE	385	135325

Each of these editors reuse common Verilog components (that is to say, components used by the range of applications constructed by the company). Here, for each of them, is the number of classes and the number of lines which it represents:

Product	Classes	Lines
LOV/OE	193 (44%)	59004 (40%)
LOV/FE	199 (53%)	61102 (50%)
LOV/BE	195 (50%)	62848 (46%)

Around 50% of each editor is formed of common components.

The part in common between OP/FE and OP/OE represents 289 classes (87009 lines of code). This represents 76% of the number of OP/FE classes and 72% of its number of lines. To global reuse of 53% is therefore added a local reuse of 23% (respectively 50% and 22% for lines of code).

The common part between OP/BE and OP/OE + OP/FE represent 315 classes (95752 lines of code). This represents 82% of the number of classes in OP/BE and 71% of its number of lines of code. At a reuse of 50% for OP/BE, is therefore to be added a local reuse of 32% (respectively 46% and 25% for lines of code).

The OP/OE and OP/FE and OP/BE editors manipulate formalisms which are very different. Despite this, it is despite that possible to arrive at rates of 70% (in terms of number of lines of code) thanks to the use of object-oriented techniques.

15.8.3 Productivity

The total time for implementing OP/OE (specification, design, coding, unit tests, integration, validation and user documentation) was 9783 hours.

The product represents 146970 lines of code. The apparent productivity was thus 15 lines per hour.

In reality, by means of reuse, only 87966 lines of code were developed. The real productivity was therefore 9 lines per hour.

The total time for implementing LOV/FE was 2743 hours (there was reuse also in the documentation). The apparent productivity for this product was therefore 44 lines per hour (about 3 times more than for LOV/OE).

Only 34214 lines of code were really developed. The real productivity was 12 lines per hour (1.3 times better than LOV/OE).

The total time for implementing LOV/BE was 2763 hours. The apparent productivity was 49 lines per hour.

There were really only 39573 lines written for LOV/BE. The real productivity was therefore 14 lines per hour.

The total time for implementing LOV/OMT was 15289 hours. Without reuse and with an average productivity of 10 lines per hour, it would have required 40352 hours to construct this product. Reuse has thus allowed a gain in productivity of 62%.

With practical reuse, the apparent productivity for the LOV/OMT development team is thus today of the order of 26 lines per hour or 205 lines per day. This is far from the average of 10 lines per day that is generally cited.

15.8.4 Quality

During the validation phase 184 errors were detected and corrected in the three editors in LOV/OMT. This represents one error every 2193 lines of code if we take the total number of lines in the three editors, and one error every 879 lines if we only take into account what has been developed (only 2 errors were detected in the global components).

If there was no reuse, with an average of one error every 879 lines, that is 459 errors which would have had to have been corrected in the validation phase.

15.8.5 Development

A large part of the development of LOV/OMT was implemented only for one of the editors and was immediately available for two other editors, each only costing one compilation and one validation.

For example, in version 1.2 of LOV/OMT, functions were added for alignment of drawings, coupling functions, functions for coupling to version management, improvements in graphic outputs. All of this was done once in the relevant components then was available to all the editors.

15.9 Conclusion

This experience proves that the use of object-oriented technologies works and that reuse is possible.

It was necessary to learn to control object-oriented techniques and to learn to organise oneself. This was not always easy. Some components were mistakes, and some projects were affected. Despite this, the global result is positive.

Verilog still uses this development environment. With the appearance of OMT, some extensions have been made. All analyses and designs are undertaken using OMT, and the code for classes is generated automatically in C++, C or Eiffel according to the application (the Adèle product is constructed in C++, the Geode product in C, and the LOV products in an Eiffel-like language).

15.10 Chapter Summary

We have seen in this chapter an example of the adoption of object-oriented technology and organisations that favour reuse.

The returns in terms of productivity, quality and development has been measured and are highly satisfactory.

This experience shows that object-oriented techniques (including multiple inheritance) work and are well suited to achieving good results for reuse.

Chapter Sixteen

Conclusions

16.1 To Know More

We have tackled the set of themes related to a policy of reuse in this book.

This book does not pretend to be exhaustive and to provide solutions to all problems. It has, rather, the objective of indicating problems and giving ways to find specific solutions which are suitable to each case.

The reader who wishes to go further in the study or the adoption of the techniques which have been discussed should refer to the bibliography at the end of this book.

16.2 Main Ideas

Among the ideas expressed in the above chapters, it is necessary to remember the following:

- There is no effort-free reuse without effort; one cannot begin to reuse by just moving over to the use of an object-oriented language; it is necessary to learn to use certain techniques and put in place an organisation which favours reuse;
- Object orientation is a good choice for reuse on condition that its rules are respected (encapsulation in particular);
- Object-orientation works: the problems that we have mentioned, in particular those concerning multiple inheritance, are those of C++ and some compilers, and not those of object-oriented techniques in general. It is a mistake to identify object-orientation with C++ in its current form (developments will take place);
- Copy is the worst reuse technique. A good reaction consists of considering that one does not reuse anymore from the moment when information is copied;
- The use of methods and tools for the analysis and design of software simplifies the adoption of reuse;
- Reuse cannot be considered if a configuration management system is not used (at least for reusable components);

- The quality of components is a trump card for the success of a re-utilisation policy;
- New jobs are to be created if one wishes to reuse software (library, component manufacturer).

16. 3 Acknowledgements

Thanks to Rodolphe Arthaud [Arthaud 95] for his invaluable remarks and suggestions during the writing of this book.

Equally, I would like to thank all those who have assisted the implementation of everything relating to reuse at Verilog.

The OMT diagrams were created with the ObjectPARTNER tool from Verilog.

References

[Aksit 92] M Aksit L. Bergmans, Obstacles in object-oriented software development, *Proceedings OOPSLA*, 1992.

[Alabiso 88] B. Alabiso, Transformation of data flow analysis models to object-oriented design, *OOPSLA*, San Diego, September ,1988.

[Anderson 90] B. Anderson, S. Gossain, *Software reusability using object oriented programming*, University of Southampton, 1990.

[Arango 88] Gujllermo Arango, *Domain engineering for software reuse*, PhD Thesis, Dept Information and Computer Science, Univ of California, 1988.

[Arango 92] Guillermo Arango, *Domain analysis methods*, Schiumberger Laboratory for Computer Science, Austin, Texas, 1992.

[Arnold 87] S. P. Arnold, S. L. Stepoway, The reuse system: cataloguing and retrieval of reusable software, *Proceedings COMPCON '87*, IEEE XS Press, 1987.

[Arthaud 95] Rodolphe Arthaud, OMT-RT: extensions of OMT for better describing behavior, *TOOLS 16*, Prentice Hall 1995.

[Balda 90] D. M. Balda, D. A. Gustafson, Cost-estimation models for the reuse and prototype software development, *ACM SIGSOFT*, July, 1990.

[Barman 89] M. A. Barman, Shifting paradigms for software development, *Proceedings of the Third International Workshop on Computer-Aided Software Engineering*, 1989.

[Barnes 88] Bruce B. Barnes, Thomas Durek, John Gaffney, Arthur Pyster, A framework and economic foundation for software reuse, in *Software Reuse: Emerging Technology*, Computer Society Press, 1988.

[Barnes 91] Bruce B. Barnes, Terry B. Bollinger, Making reuse cost-effective, *IEEE Software*, 1991.

[Barnes 93] C. M. Barnes, B. R. Swim, Inheriting software metrics, *Journal of object-oriented Programming*, Vol. 6 No. 7, 1993.

[Basili 84] V. R. Basili, D. M. Weiss, A methodology for collecting valid software engineering data, *IEEE Transactions on Software Engineering*, Vol 10, No 6,1984.

[Basili 90] V. R. Basili, Viewing maintenance as reuse-oriented software development, *IEEE Software*, Vol 7, No 1, January 1990.

[Berlin 90] L. Berlin, When objects collide: experiences with reusing multiple class hierarchies, *ACM OOPSLA ECOOP* '90 Conference Proceedings, October 1990.

[Bergstein 91] P. Bergstein, K. J. Lieberherr, Incremental class dictionary learning and optimization, *Proceedings ECOOP*, 1991.

[Bezivin 94] J. Bezivin, J. Lanneluc, R. Lemesle, Representing knowledge in the object-oriented lifecycle, *TOOLS Pacific '94*, Prentice Hall.

[Bieman 91] M. Bieman, *Deriving measures of software reuse in object oriented systems*, Technical Report Cobeado State University, July 1991.

[Biggerstaff 87] Ted J. Biggerstaff, C. Richter, Reusability framework, assessment and directions, *IEEE Software*, March 1987.

[Biggerstaff 89a] Ted J. Biggerstaff, Design recovery for maintenance and reuse, *Computer*, July, 1989.

[Biggerstaff 89b] Ted J. Biggerstaff, A. J. Perlis, *Software reusability*, Vol. I and II, ACM Press, 1989.

[Blair 91] G. Blair, J. Gallagher, D. Hutchinson, D. Shepherd, *Object-oriented languages, systems and applications*, Pitman Publishing 1991.

[Boehm 81] Barry W. Boehm, *Software engineering economics*, Prentice-Hall, 1981.

[Boehm 87] Barry W. Boehm, Improving software productivity, *IEEE Software*, September, 1987.

[Boehm 88] Barry W. Boehm, *A spiral model of software development and enhancement*, IEEE, May, 1988.

[Boehm 89] Barry W. Boehm, Applying process programming to the spiral model, *Proceedings of the 4th International Software Process Workshop*, 1989.

[Boehm 91] Barry W. Boehm, Software risk management: principles and practices, *IEEE Software*, Janvier 1991.

[Booch 87] Grady Booch, Software components with Ada, Benjamin Cummings, 1987.

[Booch 90] Grady Booch, M. Vilot, *Design strategy, analysis, and the software lifecycle*, C++ Report, Vol 2, No 7, July/August, 1990.

[Booch 91] Grady Booch, *Object-oriented design with applications*, Benjamin Cummings, 1991.

[Booch 93]Grady Booch, *Object-oriented analysis and design with applications*, Addison-Wesley 1993.

[Brooks 87] F. Brooks, No silver bullet: essence and accidents of software engineering, *Computer*, April 1987.

[Brown 92] Alan J. Brown, *The use of non-formal information in reverse engineering and reuse*, PhD thesis Department of Computer Science, Brunel University, 1992.

[Burson 90] Scott Burson, Gordon B. Kotik, Lawrence Z. Markozian, A program transformation approach to automatic software re-engineering, *COMPSAC-90*, 1990.

[Burton 87] B. A. Burton, R. W. Aragon, S. A. Bailey, K. D. Koebler, L. A. Mayes, The reusable software library, *IEEE Software*, July 1987.

[Caldiera 91] G. Caldiera, V. R. Hasili, Identifying and qualifying reusable software components, *Computer*, Vol. 24, No. 2, February 1991.

[Carter 90] C. Carter, Object-oriented design: a common sense fusion of methods, *Stp UK User Group Conference*, 1990.

[CCITT 88] Specification and description language (SDL). Recommendation Z1OO, *Technical report CCITT*, 1988.

[Checkland 81] P. Checkland, *Systems thinking, systems practice*, John Wiley and Sons, 1981.

[Checkland 90] P. Checkland, J. Scholes, *Soft systems methodology in action*, John Wiley and Sons, 1990.

[Chen 76] P.S. Chen, The entity-relationship model - toward a unified view of data, *ACM Transactions on Database Systems*, 1, March, 1976.

[Chen 93] P.S. Chen, R. Hennicker, M. Jarke, On the retrieval of reusable components, *Proceedings of the Second International Workshop on Software, Reusability Advances in Software*, Lucca, 1993.

[Chidamber 91] Shyam R. Chidamber, Chris R. Kemerer, Towards a metrics suite for object-oriented design, *OOPSLA*, 1991.

[Chikofsky 90] Elliot J. Chikofaky, James H. Cross II, Reverse engineering and design: a taxonomy, *IEEE Software*, January 1990.

[Coad 90] Peter Coad, Edward Yourdon, *Object-oriented analysis*, Yourdon Press, Prentice Hall, Englewood Cliffs 1990.

[Coad 91] Peter Coad, Edward Yourdon, *Object-oriented design*, Yourdon Press, 1991.

[Coleman 92] D. Coleman, F. Hayes, S. Bear, Introducing objectcharts or how to use statecharts in object-oriented design, *IEEE Transactions on Software*

Engineering, Vol. 18, January, 1992.

[Coleman 94] Derek Coleman, Patrick Arnold, Stephanie Bodoff, Chris Dollin, Helena Gilchrist, Fiona Hayes, Paul Jeremes, *Object-oriented development the fusion method*, Prentice Hall 1994.

[Constantine 89] Larry L. Constantine, The object-oriented paradigm, *DCI Object-Oriented Systems Symposium*, June 1989.

[Constantine 92] Larry L. Constantine, Rewards and reuse, *Computer Language*, July 1992.

[Cook 92] W. R. Cook, Interfaces and specifications for the SmallTalk-80 collection classes, *Proceedings OOPSLA*, 1992.

[Coulange 93] Bernard Coulange, Alain Roan, Object-oriented techniques at work: facts and statistics, *TOOLS 10*, Prentice Hall 1993.

[Cowan 95] Donald D. Cowan, Carlos J. P. Lucena, Abstract data views: an interface specification concept to enhance design for reuse, *IEEE Transactions on Software Engineering*, Vol 21, No 3, March 1995.

[Cox 86] Brad J. Cox, *Object-oriented programming: an evolutionary approach*, Addison-Wesley, 1986.

[Cox 90] Brad J. Cox, There is a silver bullet: a software industrial revolution based on reusable and interchangeable part will alter the software universe, *BYTE*, October 1990.

[Daniels 90] J. Daniels, Object-oriented design: refinement or transformation, *OOPS-30*, Strand Palace, London 1990.

[Dausmann 88] M. Dausmann, Organizing component libraries, *Ada Europe Software Seminar*, June 1988.

[Davis 93] T. Davis, The reuse capability model: a basis for improving an organization's reuse capability, *Proceedings of the Second International Workshop on Software, Reusability Advances in Software*, Lucca, 1993.

[DeMarco 78] Tom DeMarco, *Structured analysis and system specification*, Yourdon Press, 1978.

[Desfray 92] Philippe Desfray, *Ingénierie des objets - approche classe-relation, application à C++*, Editions Masson, 1992.

[Deutach 89] L. P. Deutsch, Design reuse and frameworks in the SmallTalk 80 system, *Software Reusability*, Vol. 2, ACM Press 1989.

[Dionisi 93] Dominique Dionisi, *L'essentiel sur MERISE*, Eyrolles, 1993.

[Edwards 90] M. Edwards, B. Henderson-Sellers, Object-oriented systems life cycle, *Communication of the ACM*, Vol. 33, No. 9, September 1990.

[Ellis 90] Margaret. A. Ellis, B. Stroustrup, *The annotated C++ reference Manual*, Addison-Wesley 1990.

[Fafchamp 94] Danielle Fafchamp, Organizational factors and reuse, *IEEE Software*, September 1994.

[Favaro 91] John Favaro, Applications of reuse in space and industry, in *Proceedings of the First Workshop on Reusability*, July, 1991.

[Feather 83] M. S. Feather, Reuse in the context of a transformation-based methodology, *ITT Proceedings, Workshop on Reusability in Programming*, 1983.

[Fenton 91] N. E. Fenton, *Software metrics, a rigorous approach*, Chapman and Hall 1991.

[Fischer 87] G. Fischer, Cognitive view of reuse and design, *IEEE Software*, July 1987.

[Frakes 90] W. B. Frakes, B. A. Nejmeh, *An information system for software reuse, Software Reuse: Emerging Technology*, IEEE Press,1990.

[Gaffney 92] J. Gafney, R. Cruickshank, A general economic model of software reuse, *14th International Conference on Software Engineering*, Melbourne, 1992.

[Gamma 94] Erich Gamma, Richard Helm, Ralph Johnson, John Vlissides, *Design patterns elements of reusable object-oriented software*, Addison Wesley, 1994.

[Gane 79] C. Gane, T. Sarson, *Structured systems analysis*, Prentice Hall, 1979.

[Gibbs 90] S. Gibbs, D. Tsichritzis, E. Casais, O. Nierstrasz, X. Pintada, Class management for software communities, *Communication ACM*, Vol. 33, No 9,1990.

[Gillis 90] Keith D. Gillis, David G. Wright, Improving software maintenance using system-level reverse engineering, *Proceedings of the 1990 Conference on Software maintenance*, San Diego, 1990.

[Girod 91] X. Girod, *Conception par objets - MECA NO: une methode et un environnement de construction d'applications par objets*, Thèse de doctorat, Université Joseph Fourier, Grenoble 1,1991.

[Godin 93] R. Godin, B. Mili, Building and maintaining analysis-level class hierarchies using galois lattices, *ACM SIGPLAN Notices, OOPSLA '93 Proceedings*, Vol. 28, October, 1993.

[Goguen 86] J. A. Goguen, Reusing and interconnecting software components, *Computer*, February 1986.

[Goldberg 83] A. Goldberg, D. Robson, *SmallTalk80: the Language and its* implementation, Addison-Wesley, 1983.

[Goldstein 80] J. P. Goldstein, D. G. Bobrow, Description for a programming environment, *Proceedings AAAI*, 1980.

[Gossain 90] S. Gossain, B. Anderson, An iterative-design model for reusable object-oriented software, *ACM SIGPLAN Notices*, Vol. 25, No. 10, October 1990.

[Graham 91] Ian Graham, *Object-oriented methods*, Addison-Wesley, 1991.

[Griss 93] M. L. Griss, Software reuse: from library to factory, *IBM Systems Journal*, Vol. 32, No. 4,1993.

[Griss 94] M. Griss, J. Favaro, P. Walcon, *Managerial and organizational issues in Starting and Running a Software Reuse Program*, Elis Horwood, 1994.

[Gruman 88] G. Gruman, Early reuse practices lives up to its promise, *IEEE Software*, November 1988.

[Hall 89] Patrick A. Hall, Cornelia Boldyreff, Software reuse overview, in *Reuse, Maintenance and Reverse Engineering of Software*, Unicom Seminars Ltd, Uxbridge, GB, 1989.

[Hall 92] Patrick A. Hall, *Software reuse and reverse engineering in/practice*, Chapman-Hall, 1992.

[Ball 93a] Patrick A. Hall, R. Weedon, Object-oriented module interconnection languages, *Proceedings of the Second International Workshop on Software, Reusability Advances in Software*, Lucca, 1993.

[Hall 93b] R. J. Hall, Generalized behavior-based retrieval, *Proceedings 15th International Conference on Software Engineering*, ACM Press, May, 1993.

[Harel 87] David Harel, Statecharts: a visual formalism for complex systems, *Science of Computer Programming*, Vol. 8, 1987.

[Harmon 93] Paul Harmon, OO class libraries and extensions to OO environments, *Object Oriented Strategies*, Volume III, No. 11,1993.

[Hatley 88] D. Hatley, I. Pirbhai, *Strategies for real-time systems specification*, Dorset House, 1988.

[Helm 90] R. Helm, I. Holland, D. Gangopadhyay, Contracts: specifying behavioral compositions in OO systems, *Proceedings OOPSLA '90*, ACM Press, October 1990.

[Helm 91] Richard Helm, Yoelle S. Maarek, Integrating information retrieval and domain specific approaches for browsing and retrieval in object-oriented class libraries, *OOPSLA '91*.

[Henderson-Sellers 90] B. Henderson-Sellers, J. M. Edwards, The object-oriented systems life cycle, *Communications of the ACM*, Vol. 33, No. 9, September, 1990.

[Henderson-Sellers 91] H. Henderson-Sellers, Some metrics for object-oriented soft engineering, *Proceedings of TOOLS 6 Pacific*, 1991.

[Henderson-Sellers 93a] H. Henderson-Sellers, D. Tegarden, D. Monarchi, Object-oriented metrics, *Proceedings of ECOOP '93*, 1993.

[Henderson-Sellers 93b] H. Henderson-Sellers, The economics of reusing library classes, *Journal of Object Oriented Programming*, July/August, 1993.

[Henry 93] S. Henry, W. Li, Object-oriented metrics that predict maintainability, *Journal of Systems and Software*, Vol. 23, No. 2, November, 1993.

[Hodgson 91] Ralph Hodgson, The X-model: a process model for object-oriented software development, *Proceedings of Le genie logiciel & ses applications*, Toulouse, 1991.

[Hooper 90] J. Hooper, R. Chester, *Software reuse guidelines*, Georgia Institute of Technology, 1990.

[Hopcroft 79] J. E. Hopcroft, J. D. Ullman, *Introduction to automata theory, languages and computation*, Addison Wesley, 1979.

[Horowitz 84] E. Horowitz, J. B. Munson, An expansive view of reusable software, *IEEE Transactions on Software Engineering*, Vol. 10, No. 5, 1984.

[Isoda 91] S. Isoda, An experience of software reuse activities, *Proceedings of the First International Workshop on Software Reusability*, Dortmund, 1991.

[Isoda 92] S. Isoda, Experience report on a software reuse project: its structure, activities, and statistical results, *Proceedings of 14th International Conference on Software Engineering*, May, 1992.

[Jacobson 87] Ivar Jacobson, Object-oriented development in an industrial environment, *OOPSLA Conference, Special Issue of SIGPLAN Notices*, 1987.

[Jacobson 91] Ivar Jacobson, Fredrik Lindstrom, Re-engineering of old systems to an object-oriented architecture, *OOPSLA Conference, Special Issue of SIGPLAN Notices*, 1991.

[Jacobson 92] Ivar Jacobson, Magnus Christerson, Patrik Jonsson, Gunnar Overgaard, *Object-oriented software engineering*, Addison-Wesley, 1992.

[Jacobson 94] Ivar Jacobson, M. Ericsson, A. Jacobson, *The object advantage - business process re-engineering with object technology*, Addison Wesley, 1994.

[Jones 84] T. Capers Jones, Reusability in programming: a survey of the state of the art, *IEEE Transactions on Software Engineering*, Vol. 10, No 5, September 1984.

[Jones 90] G. Jones, *Methodology/environment support for reusability, Software Reuse. Emerging Technology,* Will Tracz, IEEE CS Press, 1990.

[Jones 92] R. Jones, Extended type checking in Eiffel, *Journal of Object-Oriented Programming,* May, 1992.

[Johnson 91] P. A. Johnson, C. S. Rees, Reusability through fine grain inheritance, *Software, Practice and Experience,* Vol 22, No.12, December, 1992.

[Johnson 88] Ralph E. Johnson, Brian Foote, Designing reusable classes, *Journal of Object-Oriented Programming,* June/July, 1988.

[Kaiser 87] G. E. Kaiser, D. Garlan, Melding software systems from reusable building blocks, *IEEE Software,* July 1987.

[Kang 90] K. C. Kang, *A reuse-based software development methodology, Software Reuse: Emerging Technology,* Will Tracz, IEEE CS Press, 1990.

[Katz 87] S. Katz, C. Richter, K. S. The, PARIS: A system for reusing partially interpreted schemas, *Proceedings of 9th Conference on Software Engineering,* 1987.

[Kernighan 78] B. W. Kernighan, D. M. Ritchie, *The C programming language,* Prentice Hall, 1978.

[Kiczales 92] G. Kiczales, J. Lamping, Issues in the design and documentation of class libraries, *Proceedings OOPSLA '92, SIGPLAN Notices,* ACM Press, Vol 27, No 10, October 1992.

[Korson 90] T Korson, J. McGregor, Understanding object-oriented: a unifying paradigm, *Communications of the ACM,* 33, September 1990.

[Korson 93] T. Korson, J. D. McGregor, Technical criteria for the specification and evaluation of object-oriented libraries, *Proceedings of Object Expo Europe,* 1993.

[Krueger 92] C. W. Krueger, Software reuse, *ACM Computing Surveys,* Vol. 24, No. 2, June, 1992.

[Kruzela 91] Ivan Krozela, Human aspects and organizational issues of software reuse, *Unicom Seminars Ltd,* Uxbridge, 1991.

[Lanergan 84] R. G. Lanergan, C. A. Grasso, Software engineering with reusable design and code, *IEEE Transactions on Software Engineering,* Vol. 10, No. 5, 1984.

[Laranjeira 90] L. A. Laranjeira, Software size estimation of object-oriented systems, *IEEE Transactions on Software Engineering,* Vol. 16, No. 5, 1990.

[Laski 93] J . Laski, W. Szermer, Regression analysis of reusable program components, *Proceedings of the Second International Workshop on Software,*

Reusability Advances in Software, Lucca, 1993.

[Lejter 92] M. Lejter, S. Meyers, S. P. Reiss, Support for maintaining object-oriented programs, *IEEE Transactions on Software Engineering*, 18, 1992.

[Lieberherr 89] Karl J. Lieberherr, I. M. Holland, Assuring good style for object oriented programs, *IEEE Software*, September 1989.

[Lieberherr 91] Kark J. Lieberherr, Paul Bergatein, Ignacio Silva-Lepe, Prom objects to classes: algorithms for object-oriented design, *Journal of Software Engineering*, July 1991.

[Liu 90] Sying-Syang Liu, Norman Wilde, Identifying objects in a conventional procedural language: an example of data design recovery, *Conference on Software Maintenance*, IEEE Press, 1990.

[Lubars 90] M. Luhars, Wide-spectrum support for software reusability, *Software Reuse: Emerging Technology*, Will Tracz, IEEE CS Press, 1990.

[Lubars 92] M. Lubars, G. Meredith, C. Potts, C. Richter, Object-oriented analysis for evolving systems, *Proceedings 14th International Conference on Software Engineering*, ACM Press, May, 1992.

[Luqi 90] Luqi, A graph model for software evolution, *IEEE Transactions on Software Engineering*, Vol. 16, No. 8, August, 1990.

[Maarek 91] Yoelle S. Maarek, Daniel M. Berry, Gail E. Kaiser, An information retrieval approach for automatically constructing software libraries, *IEEE Transactions on Software Engineering*, Vol. 17, No. 8, August, 1991.

[Maiden 92]N. A. Maiden, A. G. Sutcliffe, Exploiting reusable specifications through analogy, Special Issue on CASE, *Communications of the ACM*, Vol. 35, No. 4, April 1992.

[Maiden 93] N. A. Maiden, A. G. Sutcliffe, People-oriented software reuse: the very thought, *Proceedings of the Second International Workshop on Software*, Reusability Advances in Software, Lucca, 1993.

[Marca 88] D. Marca, C. McGowan, *SADT: Structured Analysis and Design Technique*, Mc Graw-Hill 1988.

[Margono 92] J. Margono, T. E. Rhoads, Software reuse economics: cost program benefit analysis on a large-scale Ada project, *Proceedings 14th International Conference on Software Engineering*, ACM Press, 1992.

[Marino 90] O. Marina, F. Rechenmann, P. Uvietta, Multiple perspectives and classification mechanism in object-oriented representation, *Proceedings ECAI*, Stockholm, 1990.

[Martin 89] J. Martin, *Information engineering: a trilogy*, Volumes 1-3, Englewood Cliffs, Prentice Hall, 1989.

[Martin 92] J. Martin, J. Odell, *Object-oriented analysis and design*, Prentice-Hall 1992.

[Matsumoto 87] Y Mataumoto, *A software factory: an overall approach to software production*, IEEE, 1987.

[Matsomoto 93] Y Matsumoto, Experiences from software reuse in industrial process control applications, *Proceedings of the Second International Workshop on Software, Reusability Advances in Software*, CS Press, Lucca, 1993.

[Mayobre 91] G. Mayobre, *Using code reusability analysis to identify reusable components from the software related to an application domain*, Hewlett Packard 1991.

[McCabe 76] T. J. McCabe, A complexity measure, *IEEE Transactions on Software Engineering*, Vol. 2, No. 4, 1976.

[McCain 85a] R. McCain, Reusable software components construction: a product-oriented paradigm, *Proceedings of the 15th Computer in Aerospace Conference*, October 1985.

[McCain 85b] R. McCain, A software development methodology for reusable components, *Proceedings of 18th Conference on Systems*, 1985.

[McClure 92] C. McClure, *The three R's of software automation: re-engineering, repository, reusability*, Prentice-Hall 1992.

[Meyer 87] Bertrand Meyer, Eiffel: programming for reusability and extendability, *ACM SIGPLAN Notices 22*, February, 1987.

[Meyer 88] Bertrand Meyer, *Object-oriented software construction*, Prentice Hall, 1988.

[Meyer 89a] Bertrand Meyer, *Conception et programmation par objets pour du logiciel de qualité*, InterEditions, Paris 1989.

[Meyer 89b] Bertrand Meyer, Reusability: the case for O.O. design, *Software Reusability*, Vol. 2, ACM Press 1989.

[Meyer 89c] Bertrand Meyer, The new culture of software development: reflections on the practice of object-oriented design, *TOOLS '89*, Paris, November 1989.

[Meyer 90] Bertrand Meyer, Lessons learned from the design of the Eiffel libraries, *Communications of the ACM*, Vol. 33, No 9, 1990.

[Meyer 92] Bertrand Meyer, *Eiffel: The language*, Prentice Hall, 1992.

[Meyer 94] Bertrand Meyer *Reusable software: the base object-oriented component libraries*, Prentice Hall 1994.

[Micallef 88] Josephine Micallef, Encapsulation, reusability and extensibility in object-oriented languages, *Journal of Object-Oriented Programming*, 1, April, 1988.

[Mili 92] H. Mili, A. E. El Wahidi, Y. Intrator, Building a graphical interface for an OO tool for software reuse, *Proceedings TOOLS USA*, 1992.

[Mili 93] H. Mili, H. Li, Data abstraction in softclass, an OO case tool for software reuse, *Proceedings TOOLS*, 1993.

[Mili 94a] H. Mili, R. Mili, R. Mittermeir, Storing and retrieving software components: a refinement-based approach, *Proceedings of 16th International Conference on Software Engineering*, May, 1994.

[Mili 94b] H. Mili, O. Marcotte, A. Kabbaj, Intelligent component retrieval for software reuse, *Proceedings of 3rd Maghrebian Conference on Artificial Intelligence and Software Engineering*, April 1994.

[Mili 94c] H. Mili, R. Rada, W. Wang, K. Strickland, C. Holdyreff, Witt, J. Heger, W. Scherr, P. Elzer, Practitioner and softclass: a comparative study of two software reuse research projects, *Systems and Software*, Vol. 27, May, 1994.

[Mili 95] H. Mili, F. Mili, A Mili, Resuing sofware: issues and research directions, *IEEE Transactions on Software Engineering*, Vol. 21, No. 6, June, 1995.

[Morel 93] J. M. Morel, J. Faget, The REBOOT environment, *Proceedings of the Second International Workshop on Software, Reusability Advances in Software*, Lucca, 1993.

[Mostow 87] J. Mostow, M. Barley, Automatic reuse of design plans, *Proceedings of International Conference on Engineering*, 1987.

[Neighbors 81] J. M. Neighbors, *Software construction using components*, Ph.D. Thesis, Dept. of Information and Computer Science, University of California, Irvine, 1981.

[Neighbors 84] J. M. Neighbors, The DRACO approach to constructing software from reusable components, *IEEE Transactions on Software Engineering*, September, 1984.

[Nerson 92a] J. M. Nerson, Extending Eiffel toward OO analysis and design, proceedings, *Tools 5*, 1992.

[Nerson 92b] J. M. Nerson, Applying OO analysis and design, *Communications of the ACM*, 1992.

[Nino 90] J. Nino, Object-oriented models for software reusability, *SOUTHEASTCON '90 Proceedings*, New Orleans USA, Vol 2, April, 1990.

[Oman 90] Paul W. Oman, Maintenance tools, *IEEE Software*, May, 1990.

[OMG 91] OMG, *The common object request broker: architecture and pecification*, Technical Rapport, Framiogham, December 1991.

[Ostertag 92] E. Ostertag, J. Hendler, R. Prieto-Diaz, C. Braun, Computing similarity in a reuse library system: an AI-based approach, *ACM Transactions on Software Engineering and Methodology*, July, 1992.

[Ould 90] M. A. Ould, *The management of risk and quality*, John Wiley and Sons, 1990.

[Page-Jones 89] M. Page-Jones, S. Weiss, Synthesis/analysis object-oriented method, *DCI Object-Oriented Systems Symposium*, June, 1989.

[Page-Jones 91] M. Page-Jones, Object-orientation: The importance of being earnest, *Object Magazine*, July-August, 1991.

[Podgurski 93] A. Podguraki, L. Pierce, Retrieving reusable software by sampling behavior, *ACM Transactions Software Engineering and Methodology*, Vol. 2, No. 3, July 1993.

[Poulin 93a] J. S. Poulin, J. M. Caruso, D.R. Hancock, The business case for software reuse, *IBM Systems Journal*, Vol. 32, No. 4,1993.

[Poulin 93b] J. S. Poulin, J. M. Caruso, A reuse metrics and return on investment model, *Proceedings of the Second International Workshop on Software, Reusability Advances in Software*, Lucca, 1993.

[Poulin 94] J. S. Poulin, Balancing the need for large corporate and small specific reuse libraries, *Proceedings of ACM Symposium on Applied Computing*, 1994.

[Prieto-Diaz 89] Ruben Prieto-Diaz, Classification of reusable modules, *Software Reusability*, Vol. 2, ACM Press 1989

[Prieto-Diaz 90a] Ruben Prieto-Diaz, Domain analysis: an introduction, *ACM SEN Notes*, 15, 1990.

[Prieto-Diaz 90b] Ruben Prieto-Diaz, Implementing faceted classification for software reuse, *Proceedings of the 12th International Conference on Software Engineering*, IEEE 1990.

[Prieto-Diaz 91a] Ruben Prieto-Diaz, Implementing faceted classification for software reuse, *Communications of the ACM*, Vol. 34, No. 5, IEEE, 1991.

[Prieto-Diaz 91b] Ruben Prieto-Diaz, *Proceedings of the first workshop on reusability*, July 1991.

[Priet-Diaz 91c] Ruben Prieto-Diaz, Making software reuse work: an implementation model, *ACM SIGSOFT Software Engineering Notes*, July1991.

[Prieto-Diaz 91d] Ruben Priet-Diaz, G. Arango, *Domain analysis and software systems modeling*, Los Alamitos, California: IEEE Computer Society Press, 1991.

[PrietoDiaz 93] Ruben Prieto-Diaz, Status report: software reusability, *Software*, Vol. 10, No. 3, May 1993.

[Ramamoorthy 88] C. V. Ramamoorthy, V. Garg, A. Prakash, Support for reusability, *IEEE Transactions on Software Engineering*, Vol. 14, No. 8, August, 1988.

[Reisig 85] W. Reisig, *Petri nets: an introduction*, Berlin, Springer-Verlag, 1985.

[Royce 70] W. Royce, Managing the development of large software systems: concepts and techniques, *Proceedings of Wescon*, 1970.

[Rosson 89] M. B. Rosson, E. Gold, Problem-solution mapping in object-oriented design, *SIGPLAN Notices*, 24,1989.

[Rumbaugh 91] James Rumbaugh, M. Blaha, W. Premerlani, F. Eddy, W. Lorensen, *Object-oriented modeling and design*, Prentice Hall, 1991.

[Schultz 85] D. J. Schultz, Standard for the software life-cycle process, *ACM SEN*, 10, 1985.

[Shlaer 88] Sally Shlaer, Stephen J. Mellor, *Object-oriented systems analysis modeling the world in data*, Prentice Hall, 1988.

[Shlaer 89] Sally Shlaer, Stephen J. Mellor, An Object-oriented approach to domain analysis, *ACM SIGSOFT SEN 14*,1989.

[Shlaer 90] Sally Shlaer, Stephen J. Mellor, Recursive design, *Computer Language*, March, 1990.

[Shlaer 91] Sally Shlaer, Stephen J. Mellor, *Object lifecycles-modeling the world in states*, Prentice Hall, 1988.

[Sixtenason 90] A. Sixtenason, W. Ye, Reuse in telecommunication domain No 5, IEEEusing object-oriented technology and Ada, *Seventh Washington Ada Symposium*, 1990.

[Snyder 86] Alan Snyder, Encapsulation and inheritance in object-oriented programming languages, *OOPSLA '86, ACM SIGPLAN*.

[STABS 92] STABS, *Reuse concepts, Volume 1 Conceptual framework for reuse processes*, February, 1992.

[Stein 87] Lynn Andrea Stein, Delegation is inheritance, *OOPSLA '87, ACM SIGPLAN 22*, December 1987.

[Stroustrup 88] B. Stroustrup, What is object-oriented programming, *IEEE Software*, May, 1988.

[Stroustrup 92] B. Stroustrup, *The C++ programming language*, 2nd Edition, Addison-Wesley, 1992.

[Sutcliffe 89] D. A. G. Sutcliffe, N. A. Maiden, Analogy in the reuse of structured specifications in a case environment, *Proceedings of the Third International Workshop on Computer-Aided Software Engineering*, 1989.

[Tracz 87] W. Tracz, Software reuse: motivators and inhibitors, *Proceedings of COPCOMS '87*, IEEE 1987.

[Tracz 88a] W. Tracz, *Software reuse: emerging technology*, IEEE Computer Society Press, 1988.

[Tracz 88b] W. Tracz, Software reuse myths, *ACM SIGSOFT, Software Engineering Notes*, 13, Janvier 1988.

[Tracz 92] W. Tracz, Software reuse technical opportunities, *Proceedings of DARPA Software Technology Conference*, Los Angeles, April, 1992.

[Tray 94] Robert Tray, Software reuse: making the concept work, *Electronic Design*, June, 1994.

[Vosniadou 89] S. Vosniadoo, A. Ortony, *Similarity and analogical reasoning*, Cambridge University Press, 1989.

[Ward 85] P. Ward, S. Mellor, *Structured development for real-time systems*, Yourdon Press/Prentice Hall 1985.

[Ward 89] P. Ward, How to integrate object orientation with structured analysis and design, *IEEE Software*, March 1989.

[Wasserman 89] A. I. Wasserman, P. A. Pircher, R. Muller, An object-oriented structured design method for code generation, *ACM Software Engineering Notices*, January, 1989.

[Wasserman 90] A. I. Wasserman, P. A. Pircher, J. Mufler, The object-oriented structured design notation for software design representation, *IEEE Computer*, Vol. 23, Mars 1990.

[Wasserman 91] A. I. Wasserman, P. A. Pircher, The spiral model for object software development, *HOTLINE on Object-Oriented Technology*, 2, January, 1991.

[Wegner 83] P. Wegner, Varieties of reusability, *ITT Proceedings of the Workshop on Reusability in Programming*, 1983.

[Wegner 88] P. Wegner, S. B. Zdonik, Inheritance as an incremental modification mechanism or what like is and isn't like, *ECOOP '88*.

[Wilde 91] Norman Wilde, Ross Huitt, Maintenance support for object-oriented programs, *Conference on Software Maintenance*, IEEE Press, 1991.

[Wirfa-Brock 89] R. Wirfa-Brock, B. Wilkerson, Variables limit reusability,

Journal of Object-Oriented Programming, June, 1989.

[Wirfa-Brock 90a] R. Wirfs-Brock, B. Wilkerson, L. Wiener, *Designing object-oriented software*, Prentice Hall, 1990.

[Wirfs-Brock 90b] R. Wirfs-Brock, R. E. Johnson, Surveying current research in object-oriented design, *COMMS, ACM*, 33,1990.

[Woodfield 87] S. N. Woodfield, D. W. Embley, D. T. Scott, Can programmers reuse software, *Software*, July 1987.

[Yap 93] L. M. Yap, H. Henderson-Sellers, *Consistency considerations of object-oriented class libraries*, Technical Report, University of New South Wales, Information Technology Research Centre, Sidney, June, 1993.

[Yourdon 89] E. Yourdon, *Modern structured analysis*, Prentice Hall, 1989.

[Yourdon 94] E. Yourdon, *Software reuse, Application Development Strategies*, Vol. VI, No. 12, Decembre 1994.

[Zaremski 93] A. M. Zaremaki, J. M. Wing, Signature matching: a key to reuse software engineering, *ACM SIGSOFT*, Vol. 18,1993.

Index